Bracken Basic Concept Scale Third Edition Receptive

Examiner's Manual

Bruce A. Bracken, Ph.D.

PsychCorp is an imprint of Pearson Clinical Assessment.

Pearson Executive Office 5601 Green Valley Drive Bloomington, MN 55437

Printed in the United States of America.

800.627.7271

www.PearsonClinical.com

0158338863

PEARSON

17 18 19 20 21 22 23 24 25 26 D E

Acknowledgments

With love to my wife, Mary Jo Bracken, and our son, Bruce A. Bracken, Jr.

Being in the position to revise for the second time an accepted instrument used with diverse populations of young children is a very pleasing professional experience. It is rewarding to recognize that a product that has been a career-long work of love has touched so many children's lives, and it has been my constant desire to make each edition of the BBCS the best it could possibly be. It is especially humbling to know that there are many professionals with the same dedication to excellence who have made and continue to make significant contributions to the success of the BBCS during the past twenty years.

I would like to thank those many individuals whose names do not appear on the test in the prominent position as author. As the author, I would like to thank those individuals involved in rendering artwork, producing the normative sample, providing statistical analyses, participating in decision-making, editing the Manual, directing the project, producing the product, marketing the instrument, and receiving and fulfilling orders for the BBCS from its inception to its current edition. In addition, I would like to thank all of the professionals who have supported the BBCS by using it in their daily practice with the young children they serve.

A wide variety of individuals were involved in ensuring that the development of *Bracken Basic Concept Scale–Third Edition: Receptive* (BBCS-3:R) proceeded smoothly and efficiently. Among those professionals are the Research Directors who coordinated the project from within the Harcourt organization and who regularly interacted with me, ensuring that everyone would be satisfied with the final product. Following Dr. Kathy Shapley's great work on the BBCS–3:R tryout and standardization, Research Directors Shannon Wang and Laura Andrews came aboard and skillfully brought the project to completion.

Heartfelt thanks go to Lois Gregory. Lois was the Research Director on the first revision of the BBCS (i.e., BBCS–R) and served as the Senior Research Director on this revision. Throughout the development of this current revision, I remained confident in the eventual outcome of the test because of Lois's direction, contributions, author communications, and her invaluable combination of experience, wisdom, common sense, diplomacy, advocacy, integrity, and charm.

As Senior Research Analyst, Dulce Mendoza has served as the liaison between the development team and the many other departments involved in the development of BBCS–3:R. She attended to the day-to-day tasks of researching and organizing everything from art development to scorer training.

No project would move forward without the help of the Project Managers. BBCS–3:R has been fortunate to benefit from the support of two dedicated Project Managers —Jean Loden and Neal Campbell—each of whom contributed to the project in countless ways.

The support of the editors during the project has been invaluable. Senior Editor Margaret Young Cooley has devoted countless hours to ensure the accuracy of the content of BBCS–3:R. Managing Editor Dawn Dunleavy's supervisory contributions are irreplaceable.

Among the most exacting and tedious aspects of test development is ensuring that a nationally representative normative sample is collected. I would like to express my appreciation to those individuals who worked diligently to provide practitioners with a BBCS normative sample of such high quality that they can have confidence that the test is appropriate for their children, regardless of where their children reside or what their demographic characteristics might be. Thank you to those individuals in Systems Development (Glen Larson and Matthew Morris) and those in Sampling responsible for data collection (Gloria Angel, Mary Jo Bilicek, Teosha Blaylock, Terri Girard, Greg Hudack, Lauren Miles, Jay Overton, Hector Solis, Darrell Stiffey, and Mario Thomas).

Clinical Handscoring Supervisor David Quintero and the Scoring team headed by Glenna Simmons provided invaluable assistance in ensuring that Record Forms were accurately scored.

Once sampling data have been collected, the data are processed, organized, analyzed, and synthesized by the professionals in the Psychometrics department. I would like to thank Dr. Jianjun Zhu, Manager of Data Analysis Operations; Dr. Charles Wilkins, Senior Psychometrician; and Ying Meng, Senior Statistics Analyst for their careful and thoughtful analysis of the data, which resulted in high quality BBCS–3:R norms, administration and interpretation rules, and reliability and validity analyses.

Bringing the BBCS–3:R to publication has been a result of the many specialists within Harcourt who have contributed to the development and production of artwork, Manual layout and editing, product development, and design. I would especially like to thank those individuals involved in Publication Operations, including Mark Cooley, Robin Espiritu, Jeann Kincaid, Cyndi Sweet, and Mirna Williams.

Finally, the contributions of the Communication and Allied Therapies Group (CATG) have been instrumental in the completion of this project. Under the leadership of Patricia Zureich, Director of CATG, this group has supported the project in every way. BBCS–3:R has benefited from the expertise and the assistance of Senior Research Director Nancy Castilleja, Research Directors Dr. Debra Garrett and Dr. Bridgett Piernik-Yoder, and Research Analysts Noelle Howland and Shawn Hardee. Executive Administrative Assistant Darlene Davis, who responded whenever there was a need, was helpful in every way, as always.

Table of Contents

List of Tables

List of Figures

Chapter 1

Overview

The *Bracken Basic Concept Scale–Third Edition: Receptive* (BBCS–3:R), a revision of the *Bracken Basic Concept Scale–Revised* (BBCS–R; Bracken, 1998b), consists of ten subtests examiners use to evaluate children's basic concept development. The BBCS–3:R is a receptive measure of children's comprehension of foundational and functionally relevant education concepts in ten important concept categories: Colors, Letters, Numbers/Counting, Sizes/Comparisons, Shapes, Direction/Position, Self-/Social Awareness, Texture/Material, Quantity, and Time/Sequence. The first five subtests make up the School Readiness Composite (SRC), which is designed to assess educationally relevant concepts children have traditionally needed to know to be prepared for early formal education. Results obtained from the BBCS–3:R guide clinicians, preschool and kindergarten teachers, and parents in developing strategies for teaching young children these vital concepts that enable them to be successful academically.

The expressive counterpart to the BBCS–3:R, the *Bracken Basic Concept Scale: Expressive* (BBCS:E; Bracken, 2006) may be used in conjunction with the BBCS–3:R to compare children's receptive comprehension of basic concepts to their ability to verbally label basic concepts. The BBCS–3:R and the BBCS:E were co-normed, meaning that both tests were administered to the same children in the normative sample. Co-norming ensures that the test norms are developed using the same reference population, thus facilitating comparisons of children's receptive and expressive basic concept abilities.

Age Range

The BBCS–3:R can be administered to children ages 3 years, 0 months through 6 years, 11 months.

Administration Time

Total BBCS–3:R administration time is 30–40 minutes, depending on the age and ability of the child tested. Administration time for the BBCS–3:R School Readiness Composite (SRC) is 10–15 minutes.

Uses

The BBCS–3:R may be used by speech-language pathologists, psychologists (clinical, developmental, and school), educational diagnosticians, early childhood teachers, and special education teachers to:

- determine the extent to which a child has acquired the basic concepts needed to be successful in formal education;
- determine the basic concepts a child has mastered and the concepts the child has not acquired;
- plan curriculum-relevant interventions;
- assess student progress as it relates to response to intervention (RTI);
- assist in identifying children with language impairments;
- assist in determining eligibility for speech-language services; and
- determine if there is a significant difference between the child's receptive and expressive levels of basic concept acquisition when used in conjunction with the BBCS:E.

The BBCS–3:R incorporates the following features.

- Assessment of 282 foundational and functionally relevant concepts in ten conceptual categories (refer to Table 1.1 for a description of each subtest).
- Use of the SRC as a screener for school readiness.
- Use of subtests 6–10 as measures of a child's understanding of basic concepts in different categories (e.g., direction/position, time/sequence).
- Alignment of subtests to state early-childhood standards (refer to Appendix G).
- Parent/Teacher Conference Form (Appendix F) to assist in reporting children's understanding of each of the 282 basic concepts to their parents and teachers.
- Colorful, stimulating, and developmentally appropriate visual stimuli, designed to capture young children's attention and interest.
- Receptive item format that does not require a verbal response (i.e., a pointing response is acceptable).
- Consistent item format, appearance, style, and response mode throughout the test.

Table 1.1 Description of BBCS–3:R

Subtest	Description	Number of Items (English)	Number of Items (Spanish)
Colors	This subtest includes colors that represent primary colors and those identified as basic color terms for all languages (Berlin and Kay, 1969).	10	10
Letters	This subtest includes upper- and lower-case letters.	15	15
Numbers/Counting	This subtest includes single- and double-digit numerals (Numbers) and assigning number value to a set of objects (Counting).	18	18
Sizes/Comparisons	This subtest includes concepts that describe one dimension (e.g., *tall* being a descriptor of vertical length or *long* being a descriptor of horizontal length), two dimensions (*short* may be a descriptor of either vertical or horizontal length), or three dimensions (concepts such as *big* and *small*, where more than two salient dimensions must be considered). This subtest also measures a child's ability to match, differentiate, or compare objects based on one or more of their salient characteristics.	22	22
Shapes	This subtest includes one-, two-, and three-dimensional shapes. Included in the one-dimensional category are linear shapes such as a *curve*, *angle*, and *diagonal*. Two-dimensional shapes are represented by concepts such as *circle*, *square*, and *triangle*, and three-dimensional shapes include concepts such as *cube* and *pyramid*.	20	20
Direction/Position	This subtest includes relational terms that describe the placement of an object relative to another object or objects (e.g., *behind, on, under*), the position of an object relative to itself (e.g., *open, closed, upside down*), or a direction of placement (e.g., *right, left, corner, center*).	62	60
Self-/Social Awareness	This subtest represents a conceptual domain that is measured infrequently by preschool and primary language scales. The Self-Awareness items of this subtest include concepts referencing emotional states (e.g., *angry, excited, tired*). The Social Awareness items describe kinship, gender, relative ages, and social appropriateness (e.g., *father, woman, young, correct*).	33	31
Texture/Material	This subtest includes concept terms that describe salient characteristics or attributes of an object (e.g., *heavy, soft, sharp*) or the basic composition of an object (e.g., *wood, glass, metal*).	29	29
Quantity	This subtest includes quantity terms. Quantity terms are those that describe the degree to which objects exist and the space that these objects occupy (e.g., *all, full, triple*). This subtest also includes items that measure a child's understanding of how quantity can be manipulated (e.g., *more than, except, divided*).	43	43
Time/Sequence	This subtest includes terms for occurrences along a temporal or sequential continuum and the degree of speed and/or order with which those events occur on the continuum (e.g., *slow, beginning, fourth*).	30	30

Goals for Revising BBCS–R

This revision of the BBCS–R was based on feedback from clinicians, diagnosticians, teachers, and experts in the areas of early childhood language and cognitive development, and in response to changes in state and federal legislation. The following goals were established for this revision.

- Update normative data.
- Update test items and artwork to reflect current societal norms and culture.

- Improve the floor of the test to better identify children in the youngest age groups who have basic concept deficits.
- Provide a method to compare children's comprehension of basic concepts with their ability to express basic concepts, as measured by the BBCS–3:R and BBCS:E.
- Reduce the number of subtests by combining concepts more appropriately.
- Organize subtest content to align with concept development as indicated in early childhood state standards.

How BBCS–3:R Compares to BBCS–R

The BBCS–3:R includes the following changes from its predecessor, the BBCS–R.

- The BBCS–R SRC was composed of six subtests; the BBCS–3:R SRC is composed of five subtests.
- The BBCS–R Sizes subtest and the Comparisons subtest were combined in the BBCS–3:R to form the Sizes/Comparisons subtest.
- The BBCS–R was composed of 11 subtests; this edition is composed of 10 subtests.
- The BBCS–R total test score was referred to as the Total Test score; the BBCS–3:R total test score is referred to as the Receptive Total Composite (Receptive TC). The Receptive TC name change is intended to clearly distinguish the Receptive total test score from the Expressive total test score (i.e., the Expressive Total Composite [Expressive TC]) of the new *Bracken Basic Concept Scale: Expressive.*
- The BBCS–R Total Test score was derived by adding all subtest **raw** scores into a total raw score; the BBCS–3:R Receptive TC score is derived by adding the subtest **scaled** scores.
- The BBCS–R provided instructions for an ipsative (intra-child) score analysis to identify significant variation among subtest scores; the BBCS–3:R provides instructions for a discrepancy analysis between the BBCS–3:R and the BBCS:E to identify significant differences that may exist between the child's receptive and expressive knowledge of basic concepts.

BBCS–3:R Spanish

The BBCS–3:R includes a translated Spanish Record Form. Examiners will find the Spanish Record Form to be similar in administration, format, and scoring to the English Record Form. Differences between BBCS–3:R Spanish and BBCS–3:R English follow.

- For many Spanish items, the verbal stimuli were changed so that gender cues are no longer provided.
- Regional vocabulary choices are encouraged on BBCS–3:R Spanish for several items, recognizing that the vocabulary children use will vary somewhat depending on the child's (or the child's parents') country of origin and/or the geographic region of the U.S. in which the child's family resides.
- Many BBCS–3:R Spanish items constitute minor adaptations rather than direct translations because the concept assessed could not be expressed in a single word in Spanish or did not convey the same meaning as the English target word.
- A few BBCS–3:R Spanish items repeat a concept used in a previous item because the words for the different English language concepts are not differentiated in Spanish (e.g., *big* and *large* are both *grande* in Spanish).

- Some concepts are not assessed in Spanish because there is no equivalent concept corresponding to the target English word. For example, in subtest 6, Item 5, *which boy has his hat off?* would translate to *which child does not have his hat on*? In this case, the translation would assess the concept of *not on* rather than *off*.

Scores

The BBCS–3:R English provides both a scaled subtest score and an overall composite score for the SRC. Subtest scaled scores are provided for subtests 6–10 and a composite score is provided for the total test (i.e., Receptive TC). Percentile ranks, concept age equivalents, and descriptive classifications are also provided for all subtests and the Receptive TC score.

The BBCS–3:R Spanish provides percent mastery scores rather than norm-referenced scores and is intended to be used as a criterion-referenced or curriculum-based measure.

Test Components

Manual

The BBCS–3:R Examiner's Manual (hereafter referred to as the *Manual*) contains administration directions, scoring guidelines, and directions for interpreting children's test performance for the BBCS–3:R English SRC and subtests 6–10; a description of the test purpose, design, and development; technical information (evidence of BBCS–3:R reliability and validity); and normative data. Chapter 6 provides information about use of the BBCS–3:R Spanish and its history and development.

Stimulus Book

The easel-backed Receptive Stimulus Book contains the full-color picture stimuli necessary to administer all test items. The ten subtests are easily located by tabs that identify the beginning of each subtest.

Record Form (English)

The English Receptive Record Form contains administration, recording, and scoring directions, and all trial and test items. Page 1 of the Record Form provides space to record the child's identifying information, raw scores, scaled scores, composite scores, and confidence intervals.

Record Form (Spanish)

The Spanish Receptive Record Form contains administration, recording, and scoring directions, and all trial and test items. The Record Form is designed to be used for pre- and post testing in a curriculum-based assessment paradigm. Page 1 of the Record Form provides space to record the number of items correct and percent mastery for each subtest, and an area to record concepts targeted for instruction and/or remediation.

Examiner Qualifications

The BBCS–3:R is intended to be administered by individuals who have experience or training in administering, scoring, and interpreting standardized tests. Such individuals may include speech-language pathologists, psychologists, educational diagnosticians, early childhood teachers, and special education teachers. The BBCS–3:R may also be administered by paraprofessionals under appropriate supervision.

Challenges in Assessing Preschool Children

Although the BBCS–3:R was designed specifically for preschool assessments, anyone attempting to assess very young children should be aware of the challenges involved in testing children of this age. Preschool children can be impulsive and distractible; cooperative one minute, but unwilling to participate thereafter. Preschool children typically sit still and pay attention for only brief periods; their attention span is often too short for examiners to conduct lengthy evaluations. They often tire quickly and become frustrated more easily than older children and may "shut down" (i.e., refuse to respond or cooperate further), perhaps in the middle of a subtest. Preschool children also sometimes perseverate when responding (e.g., give the same response option on consecutive items). These are but a few of the factors that an examiner must be aware of and accommodate when assessing preschool children. Accommodations that alter the standardized administration should not be made routinely and should be noted on the Record Form and addressed in the test report.

BBCS–3:R User's Responsibilities

It is the responsibility of the test user to ensure that test materials, including Record Forms, remain secure and are released only to professionals who will safeguard their proper use. Although review of test results with parents/caregivers is appropriate, this review should not include disclosure or copying of test items, Record Forms, or other test materials that would compromise the security, validity, or value of BBCS–3:R as a measurement tool. Under no circumstance should test materials be resold or displayed in locations where unqualified individuals can purchase or view partial or complete portions of BBCS–3:R. This restriction includes personal Internet websites and Internet auction sites. Because all test items, norms, and other testing materials are copyrighted, the Legal Affairs Department of Harcourt Assessment must approve, in writing, the copying, reproduction, or distribution of any test materials. The only exceptions to this requirement are the copying of a completed Score Summary of the Record Form (page 1) for the purpose of conveying a child's records to another qualified professional and the copying of Appendix F, the Parent/Teacher Conference Form. These user responsibilities, copyright restrictions, and test security issues are consistent with the guidelines set forth in the *Standards for Educational and Psychological Testing* (American Educational Research Association, American Psychological Association, and National Council on Measurement in Education, 1999).

Administration and Scoring

General administration directions and specific scoring instructions for each of the BBCS–3:R subtests are presented in this chapter. To obtain valid scores on BBCS–3:R you must use sound clinical assessment practices, adhere to the standardized administration procedures, record and score responses accurately, and interpret obtained scores according to the guidelines outlined in chapter 3.

Testing Considerations and Procedures

You should have experience or training in administering, scoring, and interpreting results of standardized tests before attempting to administer, score, or interpret BBCS–3:R. You should also have experience or training in testing children whose ages, linguistic and cultural backgrounds, and clinical history are similar to those of the children you are testing.

Before you administer BBCS–3:R you should:

- thoroughly study the administration and scoring directions for each subtest you will administer, and
- practice administering the test.

Follow all instructions precisely to maintain a standardized test administration and make appropriate comparisons and interpretations based on the results. Modifications of standardized administration procedures could invalidate test results. Read the Cultural Diversity section and the Special Testing Considerations section in this chapter for more information.

Testing Environment and Seating Arrangement

You should administer BBCS–3:R in a quiet, well-lit room that is free from interruptions and distractions. The physical arrangement of the room will be determined, to some degree, by the child. The child may be seated or standing next to or across the corner of the table from you, or you may both sit on the floor. The child should not be seated on the opposite side of the table from you because it is important that the Stimulus Book be visible to both you and the child.

Establishing Rapport

It is important to establish and maintain rapport with examinees, especially young children who are not familiar with formal testing situations. Establishing and maintaining good rapport facilitates the child's interest and cooperation during test administration. Take time to make the child comfortable by talking with the child or engaging him or her in play before beginning test administration.

If a parent or other caregiver accompanies the child during the testing session, advise the adult to sit out of the child's view and to refrain from talking, repeating, or rewording questions. It may be important to reassure the caregiver that you will address any questions he or she may have after the testing session.

Encouragement/Reinforcement

Once you have established rapport and have begun testing, you should be continuously aware of and sensitive to the child's mood or affect. As a child progresses from easy to difficult items through each subtest, be prepared to reinforce the child's effort and cooperation in order to maintain rapport. You may make general encouraging comments or reinforcing statements such as, "I like the way you're working." You should not, however, tell the child if his or her responses are right or wrong, or how many items he or she answered correctly.

Rest Periods/Breaks

Most children in the age range assessed by BBCS–3:R can attend to and actively participate in the assessment without requiring a break. However, if the child needs a short break (for a drink of water, restroom break, etc.) during testing, strive to finish the subtest being administered before stopping.

Cultural Diversity

The great diversity and dynamic nature of American culture and the many languages spoken in the United States preclude compiling a list of adaptations for test administration that applies to all children of diverse cultures. It is important to be sensitive to issues affecting children and their families during testing, as well as when you report test results and make recommendations for intervention. Wyatt, et al. (2001) describe a number of different factors that may adversely affect test administration and interpretation for children of culturally and/or linguistically diverse backgrounds.

- There may be differences between your communicative style and that of the child you are testing. Such differences can cause misinterpretations of verbal and nonverbal behaviors and, ultimately, result in scores that do not reflect the child's true abilities.
- A child may lack familiarity with specific item content (pictures, vocabulary, items, or topics) or tasks.
- Test items may reflect values and beliefs that are culturally specific and do not apply to the cultural background of the child being tested. See chapter 5 for a discussion of BBCS–3:R bias research.

Failure to take such factors into account can lead to less accurate assessment results, and in extreme cases, a possible misdiagnosis. These issues, however, have been addressed in the design of BBCS–3:R, as well as in the earlier editions, BBCS and BBCS–R.

- BBCS–3:R is a receptive measure that requires only a pointing response, thereby minimizing differences in children's communication styles or behaviors.
- BBCS–3:R has full-color visual stimuli that picture people of different racial/ethnic groups and objects common in most cultures. The vocabulary (i.e., basic concepts) assessed on the BBCS–3:R was designed to be as universal across languages and cultures as possible, and item contexts were designed to avoid culture-specific activities.

Several researchers have proposed different approaches to minimizing potential bias in assessing language, including non-standardized test administration. Although standardized test administration is highly encouraged, in those rare situations in which this is not feasible, the following procedures may be helpful when using BBCS–3:R:

- allow extended response time;
- reword test instructions;
- continue to test beyond the discontinue point;
- ask a child to explain incorrect responses; and
- extend testing to determine the degree of understanding the child has of the concepts being presented (i.e., the child may be able to identify obvious examples of a concept but have difficulty with less obvious examples).

Additional suggestions for test modification and adaptation can be found in Kayser (1989), Kayser (1995), Langdon and Merino (1992), McCauley (2001), and Wyatt, et al. (2001).

Because it is inappropriate to use normative test scores when test administration has been modified, use a descriptive approach to report the child's test performance and reactions to test items during the assessment. Wyatt, et al. recommend including a cautionary statement and descriptions of any test administration or scoring procedure modifications when reporting test results.

Special Testing Considerations

Children With Color Blindness

In cases in which the child being tested has either partial or total color blindness, it is unreasonable to expect the child to be able to identify the color items in subtest 1. Failure of items on the Colors subtest could significantly lower the child's SRC subtest/composite score as well as the Receptive TC due to the child's physical disability rather than a lack of conceptual knowledge. Therefore, a prorating procedure has been established so that children with color blindness are not penalized on the BBCS-3:R due to their inability to distinguish basic colors.

Prorated scores were developed based on the observed means of subtests 2–5 to determine the expected number of colors correctly identified by children in the normative sample. Table 2.1 lists these scores. If a child is diagnosed with color blindness, do *not* administer the Colors subtest. Instead, administer subtests 2–5, sum the Raw Scores from those subtests, and obtain the appropriate prorated score from the second column of Table 2.1. Use this prorated score in place of the subtest 1 Colors score in the computation of the SRC raw score and the Receptive TC raw score.

Note. None of the children in the normative sample were reported by their parents to have color blindness; however, the possibility exists that some of the children had not yet been diagnosed.

Table 2.1 Prorated Colors Subtest Score for Children With Color Blindness

Obtained SRC (Subtests 2–5) Raw Score Total	Prorated Colors Subtest Score for Children With Color Blindness
0–3	0
4–11	1
12–18	2
19–26	3
27–33	4
34–41	5
42–48	6
49–56	7
57–63	8
64–71	9
72–75	10

Out-of-Age-Range Administration

The BBCS–3:R was normed on children between the ages of 3 years, 0 months and 6 years, 11 months. For children who are chronologically 7 years, 0 months of age or older but appear to be functioning at a younger developmental level, examiners may administer the BBCS–3:R according to standardized procedures. In such cases, examiners should use the obtained raw scores for curriculum-based or criterion-referenced purposes to describe the child's current level of concept knowledge. (See chapter 3 for a discussion of curriculum-based and criterion-referenced information.) Although it is inappropriate to convert the raw scores to standard scores or percentile ranks in out-of-level testing (because the normative sample did not include children older than 6 years, 11 months, 30 days), examiners can refer to Appendix D to obtain subtest and total test age equivalents and use them to describe the child's concept age. Examiners may use similar procedures when they want to test a younger child, such as a child 2 years, 6 months, who appears to be functioning at an older developmental level. See chapter 7 for results of the study with children ages 7 years, 1 month to 12 years, 8 months diagnosed with intellectual disability.

Special Needs Administration

When testing a child with special needs, the examiner should learn about the child's preferred mode of communication and physical capabilities beforehand to prevent or minimize administration difficulties. If a child is physically incapable of pointing to the pictures to indicate his or her choice, ask the child to verbally indicate his or her choice by saying the number that appears below each picture (1, 2, 3, or 4). For items that offer more than four choices, examiners can point to each of the options and ask the child to respond to each pictured option with either a "yes" or "no." If a child cannot respond verbally or by pointing, other options such as eye gaze or eye blinks can be used to indicate choices.

Children who have difficulty attending or who are easily distracted should be tested in an environment as free of distracting elements as possible. Some children may require testing over a period of days instead of completing the test in one session. In this case, examiners should complete testing subtest by subtest. Always balance the child's needs with the standardized test administration procedures and note any adjustments that are made to accommodate the child's needs.

Although examiners can adapt any subtest for children with special needs by modifying administration procedures (e.g., providing additional cues or repeating item stimuli more than is allowed in the standardized test procedure), the examiner must use the obtained raw scores only as criterion-referenced indications of the child's concept development. When test modifications (other than testing over a period of days) are made, raw scores should not be converted to scaled scores, composite scores, or percentile ranks.

Getting Acquainted With the Testing Materials

Before administering the BBCS–3:R, familiarize yourself with the Manual, Stimulus Book, and Record Form. The administration directions for the subtests are in the Record Form.

Calculating Chronological Age

Calculate the child's chronological age by subtracting his or her birth date from the test date. When doing so, remember:

- when borrowing days from months, always borrow 30 days regardless of the month;
- when borrowing months from years, always borrow 12 months;
- do not round days of age up or down to the nearest month; and
- if a child requires two testing sessions, use the first testing date for the age calculation.

For example, if a child is tested on September 18, 2006, and his or her birth date is September 20, 2002, the child's chronological age at the time of testing is calculated to be 3 years, 11 months, 28 days. The child's age is not rounded up to 4 years, 0 months (refer to Figure 2.1).

	Year	Month	Day
Date of Test	~~06~~ 05	20 ~~9~~ ~~8~~	~~18~~ 48
Date of Birth	02	9	20
Chronological Age	3	11	28

Figure 2.1 Calculating Chronological Age

Subtest Administration

Trial Items

Before administering test items, present the trial items to the child. Trial items introduce the test task to the child and allow him or her to practice and become familiar with the nature of the test. If the child is unable to respond to the trial items or doesn't understand the task, you may encourage, demonstrate, repeat, and prompt as needed to teach the task. Do not proceed to the test items until you are certain that the child understands the task demands and expectations.

School Readiness Composite (SRC) Subtests 1–5

Turn to subtest 1 Colors in the Stimulus Book and begin testing. For subtests 1–5, always begin with the first item of each subtest. Administer items and record responses in order until the child completes the last item of the subtest or has obtained scores of zero (i.e., incorrect or no response) on three consecutive items (discontinue point). After the child has reached the discontinue point or has completed a subtest, proceed to Item 1 of the next subtest.

To score an item, circle 1 if the child responds correctly or 0 if the child responds incorrectly or does not respond. Count the number of correct responses and write the number in the space provided for each subtest.

See Figure 2.2 for examples of recording responses, reaching a discontinue point, and scoring the SRC (subtests 1–5).

Subtest 4 Sizes/Comparisons

Say, **Look at all of the pictures. Show me. . .**

Item	Response	Score
1. which animal is **big**	1 2 3 4 NR	1 0
2. which dog is **small**	1 2 3 4 NR	1 0
3. which girl has **long** hair	1 2 3 4 NR	1 0
4. which ball is **little**	1 2 3 4 NR	1 0
5. which animals are **not the same**	1 2 3 4 NR	1 0
6. which girl has **short** pants	1 2 3 4 NR	1 0
7. which shoes **match**	1 2 3 4 NR	1 0
8. which fruits are **different**	1 2 3 4 NR	1 0
9. which fence is **tall**	1 2 3 4 NR	1 0
10. which water is **deep**	1 2 3 4 NR	1 0
11. which rock is **large**	1 2 3 4 NR	1 0
12. which balloons are the **same**	1 2 3 4 NR	1 0
13. which boats are **alike**	1 2 3 4 NR	1 0
14. which boat is **wide**	1 2 3 4 NR	1 0
15. which shoe fits **exactly**	1 2 3 4 NR	1 0
16. which person is reading something **other than** a book	1 2 3 4 NR	1 0
17. which animals are **similar**	1 2 3 4 NR	1 0
18. which cans are of **equal** size	1 2 3 4 NR	1 0
19. which book is **thin**	1 2 3 4 NR	1 0
20. which ribbon is **narrow**	1 2 3 4 NR	1 0
21. which glasses have **unequal** amounts of juice	1 2 3 4 NR	1 0
22. which water is **shallow**	1 2 3 4 NR	1 0
	Raw Score	10

Subtest 5 Shapes

Say, **Look at all of the pictures. Show me. . .**

Item	Response	Score
1. the **star**	______ NR	1 0
2. the **heart**	1 2 3 4 NR	1 0
3. the **circle**	______ NR	1 0
4. which children are in a **line**	1 2 3 4 NR	1 0
Items 5–6		
5. the **square**	rectangle NR	1 0
6. the **triangle**	______ NR	1 0
7. the **cone**	1 2 3 4 NR	1 0
8. which one is **round**	1 2 3 4 NR	1 0
Items 9–11		
9. the **diamond**	______ NR	1 0
10. the **oval**	______ NR	1 0
11. the **rectangle**	circle NR	1 0
12. the **check mark**	1 2 3 4 NR	1 0
13. which ducks are in a **row**	1 2 3 4 NR	1 0
14. the **pyramid**	1 2 3 4 NR	1 0
15. the **cylinder**	1 2 3 4 NR	1 0
16. the **cube**	1 2 3 4 NR	1 0
17. the **curve**	1 2 3 4 NR	1 0
18. the **column**	1 2 3 4 NR	1 0
19. the **diagonal**	1 2 3 4 NR	1 0
20. the **angle**	1 2 3 4 NR	1 0
	Raw Score	9

Discontinue Point

Figure 2.2 Recording Responses, Reaching a Discontinue Point, and Scoring SRC Subtests

Subtests 6–10

Determine the Start Point

To determine a child's start point (letter or starting items) for subtests 6–10, calculate the School Readiness Composite (SRC) Raw Score by adding the raw scores for subtests 1–5 and writing the sum in the space provided on page 4 of the Record Form (see Figure 2.3). Use either the Start Point Table on page 4 of the Record Form or Table 2.2 and scan across the table to locate the child's SRC Raw Score. Look down the column to determine the corresponding letter or number of the starting items for subsequent subtests. The Start Point Table on page 4 of the Record Form presents the letters that indicate the start points for subtests 6–10. Table 2.2 reports both the letter and number of the starting item for each subtest that corresponds to the SRC Raw Score.

Table 2.2 Start Points for Subtests 6–10

SRC Raw Score	0–25	26–40	41–50	51–60	61–70	71–75	76–79	80–85
Start Point Letter/Item Number	A	B	C	D	E	F	G	H
6 Direction/Position	1	1	6	9	12	19	25	39
7 Self-/Social Awareness	1	4	4	7	11	14	19	27
8 Texture/Material	1	1	1	3	6	9	11	16
9 Quantity	1	1	1	4	8	9	14	18
10 Time/Sequence	1	1	1	1	1	5	8	11

Note. SRC = School Readiness Composite

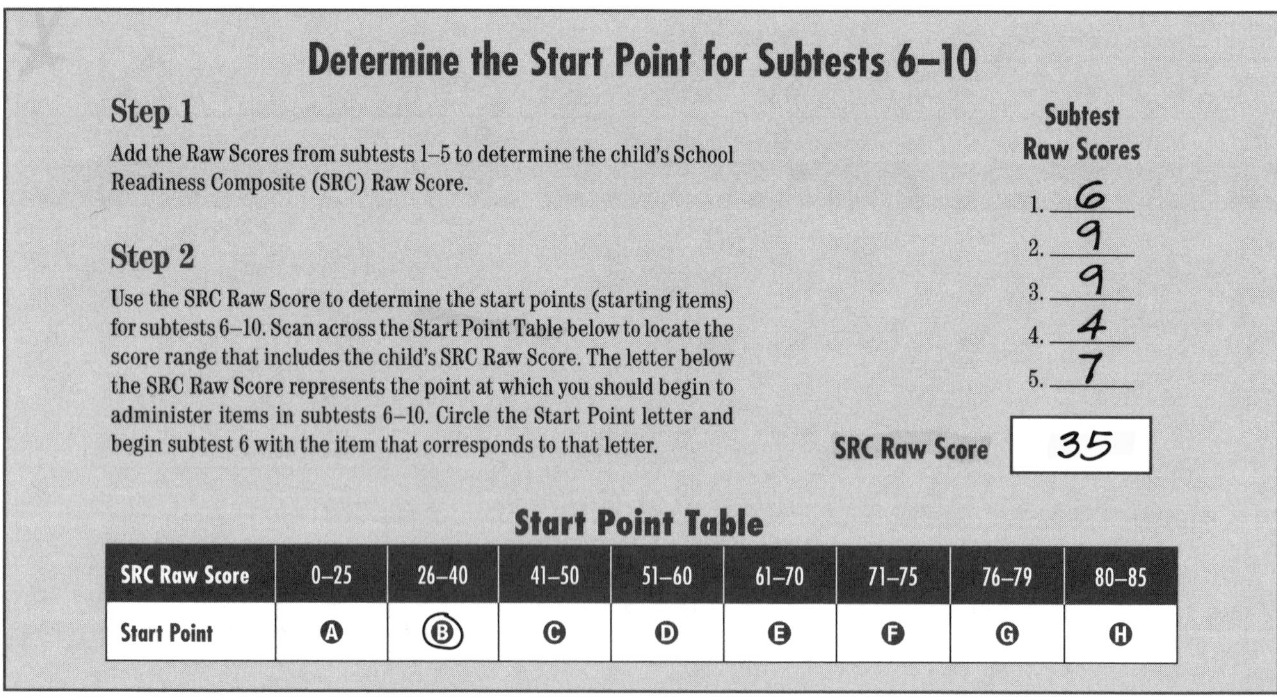

Figure 2.3 Calculating the SRC Raw Score and Determining the Start Point for Subtests 6–10

Once you have determined the start point for subtests 6–10, proceed to subtest 6 and administer the starting item for that subtest. Administer the items in order until the child obtains scores of zero (i.e., incorrect or no response) on three consecutive items (discontinue point) or completes the subtest. After the child has reached the discontinue point or completed the subtest, proceed to the start point of the next subtest.

Clinician's Note: The recommended start points are based on data from the normative sample. In rare cases, the recommended start point may not be optimal for the child you are testing. If after administering the Direction/Position subtest you find that the start point overestimates or underestimates the child's ability (i.e., you needed to test backward or forward to establish a true basal), you may wish to start at an earlier or later point in subsequent subtests.

Establish a Basal

Administer items from the start point forward until you establish a basal. A basal is achieved when the child responds correctly to three consecutive items. If the child does not respond correctly to three items in a row from the start point forward, test backward from the start point until the child does respond correctly to three consecutive items (a basal). Some children will not achieve a basal (i.e., items are administered back to Item 1 without the child responding correctly to three consecutive items). If a child does not establish a basal, you may still convert all earned raw scores into scaled scores.

Establish a Discontinue Point

After you establish a basal (or have administered all items below the start point in an attempt to establish a basal), continue to test forward until you administer all items of the subtest or establish a discontinue point. A discontinue point is achieved when the child obtains scores of zero (i.e., incorrect or no response) on three consecutive items. If the child obtains three consecutive scores of zero prior to reaching a basal, then the discontinue point has been established. In this case, once you have tested backward to establish a basal, you may discontinue the subtest. Keep in mind that some children may not establish a discontinue point (i.e., you may administer the remaining items in the subtest without the child responding incorrectly on three consecutive items).

Calculating Subtest Raw Scores

The child's raw score on subtests 6–10 equals the total number of correct responses before the discontinue point. This means that all items below the basal are counted as correct even though they were not administered. If a discontinue point is determined while establishing a basal, do not include correctly answered items beyond the discontinue point in the calculation of the child's raw score. If neither a basal nor a discontinue point can be established for a subtest (i.e., all subtest items were administered), the child's raw score equals the total number of correct responses (i.e., all items passed).

Examples of Establishing a Basal and a Discontinue Point, and Calculating Subtest Raw Scores

Figures 2.4–2.11 are examples of establishing basals and discontinue points for subtests 6–10. The start point in each example is indicated by the ▶ symbol. Figure 2.4 is an example of beginning subtest 8 at start point F (Item 9) and testing until the basal (three consecutive items correct) and discontinue point (three consecutive scores of zero) are established. The subtest raw score of 14 is calculated by adding the highest basal item number (11) to the number of items answered correctly (3) between that item and the discontinue point item set (Items 16–18). All items not administered preceding the basal are counted as correct.

Subtest 8 **Texture/Material**

Say, **Look at all of the pictures. Show me. . .**

	Item	Response					Score	
Ⓐ Ⓑ Ⓒ								
1.	which shoe is **wet**	1	**2**	3	4	NR	1	0
2.	which one is **heavy**	1	2	3	**4**	NR	1	0
Ⓓ								
3.	which child is making a **loud** noise	**1**	2	3	4	NR	1	0
4.	which paint is **dark**	1	2	3	**4**	NR	1	0
5.	which one is **quiet**	1	2	3	**4**	NR	1	0
Ⓔ								
6.	which one is **soft**	1	**2**	3	4	NR	1	0
7.	which one is made of **wood**	1	**2**	3	4	NR	1	0
8.	which one is **sharp**	1	2	**3**	4	NR	1	0
▶Ⓕ								
9.	which one is **hard**	~~1~~	2	3	4	NR	(1)	0
10.	which one is made of **glass**	1	2	3	~~4~~	NR	(1)	0
Ⓖ								
11.	which one is **shiny**	1	~~2~~	3	4	NR	(1)	0
12.	which crayon is a **light** color	~~1~~	2	3	4	NR	(1)	0
13.	which one is **boiling**	1	2	~~3~~	4	NR	(1)	0
14.	which road is **flat**	~~1~~	2	3	**4**	NR	1	(0)
15.	which light is **bright**	1	2	3	~~4~~	NR	(1)	0
Ⓗ								
16.	which one is a **gas**	1	**2**	~~3~~	4	NR	1	(0)
17.	which one is made of **metal**	~~1~~	**2**	3	4	NR	1	(0)
18.	which cat sees its **reflection**	1	~~2~~	**3**	4	NR	1	(0)
19.	which rock is **smooth**	1	2	3	**4**	NR	1	0
20.	which one is made of **cloth**	1	2	**3**	4	NR	1	0
21.	which one is **rough**	**1**	2	3	4	NR	1	0
22.	which drink is **clear**	1	**2**	3	4	NR	1	0
23.	which one is **dry**	**1**	2	3	4	NR	1	0
24.	which rope is **tight**	**1**	2	3	4	NR	1	0
25.	which rope is **loose**	1	**2**	3	4	NR	1	0
26.	which one is **light**	**1**	2	3	4	NR	1	0
27.	which one is **solid**	1	2	**3**	4	NR	1	0
28.	which knife is **dull**	1	2	**3**	4	NR	1	0
29.	which one is **liquid**	1	2	3	**4**	NR	1	0

Basal (items 9–13)

Discontinue Point (items 16–18)

Raw Score 14

Figure 2.4 Testing Forward to Establish a Basal and a Discontinue Point

Figure 2.5 is an example of beginning subtest 8 at start point F (Item 9) and testing backward to establish a basal because the child obtained a score of zero on the second item administered. After the basal was established, the examiner went back to the highest-numbered item administered (Item 10) and continued testing forward to establish the discontinue point. The subtest raw score of 12 was calculated by adding the highest basal item number (9) to the number of items answered correctly (3) between that item and the discontinue point item set (Items 16–18).

Subtest 8 **Texture/Material**

Say, **Look at all of the pictures. Show me. . .**

Item	Response	Score
A B C		
1. which shoe is **wet**	1 2 3 4 NR	1 0
2. which one is **heavy**	1 2 3 4 NR	1 0
D		
3. which child is making a **loud** noise	1 2 3 4 NR	1 0
4. which paint is **dark**	1 2 3 4 NR	1 0
5. which one is **quiet**	1 2 3 4 NR	1 0
E		
6. which one is **soft**	1 2 3 4 NR	1 0
7. which one is made of **wood**	1 2 3 4 NR	1 0
8. which one is **sharp**	1 2 3 4 NR	1 0
F		
9. which one is **hard**	1 2 3 4 NR	1 0
10. which one is made of **glass**	1 2 3 4 NR	1 0
G		
11. which one is **shiny**	1 2 3 4 NR	1 0
12. which crayon is a **light** color	1 2 3 4 NR	1 0
13. which one is **boiling**	1 2 3 4 NR	1 0
14. which road is **flat**	1 2 3 4 NR	1 0
15. which light is **bright**	1 2 3 4 NR	1 0
H		
16. which one is a **gas**	1 2 3 4 NR	1 0
17. which one is made of **metal**	1 2 3 4 NR	1 0
18. which cat sees its **reflection**	1 2 3 4 NR	1 0
19. which rock is **smooth**	1 2 3 4 NR	1 0
20. which one is made of **cloth**	1 2 3 4 NR	1 0
21. which one is **rough**	1 2 3 4 NR	1 0
22. which drink is **clear**	1 2 3 4 NR	1 0
23. which one is **dry**	1 2 3 4 NR	1 0
24. which rope is **tight**	1 2 3 4 NR	1 0
25. which rope is **loose**	1 2 3 4 NR	1 0
26. which one is **light**	1 2 3 4 NR	1 0
27. which one is **solid**	1 2 3 4 NR	1 0
28. which knife is **dull**	1 2 3 4 NR	1 0
29. which one is **liquid**	1 2 3 4 NR	1 0
	Raw Score	12

Basal

Discontinue Point

Figure 2.5 Testing Backward to Establish a Basal and Then Progressing Forward to Establish a Discontinue Point

Figure 2.6 is an example of beginning subtest 8 at start point G (Item 11) and testing backward to establish a basal because the child obtained a score of zero on the starting item. In the process of establishing a basal, a discontinue point was also established. The subtest raw score of 6 was calculated by adding the highest basal item number (4) to the number of items answered correctly (2) between that item and the discontinue point item set (Items 8–10).

Subtest 8 **Texture/Material**

Say, **Look at all of the pictures. Show me. . .**

Item	Response	Score
A B C		
1. which shoe is **wet**	1 2 3 4 NR	1 0
2. which one is **heavy**	1 2 3 4 NR	1 0
D		
3. which child is making a **loud** noise	1 2 3 4 NR	1 0
4. which paint is **dark**	1 2 3 4 NR	1 0
5. which one is **quiet**	1 2 3 4 NR	1 0
E		
6. which one is **soft**	1 2 3 4 NR	1 0
7. which one is made of **wood**	1 2 3 4 NR	1 0
8. which one is **sharp**	1 2 3 4 NR	1 0
F		
9. which one is **hard**	1 2 3 4 NR	1 0
10. which one is made of **glass**	1 2 3 4 NR	1 0
▶ **G**		
11. which one is **shiny**	1 2 3 4 NR	1 0
12. which crayon is a **light** color	1 2 3 4 NR	1 0
13. which one is **boiling**	1 2 3 4 NR	1 0
14. which road is **flat**	1 2 3 4 NR	1 0
15. which light is **bright**	1 2 3 4 NR	1 0
H		
16. which one is a **gas**	1 2 3 4 NR	1 0
17. which one is made of **metal**	1 2 3 4 NR	1 0
18. which cat sees its **reflection**	1 2 3 4 NR	1 0
19. which rock is **smooth**	1 2 3 4 NR	1 0
20. which one is made of **cloth**	1 2 3 4 NR	1 0
21. which one is **rough**	1 2 3 4 NR	1 0
22. which drink is **clear**	1 2 3 4 NR	1 0
23. which one is **dry**	1 2 3 4 NR	1 0
24. which rope is **tight**	1 2 3 4 NR	1 0
25. which rope is **loose**	1 2 3 4 NR	1 0
26. which one is **light**	1 2 3 4 NR	1 0
27. which one is **solid**	1 2 3 4 NR	1 0
28. which knife is **dull**	1 2 3 4 NR	1 0
29. which one is **liquid**	1 2 3 4 NR	1 0
	Raw Score	6

Basal

Discontinue Point

Figure 2.6 Testing Backward to Establish a Basal and a Discontinue Point

Figure 2.7 is an example of beginning subtest 8 at start point F (Item 9) and testing forward to establish a basal and discontinue point. The subtest raw score of 11 in this case is the highest basal item number (11).

Subtest 8 **Texture/Material**

Say, **Look at all of the pictures. Show me. . .**

	Item	Response					Score	
Ⓐ Ⓑ Ⓒ								
1.	which shoe is **wet**	1	**2**	3	4	NR	1	0
2.	which one is **heavy**	1	2	3	**4**	NR	1	0
Ⓓ								
3.	which child is making a **loud** noise	**1**	2	3	4	NR	1	0
4.	which paint is **dark**	1	2	3	**4**	NR	1	0
5.	which one is **quiet**	1	2	3	**4**	NR	1	0
Ⓔ								
6.	which one is **soft**	1	**2**	3	4	NR	1	0
7.	which one is made of **wood**	1	**2**	3	4	NR	1	0
8.	which one is **sharp**	1	2	**3**	4	NR	1	0
► Ⓕ								
9.	which one is **hard**	~~1~~	2	3	4	NR	(1)	0
10.	which one is made of **glass**	1	2	3	~~4~~	NR	(1)	0
Ⓖ								
11.	which one is **shiny**	1	~~2~~	3	4	NR	(1)	0
12.	which crayon is a **light** color	**1**	2	~~3~~	4	NR	1	(0)
13.	which one is **boiling**	1	~~2~~	**3**	4	NR	1	(0)
14.	which road is **flat**	1	2	~~3~~	**4**	NR	1	(0)
15.	which light is **bright**	1	2	3	**4**	NR	1	0
Ⓗ								
16.	which one is a **gas**	1	**2**	3	4	NR	1	0
17.	which one is made of **metal**	1	**2**	3	4	NR	1	0
18.	which cat sees its **reflection**	1	2	**3**	4	NR	1	0
19.	which rock is **smooth**	1	2	3	**4**	NR	1	0
20.	which one is made of **cloth**	1	2	**3**	4	NR	1	0
21.	which one is **rough**	**1**	2	3	4	NR	1	0
22.	which drink is **clear**	1	**2**	3	4	NR	1	0
23.	which one is **dry**	**1**	2	3	4	NR	1	0
24.	which rope is **tight**	**1**	2	3	4	NR	1	0
25.	which rope is **loose**	1	**2**	3	4	NR	1	0
26.	which one is **light**	**1**	2	3	4	NR	1	0
27.	which one is **solid**	1	2	**3**	4	NR	1	0
28.	which knife is **dull**	1	2	**3**	4	NR	1	0
29.	which one is **liquid**	1	2	3	**4**	NR	1	0
							Raw Score	11

Basal (items 9–11)

Discontinue Point (items 12–14)

Figure 2.7 Establishing a Basal and Discontinue Point

Figure 2.8 is an example of establishing a basal without a discontinue point. The examiner began subtest 8 at start point H (Item 16). The child responded correctly to the first three items administered to establish a basal. The examiner administered items from that point forward, but was unable to establish a discontinue point before the end of the subtest. To calculate the subtest raw score of 24, start with the highest basal item number (18) and add to that number all of the items answered correctly (6) beyond that item.

Subtest 8 **Texture/Material**

Say, **Look at all of the pictures. Show me. . .**

	Item	Response	Score
Ⓐ Ⓑ Ⓒ			
1.	which shoe is **wet**	1 2 3 4 NR	1 0
2.	which one is **heavy**	1 2 3 4 NR	1 0
Ⓓ			
3.	which child is making a **loud** noise	1 2 3 4 NR	1 0
4.	which paint is **dark**	1 2 3 4 NR	1 0
5.	which one is **quiet**	1 2 3 4 NR	1 0
Ⓔ			
6.	which one is **soft**	1 2 3 4 NR	1 0
7.	which one is made of **wood**	1 2 3 4 NR	1 0
8.	which one is **sharp**	1 2 3 4 NR	1 0
Ⓕ			
9.	which one is **hard**	1 2 3 4 NR	1 0
10.	which one is made of **glass**	1 2 3 4 NR	1 0
Ⓖ			
11.	which one is **shiny**	1 2 3 4 NR	1 0
12.	which crayon is a **light** color	1 2 3 4 NR	1 0
13.	which one is **boiling**	1 2 3 4 NR	1 0
14.	which road is **flat**	1 2 3 4 NR	1 0
15.	which light is **bright**	1 2 3 4 NR	1 0
▶Ⓗ			
16.	which one is a **gas**	1 2 3 4 NR	(1) 0
17.	which one is made of **metal**	1 2 3 4 NR	(1) 0
18.	which cat sees its **reflection**	1 2 3 4 NR	(1) 0
19.	which rock is **smooth**	1 2 3 4 NR	(1) 0
20.	which one is made of **cloth**	1 2 3 4 NR	(1) 0
21.	which one is **rough**	1 2 3 4 NR	1 (0)
22.	which drink is **clear**	1 2 3 4 NR	(1) 0
23.	which one is **dry**	1 2 3 4 NR	(1) 0
24.	which rope is **tight**	1 2 3 4 NR	1 (0)
25.	which rope is **loose**	1 2 3 4 NR	1 (0)
26.	which one is **light**	1 2 3 4 NR	(1) 0
27.	which one is **solid**	1 2 3 4 NR	1 (0)
28.	which knife is **dull**	1 2 3 4 NR	(1) 0
29.	which one is **liquid**	1 2 3 4 NR	1 (0)
		Raw Score	24

Basal

Figure 2.8 Establishing a Basal Without a Discontinue Point

Figure 2.9 is an example of establishing a discontinue point without a basal. The examiner began subtest 8 at start point F (Item 9). The child responded correctly on that item, but incorrectly on the next item. The examiner went back to Item 8 and tested backward to establish a basal. The child never obtained three consecutive correct responses and so did not establish a basal. Instead the child responded incorrectly to three items in a row, establishing a discontinue point below the start point. In this case, the subtest raw score of 3 was calculated by adding all the items answered correctly, beginning with Item 1, to the discontinue point item set. Remember, do not give credit for any item beyond the discontinue point (i.e., the child does not receive credit for Item 9 because it is beyond the discontinue point).

Subtest 8 **Texture/Material**

Say, **Look at all of the pictures. Show me. . .**

Item	Response	Score
A B C		
1. which shoe is **wet**	1 2 3 4 NR	1 0
2. which one is **heavy**	1 2 3 4 NR	1 0
D		
3. which child is making a **loud** noise	1 2 3 4 NR	1 0
4. which paint is **dark**	1 2 3 4 NR	1 0
5. which one is **quiet**	1 2 3 4 NR	1 0
E		
6. which one is **soft**	1 2 3 4 NR	1 0
7. which one is made of **wood**	1 2 3 4 NR	1 0
8. which one is **sharp**	1 2 3 4 NR	1 0
▶ **F**		Discontinue Point
9. which one is **hard**	1 2 3 4 NR	1 0
10. which one is made of **glass**	1 2 3 4 NR	1 0
G		
11. which one is **shiny**	1 **2** 3 4 NR	1 0
12. which crayon is a **light** color	**1** 2 3 4 NR	1 0
13. which one is **boiling**	1 2 **3** 4 NR	1 0
14. which road is **flat**	1 2 3 **4** NR	1 0
15. which light is **bright**	1 2 3 4 NR	1 0
H		
16. which one is a **gas**	1 **2** 3 4 NR	1 0
17. which one is made of **metal**	1 **2** 3 4 NR	1 0
18. which cat sees its **reflection**	1 2 **3** 4 NR	1 0
19. which rock is **smooth**	1 2 3 **4** NR	1 0
20. which one is made of **cloth**	1 2 **3** 4 NR	1 0
21. which one is **rough**	**1** 2 3 4 NR	1 0
22. which drink is **clear**	1 **2** 3 4 NR	1 0
23. which one is **dry**	**1** 2 3 4 NR	1 0
24. which rope is **tight**	**1** 2 3 4 NR	1 0
25. which rope is **loose**	1 **2** 3 4 NR	1 0
26. which one is **light**	**1** 2 3 4 NR	1 0
27. which one is **solid**	1 2 **3** 4 NR	1 0
28. which knife is **dull**	1 2 **3** 4 NR	1 0
29. which one is **liquid**	1 2 3 **4** NR	1 0
	Raw Score	3

Figure 2.9 Establishing a Discontinue Point Without a Basal

Figure 2.10 is an example of when no basal and discontinue point are established. The examiner began subtest 8 at start point G (Item 11), but no basal was obtained, even by testing backward to Item 1. The examiner tested forward from the highest administered item (Item 13), but was unable to establish a discontinue point. Because no basal or discontinue point was established for the subtest, the subtest raw score of 16 was computed by adding all of the items answered correctly.

Subtest 8 **Texture/Material**

Say, **Look at all of the pictures. Show me. . .**

	Item	Response	Score
Ⓐ Ⓑ Ⓒ			
1.	which shoe is **wet**	1 2 3 4 NR	1 0
2.	which one is **heavy**	1 2 3 4 NR	1 0
Ⓓ			
3.	which child is making a **loud** noise	1 2 3 4 NR	1 0
4.	which paint is **dark**	1 2 3 4 NR	1 0
5.	which one is **quiet**	1 2 3 4 NR	1 0
Ⓔ			
6.	which one is **soft**	1 2 3 4 NR	1 0
7.	which one is made of **wood**	1 2 3 4 NR	1 0
8.	which one is **sharp**	1 2 3 4 NR	1 0
Ⓕ			
9.	which one is **hard**	1 2 3 4 NR	1 0
10.	which one is made of **glass**	1 2 3 4 NR	1 0
Ⓖ			
11.	which one is **shiny**	1 2 3 4 NR	1 0
12.	which crayon is a **light** color	1 2 3 4 NR	1 0
13.	which one is **boiling**	1 2 3 4 NR	1 0
14.	which road is **flat**	1 2 3 4 NR	1 0
15.	which light is **bright**	1 2 3 4 NR	1 0
Ⓗ			
16.	which one is a **gas**	1 2 3 4 NR	1 0
17.	which one is made of **metal**	1 2 3 4 NR	1 0
18.	which cat sees its **reflection**	1 2 3 4 NR	1 0
19.	which rock is **smooth**	1 2 3 4 NR	1 0
20.	which one is made of **cloth**	1 2 3 4 NR	1 0
21.	which one is **rough**	1 2 3 4 NR	1 0
22.	which drink is **clear**	1 2 3 4 NR	1 0
23.	which one is **dry**	1 2 3 4 NR	1 0
24.	which rope is **tight**	1 2 3 4 NR	1 0
25.	which rope is **loose**	1 2 3 4 NR	1 0
26.	which one is **light**	1 2 3 4 NR	1 0
27.	which one is **solid**	1 2 3 4 NR	1 0
28.	which knife is **dull**	1 2 3 4 NR	1 0
29.	which one is **liquid**	1 2 3 4 NR	1 0
		Raw Score	16

Figure 2.10 No Basal and Discontinue Point Established

Double Discontinue Points

When establishing a basal and discontinue point, it is possible for a child to have more than one discontinue point. The *true* discontinue point is considered to be the earliest or lowest point at which the child responds incorrectly to three items in a row. Due to guessing, it is possible for children to answer items correctly 25% of the time by chance and pass items beyond their true discontinue points. For this reason, correct items beyond the true discontinue point item set should not be counted as correct (i.e., added to the total raw score).

Figure 2.11 is an example of when two discontinue points are established before the basal is established. The examiner began subtest 8 at start point H (Item 16). The child responded incorrectly on the first item, so the examiner tested backward to establish the basal. In the process of establishing the basal, two sets of three consecutive incorrect responses occurred (Items 12–14 and Items 7–9). The lowest discontinue point (Items 7–9) is considered to be the true discontinue point. The subtest raw score of 5 was calculated by adding the highest item number of the basal (Item 4) and the number of items answered correctly (1) between that point and the true discontinue point item set. Do not credit any items correct (e.g., Item 10) after the discontinue point item set (Items 7–9).

Subtest 8 **Texture/Material**

Say, **Look at all of the pictures. Show me. . .**

	Item	Response					Score	
A B C								
1.	which shoe is **wet**	1	**2**	3	4	NR	1	0
2.	which one is **heavy**	1	2	3	**4**	NR	1	0
D								
3.	which child is making a **loud** noise	**1**	2	3	4	NR	1	0
4.	which paint is **dark**	1	2	3	**4**	NR	1	0
5.	which one is **quiet**	1	2	**3**	4	NR	1	0
E								
6.	which one is **soft**	1	**2**	3	4	NR	1	0
7.	which one is made of **wood**	1	**2**	3	4	NR	1	0
8.	which one is **sharp**	1	2	**3**	4	NR	1	0
F								
9.	which one is **hard**	**1**	2	3	4	NR	1	0
10.	which one is made of **glass**	1	2	3	**4**	NR	1	0
G								
11.	which one is **shiny**	1	**2**	3	4	NR	1	0
12.	which crayon is a **light** color	**1**	2	3	4	NR	1	0
13.	which one is **boiling**	1	2	**3**	4	NR	1	0
14.	which road is **flat**	1	2	3	**4**	NR	1	0
15.	which light is **bright**	1	2	3	**4**	NR	1	0
▶ H								
16.	which one is a **gas**	1	**2**	3	4	NR	1	0
17.	which one is made of **metal**	1	**2**	3	4	NR	1	0
18.	which cat sees its **reflection**	1	2	**3**	4	NR	1	0
19.	which rock is **smooth**	1	2	3	**4**	NR	1	0
20.	which one is made of **cloth**	1	2	**3**	4	NR	1	0
21.	which one is **rough**	**1**	2	3	4	NR	1	0
22.	which drink is **clear**	1	**2**	3	4	NR	1	0
23.	which one is **dry**	**1**	2	3	4	NR	1	0
24.	which rope is **tight**	**1**	2	3	4	NR	1	0
25.	which rope is **loose**	1	**2**	3	4	NR	1	0
26.	which one is **light**	**1**	2	3	4	NR	1	0
27.	which one is **solid**	1	2	**3**	4	NR	1	0
28.	which knife is **dull**	1	2	**3**	4	NR	1	0
29.	which one is **liquid**	1	2	3	**4**	NR	1	0
							Raw Score	5

Basal

Discontinue Point

Figure 2.11 Establishing Double Discontinue Points

Other Basal and Discontinue Point Considerations

Basal and discontinue point rules are effective ways to shorten test administration time and to help ensure that a child is not being tested on items of inappropriate difficulty (too easy or too difficult). Although it is unlikely that a child will fail many items below the basal or pass many items beyond the discontinue point, there may be isolated concepts below the basal that are problematic for the child or concepts above the discontinue point that the child has already mastered. It is also possible that, because of the multiple-choice format of the test, a child could correctly guess some items (about one out of four) beyond the discontinue point. Similarly, children occasionally can be expected to correctly guess the meaning of a concept based on limited contextual knowledge, yet not have sufficient knowledge to use the concept appropriately in all instances. Clinicians and teachers should be able to quickly identify these concepts during instruction.

Clinician's Note: Although testing a child on all the items may be useful for diagnostic and prescriptive purposes, scores compared to the norms must always be obtained by strictly following the administration and scoring procedures described in this Manual.

Completing the Score Summary

Use the following steps to complete the Score Summary on page 1 of the Record Form. Refer to Figure 2.12 for an example of a completed Score Summary for a child 4 years, 5 months of age.

Step 1. Recording Raw Scores

School Readiness Composite (SRC): Subtests 1–5

Calculate the School Readiness Composite (SRC) raw score by adding the raw scores for subtests 1–5. Record this sum in *two* places in the Score Summary section—the box provided for the SRC Raw Score in the Subtest section (refer to A in Figure 2.12) and the box provided for the Receptive SRC Raw Score in the Composite section (refer to B in Figure 2.12).

Clinician's Note: The School Readiness Composite (SRC) can be converted to both a subtest scaled score and a composite score. When the SRC is used as a subtest to evaluate a child's skills and converted to a scaled score, it is referred to as the SRC (School Readiness Composite) and contributes equally to the sum of subtest scaled scores used to determine the Receptive Total Composite. When the SRC is considered at the composite level and converted to a composite score, it is referred to as the Receptive SRC (Receptive School Readiness Composite) and serves as an independent measure of the child's understanding of those academic concepts children have traditionally needed to know to be adequately prepared for early formal education.

Subtests 6–10

Record the raw score for each subtest administered in the corresponding Raw Score column in the Subtest section (refer to C in Figure 2.12).

Step 2. Converting the SRC and Subtest Raw Scores to Scaled Scores

Convert the SRC and individual subtest raw scores (subtests 6–10) to norm-referenced scaled scores by locating the age-appropriate Subtest Scaled Score table in Appendix A. Locate the child's raw score for each subtest in the appropriate column and read the corresponding scaled score equivalent to the right or left. Record it in the Scaled Score column of the Score Summary Subtest section on page 1 of the Record Form (refer to D in Figure 2.12).

Step 3. Determining Subtest Scaled Score Confidence Intervals

Obtain a confidence interval for the SRC and subtests 6–10 scaled scores by using the bottom portion of the age-appropriate Subtest Scaled Score table in Appendix A. Select the desired level of confidence (i.e., 90% or 95%) and read across the row to locate the number (referred to as the critical value) of scaled score points used to determine the confidence interval for each subtest. Record the level of confidence at the top of the Scaled Score Confidence Interval column in the Score Summary Subtest section (refer to E in Figure 2.12). Record the critical value in the Scaled Score Points (+/–) column for each subtest. Compute the lower limit of the confidence interval by subtracting the scaled score points from the subtest scaled score, and calculate the upper limit of the confidence interval by adding the scaled score points to the subtest scaled score. Record this score range in the Scaled Score Confidence Interval column (refer to F in Figure 2.12).

Step 4. Determining Subtest Percentile Ranks and Confidence Intervals

Convert the SRC and individual subtest scaled scores to percentile ranks using the same age-appropriate table in Appendix A used to convert raw scores to scaled scores. Locate the child's scaled score in the Scaled Score column and read across to the corresponding percentile rank in the Percentile Rank column. Record this number in the Percentile Rank column (refer to G in Figure 2.12).

Establish a confidence interval around each percentile rank using Appendix A or Appendix E to locate the percentile ranks associated with the lower and upper limits of the confidence interval for each subtest scaled score. Record those percentile ranks in the Percentile Rank Confidence Interval column (refer to H in Figure 2.12).

Step 5. Determining Descriptive Classifications

Determine the descriptive classification for the SRC and subtest scaled scores by using the same table in Appendix A that you used to determine the scaled scores. Locate the child's scaled score in the appropriate column for each subtest and read across the row to find the corresponding descriptive classification (Very Advanced, Advanced, Average, Delayed, or Very Delayed). Record the classification for each subtest in the Descriptive Classification column (refer to I in Figure 2.12).

Step 6. Determining Concept Age Equivalents

Determine concept age equivalents using Appendix D. Locate the child's raw score for the SRC or individual subtests in the appropriate Subtest Raw Score column and read across to the Concept Age Equivalent column which lists age in years and months (i.e., 6:11 is 6 years, 11 months old). That age is the child's concept age equivalent for that particular subtest. Record the age equivalent for each subtest in the Concept Age Equivalent column (refer to J in Figure 2.12).

Clinician's Note: The same numerical score on one subtest will not yield the same concept age equivalent as another subtest. For example, a raw score of 28 on Direction/Position yields a concept age equivalent of 4:5, but a raw score of 28 on Quantity yields a concept age equivalent of 5:11. Similarly, the same scaled score on one subtest will not result in the same age equivalent on other subtests.

Step 7. Determining Composite Scores

The Receptive Total Composite (Receptive TC) and the Receptive School Readiness Composite (Receptive SRC) are determined by different methods. The Receptive TC is derived from the sum of subtest **scaled** scores. In comparison, the Receptive SRC is derived from the sum of subtest **raw** scores.

Receptive Total Composite (Receptive TC)

The Receptive TC serves as the measure of a child's understanding of all foundational and functionally relevant education concepts in ten important concept categories: colors, letters, numbers/counting, sizes/comparisons, shapes, direction/position, self-/social awareness, texture/material, quantity, and time/sequence. To determine the Receptive TC, add the SRC scaled score and subtest scaled scores (6–10). Record this sum in the Sum of Scaled Scores box in the Score Summary (refer to K in Figure 2.12). Use Appendix B to convert the sum to its corresponding composite score. Locate the sum of the scaled scores in the first column (Sum of Scaled Scores) and read across to the Composite Score column to find the corresponding Receptive TC.

Receptive School Readiness Composite (Receptive SRC)

The Receptive SRC serves as an independent measure of the child's understanding of those educationally relevant concepts children traditionally have been expected to know to be prepared for early formal education (i.e., colors, letters, numbers, counting, sizes, comparisons, shapes). To determine the Receptive SRC, refer to the age-appropriate table in Appendix C. Locate the Receptive SRC raw score in the second column and read across to the corresponding Composite Score.

Step 8. Determining Receptive TC Confidence Interval, Percentile Rank, Descriptive Classification, and Concept Age Equivalent

The third and fourth columns of the table in Appendix B provide calculated Receptive TC confidence intervals. Select the desired confidence level (90% or 95%) and record the confidence level and the lower and upper limits of the composite score confidence interval in the Composite Score Confidence Interval (__% Level) column in the Score Summary (refer to L in Figure 2.12). Read across to the Percentile Rank and Descriptive Classification columns to locate the corresponding Receptive TC percentile rank and descriptive classification, respectively. Record the values in the appropriate columns of the Score Summary (refer to M and N in Figure 2.12).

Establish a Receptive TC percentile rank confidence interval using Appendix B or Appendix E. Locate the percentile ranks associated with the lower and upper limits of the composite score confidence interval (i.e., the values recorded in the Composite Score Confidence Interval column) and record the percentile ranks in the Percentile Rank Confidence Interval column (refer to O in Figure 2.12).

Determine the Receptive TC concept age equivalent by adding the raw scores for the SRC and subtests 6–10 and using Appendix D. Locate the child's total test raw score in the Receptive TC Raw Score column and read across to the Concept Age Equivalent column, which lists age in years and months (i.e., 6:11 is 6 years, 11 months old). The age located in the table represents the child's concept age equivalent for the Receptive TC. Record the age equivalent in the Concept Age Equivalent column (refer to P in Figure 2.12).

Step 9. Determining Receptive SRC Confidence Interval, Percentile Rank, and Descriptive Classification

Establish a confidence interval around the Receptive SRC in the same manner that you established confidence intervals for the subtest scaled scores. Use the composite score points for building confidence intervals (located at the end of each table in Appendix C) for the selected confidence level (90% or 95%). Record the level of confidence and the lower and upper limits of the confidence interval in the Composite Score Confidence Interval (__% Level) column (refer to Q in Figure 2.12).

Read across to the third and fourth columns in Appendix C to locate the percentile rank and descriptive classification, respectively. Record the values in the Receptive SRC row of the Score Summary (refer to R and S in Figure 2.12). Establish the Receptive SRC percentile rank confidence interval in the same manner that you established the Receptive TC percentile rank confidence interval (use Appendix C or Appendix E).

Subtest Raw Scores of Zero

It is possible for a child with a raw score of zero to achieve a subtest scaled score. If the child earns a subtest raw score of zero, the resulting scaled score should not be considered an accurate indicator of the child's knowledge in this conceptual domain. Nor does a raw score of zero on any subtest indicate that the child entirely lacks the ability measured by the subtest. It indicates, rather, that the child's ability cannot be accurately determined by that particular set of subtest items. For example, a child may earn a raw score of zero on the Letters subtest, but still be able to correctly identify one of the letters not sampled by the subtest. If a child obtains a raw score of zero on one or two subtests that contribute to a composite score, you can still derive the composite score by using the appropriate norms tables. However, if three or more subtests that contribute to a composite score have raw scores of zero, you cannot derive composite scores because there is insufficient information to determine the child's true conceptual knowledge.

To convert a raw score of zero to a scaled score, the raw score must be an *earned* score of zero. An earned score means that items that were administered were scored zero until the discontinue rule was met. A child who cannot be trained to take the subtest items does not get a raw score of zero on the subtest; rather, it should be noted on the Record Form that the child was unable to be trained in the subtest task, the subtest was discontinued, and a raw score could not be obtained.

Step 10. Plotting Subtest Scaled Scores, Composite Scores, and Confidence Intervals

Both the subtest and composite scores may be plotted on the graphs provided in the Score Profile on page 1 of the Record Form (refer to T in Figure 2.12). Mark an X on the dot that corresponds to each composite score. You can place bars at the upper and lower limits of the confidence interval around each score. Plot the subtest scaled scores in the same manner.

Receptive Record Form

Name Marissa Amonee ☐ M ☒ F

School/Agency Keller Elementary Grade PK

Teacher M. Craig Examiner L. Pease

	Year	Month	Day
Date of Test	06	9	11
Date of Birth	02	4	8
Chronological Age	4	5	3

Score Summary

Subtest	Raw Score	Scaled Score	Scaled Score Points +/-	Scaled Score Confidence Interval (95% Level) [E]	Percentile Rank	Percentile Rank Confidence Interval	Descriptive Classification	Concept Age Equivalent
1–5 SRC [A]	24	6	1	5 to 7	9	5 to 16	Delayed	3:1
6 Direction/ Position	20	8	1	7 to 9	25	16 to 37	Average	3:9
7 Self-/Social Awareness	13 [C]	6 [D]	1	5 to 7 [F]	9 [G]	5 to 16 [H]	Delayed [I]	3:3 [J]
8 Texture/ Material	3	5	2	3 to 7	5	1 to 16	Delayed	<3:0
9 Quantity	5	6	1	5 to 7	9	5 to 16	Delayed	3:0
10 Time/ Sequence	3	6	2	4 to 8	9	2 to 25	Delayed	3:1
Sum of Scaled Scores* [K]		37						

Composite	Raw Score	Composite Score*	Composite Score Points +/-	Composite Score Confidence Interval (95% Level) [L]	Percentile Rank [M]	Percentile Rank Confidence Interval [O]	Descriptive Classification [N]	Concept Age Equivalent [P]
Receptive TC*	68	76		72 to 81 [Q]	5 [R]	3 to 10	Delayed [S]	3:2
Receptive SRC* [B]	24	79	6	73 to 85	8	4 to 16	Delayed	

*Receptive TC based on sum of subtests 1–10 **scaled** scores; Receptive SRC based on sum of subtests 1–5 **raw** scores.

Discrepancy Comparison

	Score 1	Score 2	Difference	Critical Value*	Significant Difference? (Y or N)*	Prevalence in Normative Sample*	Level of Significance
Receptive TC–Expressive TC							.15/.05
Receptive SRC–Expressive SRC							.15/.05

*See Tables 3.4 and 3.5.

Score Profile

Chart columns: Subtest Scaled Scores (SRC (1–5), 6, 7, 8, 9, 10); Descriptive Classification; Composite Scores (Receptive TC, Receptive SRC). Callout [T] is above the subtest columns.

SD	Scaled Score	Descriptive Classification	Composite Score
		Very Advanced	160
		Very Advanced	155
		Very Advanced	150
+3 SD	19	Very Advanced	145
	18	Very Advanced	140
	17	Very Advanced	135
+2 SD	16	Advanced	130
	15	Advanced	125
	14	Advanced	120
+1 SD	13	Average	115
	12	Average	110
	11	Average	105
Mean	10	Average	100
	9	Average	95
	8	Average	90
−1 SD	7	Delayed	85
	6	Delayed	80
	5	Delayed	75
−2 SD	4	Very Delayed	70
	3	Very Delayed	65
	2	Very Delayed	60
−3 SD	1	Very Delayed	55
		Very Delayed	50
		Very Delayed	45
		Very Delayed	40

Figure 2.12 Completed Score Summary

Chapter 3

Interpretation

This chapter provides the information you need to interpret the results of the *Bracken Basic Concept Scale–Third Edition: Receptive* (BBCS–3:R). Directions for interpreting the norm-referenced subtest scores and composite scores are included in this chapter. Methods for determining and describing a child's strengths and weaknesses in basic concept knowledge are also presented.

Description of Scores

BBCS–3:R subtest standard scores are referred to as scaled scores, and the Receptive Total Composite (Receptive TC) and the Receptive School Readiness Composite (Receptive SRC) standard scores are referred to as composite scores. Subtests 1–5 are combined to derive the School Readiness Composite (SRC). The SRC is reported as a scaled score and as a composite score (Receptive SRC). Both scaled scores and composite scores are standard scores that have been placed on specific scales; a scale with a range of 1–19 for scaled scores and a scale with a range of 40–160 for composite scores. Both types of scores provide normative information about the child.

Subtest Scaled Scores

BBCS–3:R subtest scaled scores provide measures of a child's understanding of basic concepts in different categories (e.g., direction/position, time/sequence). Subtest scaled scores are normative scores used specifically to compare the child's test performance to the performances of children of the same-age peer group. These scores are derived from the subtest raw scores and are converted to a score scale with a mean (*M*) of 10, a standard deviation (*SD*) of 3, and a score range of 1–19. A scaled score of 10 corresponds to the average performance of children within a given age group. Scaled scores of 7 and 13 are 1 *SD* below and above the mean, respectively. Approximately two-thirds of children of a given age group obtain scaled scores between 7 and 13, which is considered the range of average performance. The relationship between BBCS–3:R subtest scaled scores, distances from the mean, and percentile ranks, in terms of standard deviation units are illustrated in Table 3.1. Use the tables in Appendix A to convert each subtest raw score to its corresponding scaled score.

Table 3.1 Distance From the Mean of Subtest Scaled Scores

Scaled Score	Distance From Mean	Percentile Rank
19	+3 *SD*	99.9
16	+2 *SD*	98
13	+1 *SD*	84
10	Mean	50
7	–1 *SD*	16
4	–2 *SD*	2
1	–3 *SD*	0.1

SRC Scaled and Receptive SRC Composite Scores

The School Readiness Composite (SRC) is composed of subtests 1–5 and represents conceptual knowledge that is closely aligned with early childhood experiences and curricula (i.e., colors, letters, numbers/counting, sizes/comparisons, and shapes). As such, the SRC is a good descriptor of children's school-related concept development and a good indicator of the academic preparation a child has received prior to beginning formal schooling. That is, it is more common for children who have attended preschool programs or who have parents who have systematically exposed their children to rudimentary educational concepts to demonstrate advanced concept development on the SRC. Similarly, children who have not attended preschool programs and whose parents have not taught these concepts to them are more likely to score in the average to delayed ranges of concept development (Breen, 1984; Sterner and McCallum, 1988; Zucker and Riordan, 1990).

Because the School Readiness Composite may be reported as either a scaled score (SRC) or as a composite score (Receptive SRC), you may use whichever score scale is most useful for you to describe the child's skills normatively. For example, you may choose to report the scaled score when scaled scores are reported from other BBCS–3:R subtests or subtests on other instruments that the child has been administered (e.g., *Wechsler Preschool and Primary Scales of Intelligence®–Third Edition* [WPPSI–III; Wechsler, 2002] Receptive Vocabulary subtest). You may choose to report the child's composite score when you want to compare it to his or her composite or index score on other instruments (e.g., *Preschool Language Scale–Fourth Edition* [PLS–4; Zimmerman, Steiner, and Pond, 2002] Total Language Score). Scaled scores are distributed across a narrower scale range of 1–19. SRC scaled scores between 7 and 13 represent average development, scores of 13 and above represent advanced development, and scores of 7 and below indicate delayed development. Composite scores are distributed across a wider scale range of 40–160; this allows for more precise measurement of a child's abilities. For this reason, the Receptive SRC is the recommended score. Receptive SRC composite scores that range between 85 and 115 (± 1 *SD*) represent average development, scores of 115 and above represent advanced development, and scores of 85 and below indicate delayed development.

Subtests 1–5 are combined and treated collectively as the School Readiness Composite (SRC) for several reasons. First, the first five subtests collectively represent the "readiness" concepts that parents and preschool/kindergarten programs have traditionally taught children in preparation for formal education. Second, this grouping is more psychometrically sound as a total entity than any of the individual subtests that are included within it because there are more items combined to form the SRC than are represented in any one subtest. Combining the items across the first five subtests provides a more even distribution of raw scores than the individual subtest distributions. Although the SRC should not be interpreted as a compilation of all the concepts necessary for a child's success in school, the SRC has been shown to predict school success and school readiness (Panter, 1997).

Subtests 6–10 assess conceptual content that parents frequently do not teach to their children in a systematic manner; each subtest assesses from 29–62 concepts. Although these latter subtests vary somewhat in their respective technical qualities, each subtest is reliable across the age range and is very well-suited for individual normative interpretation.

Receptive Total Composite (Receptive TC) Score

BBCS–3:R includes a Receptive Total Composite (Receptive TC) score that provides information about a child's overall conceptual development as assessed receptively. The Receptive TC score is formed by summing the scaled scores of the SRC and remaining subtests (6–10) and converting the sum to a composite score using the table in Appendix B. Receptive TC scores are norm-referenced and enable you to compare a given child's performance to the performances of other children in the same age group. BBCS–3:R composite scores are based on a scale with a mean (*M*) of 100 and a standard deviation (*SD*) of 15. A score of 100 on this scale represents the average performance for children within a given age group. Figure 3.1 shows the relationship between the BBCS–3:R composite scores and a normal distribution of scores. Scores of 85 and 115 correspond to 1 *SD* below and above the mean, respectively. Given the nature of a normal distribution of scores, approximately two-thirds of children in a given age group obtain a BBCS–3:R composite score in this range, which is considered the range of average performance for that age group. Table 3.2 shows the relationship between composite scores, distances from the mean, and percentile ranks, as expressed in standard deviation units.

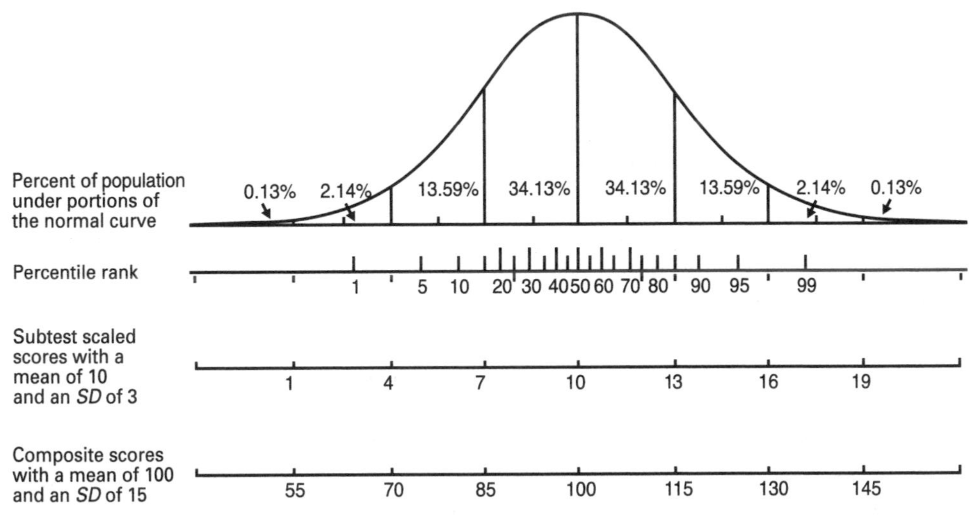

Figure 3.1 Normal Curve With BBCS–3:R Scaled and Composite Scores and Percentile Ranks Indicated

Table 3.2 Distance From the Mean of Composite Scores

Composite Score	Distance From Mean	Percentile Rank
145	+3 *SD*	99.9
130	+2 *SD*	98
115	+1 *SD*	84
100	Mean	50
85	−1 *SD*	16
70	−2 *SD*	2
55	−3 *SD*	0.1

Using Confidence Intervals to Reflect Confidence in Obtained Scores

Even in highly reliable tests such as the BBCS–3:R, there is some degree of error reflected in the score a child obtains on the test. If a test were perfectly reliable (without any measurement error) and if children could be counted on to respond in a perfectly reliable manner, a child would always obtain the same score if given the test repeatedly. This hypothetically perfect score is called a *true* score and represents what the child's true ability would be under perfect conditions. Because no test is perfectly reliable and children's behavior is not perfectly consistent, the true score is expected to be within a range of scores that reflects the expected amount of measurement error at given probability levels.

When interpreting BBCS–3:R scores, it is important to consider the amount of measurement error present within the test at different age levels. Because measurement error is randomly distributed, the mean of any hypothetical error distribution is equal to zero. The standard error of measurement (*SEM*) is the standard deviation of such an error distribution and represents the amount of measurement error variability that exists for a test in standard score units. The more reliable the test, the smaller the *SEM*; the smaller the *SEM*, the more confidence you can have in the obtained test score, and the narrower the confidence interval built around the obtained score.

The standard error of measurement for BBCS–3:R scaled and composite scores can be used to construct confidence intervals (or ranges) around a child's obtained scores. Such confidence intervals provide a range of scores that likely contain the hypothetical true score within some predetermined level of probability (e.g., 90% confidence). Presenting parents or teachers with confidence intervals, rather than focusing on a single score, enables you to state the degree of confidence that you have in the range of scores that may be used to contribute to a classification, eligibility, or placement decision based on BBCS–3:R results. Therefore, reporting a confidence interval around a child's score is particularly important in cases where the score will contribute to classification or placement decisions. Each subtest and composite score is subject to a greater or lesser degree of measurement error, depending on the precision of the particular subtest score or composite score for a given age. In general, the BBCS–3:R scaled and composite scores are very reliable and produce small confidence intervals, even at high levels of probability, enabling examiners to have considerable confidence in the decisions they make based on BBCS–3:R results.

Because the *SEM* is based on the internal consistency reliability of each subtest or composite, the *SEM* is likely to differ across each subtest or Receptive SRC score and across all age levels. The resulting confidence intervals will also differ for each subtest across the age levels.

The reliability for the Receptive TC, however, is similar across ages, and the *SEM* is similar across ages as well. The resulting confidence intervals are nearly identical, so the normative data are presented in one table based on overall ages. For clinical utility, Receptive TC confidence intervals for the 90% and 95% levels of confidence have been calculated for you in Appendix B (refer to Figure 3.2).

The values used to construct confidence intervals are in scaled score points for the 90% and 95% levels of confidence for each subtest and are in the lower portion of each table in Appendix A. The greater confidence that you wish to apply to a score range, the greater the value and the greater the range of scores around the obtained score will be. Establishing confidence intervals around BBCS–3:R scores and using that information ensures greater reliability when you are interpreting scores.

Figure 3.2 includes three illustrations: a portion of Appendix A, showing the values for confidence interval construction (for each subtest) in scaled score points; a portion of Appendix B, showing the calculated confidence intervals; and a portion of Appendix C, showing the value in standard score points listed at the end of each table.

Confidence intervals span only the possible score range for subtest scales (i.e., the possible scaled score range is 1–19). For example, if a child 4 years, 6 months of age obtains a Direction/Position scaled score of 1 and the ± points (critical value) for building the confidence interval at 95% is ± 1, the confidence interval is 1 to 2. The minimum obtainable score in the range is 1, and it is not possible to obtain a score below 1. However, confidence interval ranges for composite scores are derived from specified confidence interval values and do not have a restricted range (i.e., scores range from 40–160). If the same child obtains a Receptive TC score of 41, the 95% confidence interval is 38 to 46. The confidence interval score range is not restricted to the range of standard scores (40–160).

You should select the level of confidence that is most appropriate for the purpose of the assessment. The 95% level results in a broader band of scores and provides you with the highest degree of confidence that the true score is actually in the range specified. Both 90% and 95% levels are commonly used by decision-making teams to inform diagnostic decisions that are intended to determine service provision and eligibility.

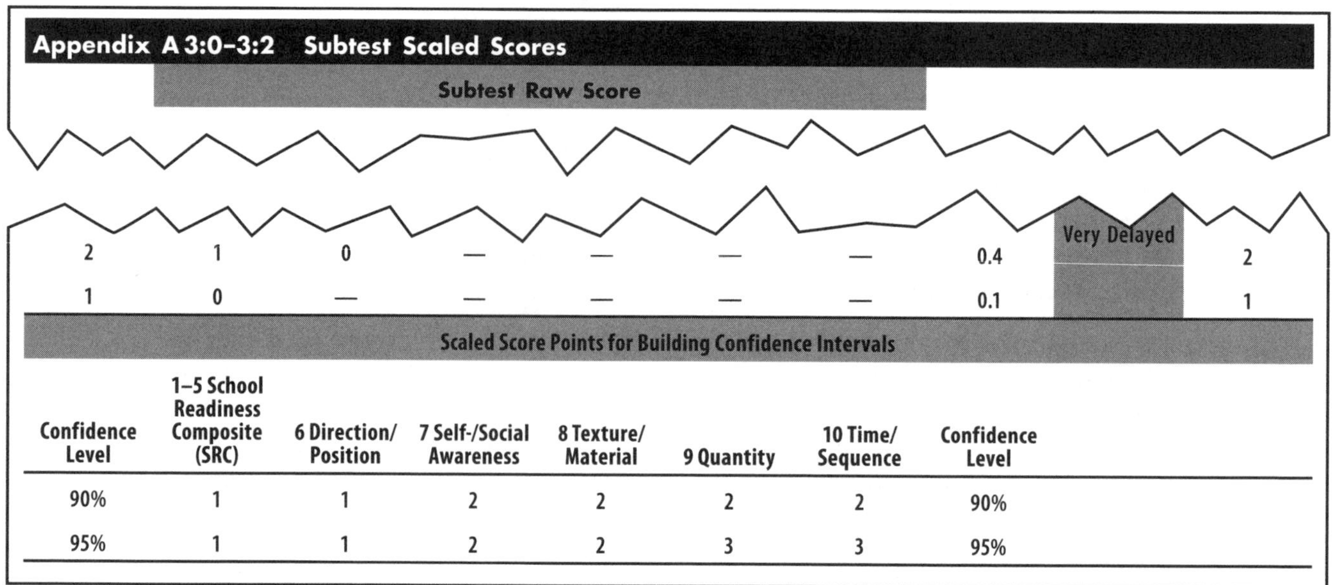

Appendix A 3:0–3:2 Subtest Scaled Scores

Subtest Raw Score

2	1	0	—	—	—	—	0.4	Very Delayed	2
1	0	—	—	—	—	—	0.1		1

Scaled Score Points for Building Confidence Intervals

Confidence Level	1–5 School Readiness Composite (SRC)	6 Direction/ Position	7 Self-/Social Awareness	8 Texture/ Material	9 Quantity	10 Time/ Sequence	Confidence Level
90%	1	1	2	2	2	2	90%
95%	1	1	2	2	3	3	95%

Appendix B Receptive Total Composite Scores

Sum of Scaled Scores	Composite Score	Confidence Interval 90%	Confidence Interval 95%	Percentile Rank	Descriptive Classification
61	101	98–104	97–105	53	Average
62	102	99–105	98–106	55	
63	103	100–106	99–107	58	
64	104	101–107	100–108	61	
65	105	101–108	101–109	63	
66	106	102–109	102–110	66	
67	107	103–110	103–111	68	
68	108	104–111	104–112	70	
69	109	105–112	105–113	73	
70	110	106–113	106–114	75	
71	112	108–115	108–116	79	
72	113	109–116	109–117	81	
73	114	110–117	110–118	82	
74	115	111–118	111–119	84	Advanced
75	116	112–119	112–120	86	
76	117	113–120	113–121	87	
77	118	114–121	114–122	88	
78	119	115–122	115–123	90	
79	120	116–123	116–124	91	

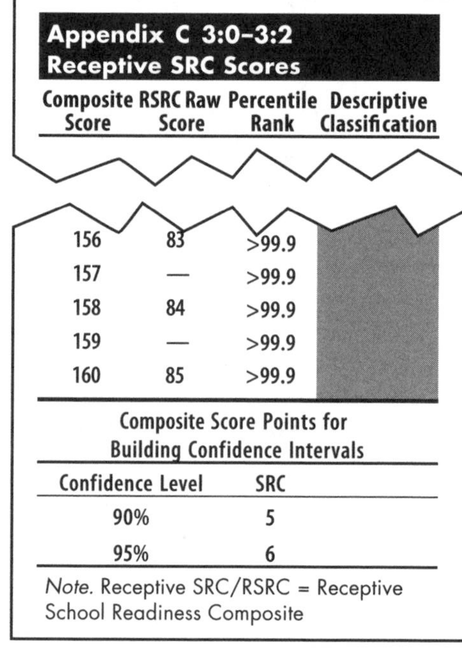

Appendix C 3:0–3:2 Receptive SRC Scores

Composite Score	RSRC Raw Score	Percentile Rank	Descriptive Classification
156	83	>99.9	
157	—	>99.9	
158	84	>99.9	
159	—	>99.9	
160	85	>99.9	

Composite Score Points for Building Confidence Intervals

Confidence Level	SRC
90%	5
95%	6

Note. Receptive SRC/RSRC = Receptive School Readiness Composite

Figure 3.2 **Critical Values in Standard Score Points Used to Build Confidence Intervals at 90% and 95% Levels of Confidence (Appendix A and Appendix C) and Calculated Confidence Intervals (Appendix B)**

Percentile Ranks

BBCS–3:R provides age-based percentile ranks for scaled and composite scores. Percentile ranks represent the child's test performance relative to test performances of children in the normative sample. For example, a percentile rank of 60 would mean that the child earned a score that was equal to or greater than 60% of children in the normative sample. Percentile ranks should not be confused with the percent of items answered correctly on a test. Figure 3.1 displays the percentile ranks associated with standard scores in a normal distribution. BBCS–3:R percentile ranks range from ≤ 0.1 to ≥ 99.9, with 50 as the percentile rank associated with the mean score. Percentile ranks are easier for parents and teachers to understand and can be especially useful for explaining a child's performance on BBCS–3:R. For example, parents are much more likely to understand that their child performed as well as or better than 25% of children of the same age in the BBCS–3:R normative sample than they are to understand that the child earned a Receptive TC of 90. A percentile rank of 25 also can be useful to illustrate that 75% of the children in the normative sample earned higher scores on the BBCS–3:R than the child under consideration.

Percentile ranks are not distributed in equal intervals as are standard scores, and they tend to cluster around the mean—the 50th percentile. Consequently, for a child within the average range of concept understanding, a change of 1 or 2 standard score points may produce a large change in his or her respective percentile rank. Conversely, for a child who earns a very low or very high standard score on a BBCS–3:R subtest, a change of 1 or 2 standard score points is likely to produce only a small change in his or her percentile rank. Appendix A and Appendix E present percentile ranks that correspond to selected subtest scaled scores and their respective distances from the mean, expressed in standard deviation units. Similarly, Appendix B, Appendix C, and Appendix E present percentile ranks that correspond to selected Receptive TC and Receptive SRC scores.

You can also establish a confidence interval around a percentile rank. Determine the percentile rank confidence interval by recording the percentile ranks associated with the lower and upper limits of the child's subtest scaled score or composite score confidence interval. For example, a child who is 4 years, 1 month of age and obtains a Texture/Material scaled score of 5 would have a confidence interval of 4 to 6 (i.e., ± 1) at the 90% level of confidence. The percentile rank corresponding to a subtest scaled score of 5 is 5, and the percentile ranks corresponding to a scaled score of 4 (lower limit of the 90% confidence interval) and 6 (upper limit of the 90% confidence interval) are 2 and 9, respectively. Therefore, the percentile rank of a subtest scaled score of 5 is 5 and the 90% confidence interval around the percentile rank of 5 is percentile rank 2 to percentile rank 9.

Concept Age Equivalents

Concept age equivalents are provided for BBCS–3:R SRC, subtests 6–10, and Receptive TC raw scores. Concept age equivalents represent the median raw score for children of given ages, indicated in years and months typical for a given raw score. For example, a raw score of 28 on the Quantity subtest converts to an age equivalent of 5 years, 11 months. Although concept age equivalents may be useful for describing a child's language skills in comparison to typical functioning for children of various ages, there are psychometric limitations to their use and interpretation.

Limitation 1

Concept age equivalents do not reflect a child's relative rank or standing within a group of age peers, and therefore lack the precise information that within-group norms provide about rank within an age range. You can make judgments about a child's relative standing only by using standard scores or percentile ranks (Lawrence, 1992; McCauley and Swisher, 1984; Wiig and Secord, 1992).

Limitation 2

Small raw score changes may sometimes result in large changes in concept age equivalents. Large differences between concept age equivalents and a child's chronological age may be obtained, but interpreting the child's language skills as being far below or far above average for his or her age may be unwarranted because the range of average scores may overlap across several adjacent age groups. For example, Noelle and Laura are both 5 years, 7 months old and were administered the Texture/Material subtest. Noelle earned a total raw score of 11 and an age equivalent of 3 years, 10 months. Laura earned a total raw score of 14 and an age equivalent of 4 years, 5 months. This does not mean that Laura's skills are 7 months more advanced than Noelle's. In fact, Noelle's and Laura's scaled scores are 9 and 10 respectively, both in the average range compared with their peers.

Limitation 3

Concept age equivalents may not be comparable across subtests (e.g., a child's percentile ranks for two subtests with the same concept age equivalent may differ substantially). For example, a child age 5 years, 2 months can obtain an age equivalent of 4 years, 10 months on both the Self-/Social Awareness subtest and the Time/Sequence subtest; however, the respective percentile ranks for these subtests are 50 and 37.

Limitation 4

A concept age equivalent that is much lower or much higher than the child's chronological age does not signify that the child's concept development level resembles that of children much younger or much older in every way. In addition, concept age equivalents at the most extreme ends of the age range are particularly difficult to interpret because they may only be reported as being less than 3 years, 0 months (< 3:0) or greater than 6 years, 11 months (> 6:11). You have no way of knowing how far below or above these extreme concept age equivalents the child's actual level of functioning might best be described.

By considering the limitations cited previously and using caution, concept age equivalents can still provide you with a helpful developmental picture of the child's current level of concept development to share with parents. However, because of the limitations associated with age equivalents, it is recommended that you use scaled scores, composite scores, or percentile ranks to compare a child's performance on the BBCS–3:R to other children of the same age. Diagnostic decisions should be made from a review of the child's standard scores and other background and qualitative information such as language samples, interviews with the child's primary caregiver/teacher, and observations of the child in different language contexts. Placement decisions or diagnoses should never be based on concept age equivalents only or for that matter on any one type of score.

BBCS–3:R concept age equivalents for SRC and subtests 6–10 raw scores, and the Receptive TC raw score are presented in Appendix D. To determine the age equivalent, locate the raw score in the specific subtest column and scan to the Concept Age Equivalent. To determine the Receptive TC concept age equivalent, locate the child's Receptive TC Raw Score and scan to the Concept Age Equivalent. See chapter 5 for a discussion of the development of BBCS–3:R concept age equivalents.

Calculating Percent Delay From a Concept Age Equivalent

Some states and agencies require quantitative criteria for placing preschool children in special services and provide examiners with the option of expressing delay as a percent of chronological age. Calculating *percent delay* is most often done by dividing the age at which an obtained raw score is the median (i.e., the concept age equivalent) by the child's chronological age and subtracting the resulting percentage from 100. Thus, a child who is 4 years, 5 months (53 months) old with a concept age equivalent of 3 years, 5 months (41 months) would be performing at 77% of "normal" ability or considered to have a 23% delay. Because state guidelines frequently specify a 25% delay as the criterion for receiving special services, a child with a 23% delay would not be recommended for services without information from other sources (e.g., parents, teachers), even if the child had significant deficits in basic concept skills. Due to the limitations inherent in using concept age equivalents, it is recommended that examiners generally avoid using percent delay to qualify children for services, and instead use standard scores or percentile ranks.

Subtest and Composite Profiles

There are several ways to consider subtest and composite scores obtained on the BBCS–3:R. The Score Profile section of the Record Form provides a graphical display of the child's performance to help you visualize the child's conceptual strengths and weaknesses within concept categories as compared to his or her age group (i.e., normative comparison). To build the conceptual profile, plot each of the child's scaled and composite scores in the appropriate Score Profile columns. Place bars at the upper and lower limits of the confidence interval around each score (refer to Figure 3.3). Scaled scores for individual subtests that are one or more standard deviations below the mean indicate areas of normative conceptual weakness while subtest scaled scores one or more standard deviations above the mean indicate areas of normative strength.

Score Profile

	Subtest Scaled Scores (SRC (1–5), 6, 7, 8, 9, 10)	Descriptive Classification	Composite Scores (Receptive TC, Receptive SRC)
		Very Advanced	160
			155
			150
+3 *SD*	19		145
	18		140
	17		135
+2 *SD*	16		130
	15	Advanced	125
	14		120
+1 *SD*	13		115
	12	Average	110
	11		105
Mean	10		100
	9		95
	8		90
−1 *SD*	7		85
	6	Delayed	80
	5		75
−2 *SD*	4		70
	3	Very Delayed	65
	2		60
−3 *SD*	1		55
			50
			45
			40

Figure 3.3 BBCS-3:R Score Profile

Descriptive Classification

In addition to plotting a child's scores to create subtest and composite profiles, you can describe the rate of a child's conceptual development as being average or within degrees of advanced development (i.e., Advanced, Very Advanced) or delayed development (i.e., Delayed, Very Delayed) by using the qualitative descriptive classifications. These informative and descriptive classifications enable you to communicate rates of development to parents and teachers in broad terms without emphasizing less easily understood measurement descriptors (e.g., standard scores, percentile ranks).

Table 3.3 presents the BBCS–3:R descriptive classifications for varying levels of conceptual development for the subtest and composite scores. The degree of developmental advance or delay is based on the normal distribution and the number of standard deviations above or below the mean that the child's score is located on the normal curve. Average or normal levels of concept development include all scores within one standard deviation above or below the mean. Scores that are one or more standard deviations above the mean represent advanced levels of development and scores one or more standard deviations below the mean represent delayed development.

Table 3.3 Descriptive Classifications

Standard Score	Scaled Score	Conceptual Development
130 and above	16–19	Very Advanced
115–129	13–15	Advanced
86–114	8–12	Average
71–85	5–7	Delayed
70 and below	1–4	Very Delayed

Discrepancy Comparison

Determining Discrepancy Comparisons Between BBCS–3:R and BBCS:E Composite Scores

The BBCS–3:R assesses a child's basic concept development using a receptive test administration format. Its counterpart BBCS:E assesses a child's basic concept development using an expressive testing format. When you administer both tests, you can use the Discrepancy Comparison section on page 1 of the Record Form to help you determine if a child has a concept deficit that is generalized across receptive and expressive skills, or if the deficit is primarily a receptive or an expressive deficit.

To complete the Discrepancy Comparison, first determine which scores you want to compare—Receptive Total Composite (Receptive TC)/Expressive Total Composite (Expressive TC) or Receptive School Readiness Composite (Receptive SRC)/Expressive School Readiness Composite (Expressive SRC). Compare the Receptive and Expressive TC scores when you want to determine the difference between the child's overall receptive and expressive basic concept development. Compare the Receptive and Expressive SRC scores when you want to determine the difference between the child's receptive and expressive knowledge of school readiness concepts.

Once you have determined which scores you want to compare, write the corresponding scores in the Score 1 and Score 2 columns of the Discrepancy Comparison section. Subtract Score 2 from Score 1. Write the difference in the Difference column, remembering to note whether the resulting value is positive or negative. Table 3.4 provides the required differences between composite scores needed for statistical significance (critical values) at the .15 and .05 level for each age. Choose the level of significance you wish to use, and circle that level in the Level of Significance column in the Discrepancy Comparison section. Find the appropriate age in Table 3.4 and the selected level of significance. Read across to the appropriate column and write the number in the Critical Value column. The difference score for each composite must be equal to or greater than the critical value to be statistically significant. Record a Y for Yes in the Significant Difference? column if the difference score is equal to or greater than the critical value. Record an N for No if the difference is less than the corresponding critical value (refer to Figure 3.4).

For all significant differences, Table 3.5 provides the percentage of children in the Descriptive sample who obtained the same or greater discrepancy between composite scores (Prevalence in Normative Sample). The values reported in Table 3.5 are separated into – and + columns, based on the directions of the difference. Locate the absolute value of the child's difference score in the Amount of Discrepancy column to the extreme right or left, and read across the row to the column that corresponds to the direction of the difference score. Enter this value in the Prevalence in Normative Sample column of the Discrepancy Comparison section of the Record Form (refer to Figure 3.4).

Discrepancy Comparison

	Score 1	Score 2	Difference	Critical Value*	Significant Difference? (Y or N)*	Prevalence in Normative Sample*	Level of Significance
Receptive TC–Expressive TC	87	80	7	6	Y	21.4	(.15)/.05
Receptive SRC–Expressive SRC	76	81	-5	4	N	–	.15/.05

*See Tables 3.4 and 3.5.

Figure 3.4 Completed Discrepancy Comparison

Interpreting Differences in Composite Scores

Once you have completed the Discrepancy Comparison section, you may analyze and interpret the test results. The Record Form provides a table to assist in the evaluation of composite score differences between the receptive and expressive tests. Mean differences between selected composite scores (i.e., Receptive TC and Expressive TC; Receptive SRC and Expressive SRC) were calculated and compared for children in the normative sample, and patterns of differences were very consistent across all of the children in the sample. For example, 93.9% of the normative sample had a difference of at least one standard score point between the Receptive TC and Expressive TC. Approximately 56% of the normative sample had a difference of five points or greater between the two scores, and 8.6% had a 15-point or greater difference between the scores; of these, 4.8% had a 15-point or greater difference, with the Receptive TC score greater than the Expressive TC score, and 3.8% had a 15-point or greater difference, with Expressive TC score greater than the Receptive TC score. Similarly, 95.4% of the normative sample had a difference of at least one standard score point between the Receptive SRC and Expressive SRC scores. Approximately 54% of the normative sample had a difference of five points or greater between the two scores, and 10.6% had a 15-point or greater difference between the scores; of these, 5.3% had a 15-point or greater difference, with the Receptive SRC score greater than the Expressive SRC score, and 5.3% had a 15-point or greater difference, with the Expressive SRC score greater than the Receptive SRC score. You can expect most of the children to whom you administer BBCS–3:R and BBCS:E to exhibit some difference between these two sets of composite scores. Table 3.4 will help determine if the difference is statistically significant (i.e., not a chance occurrence). Table 3.5 will help determine if the difference in scores occurs frequently in the normative sample.

Determining if the difference between two scores (Receptive TC and Expressive TC; Receptive SRC and Expressive SRC) is a meaningful difference rather than a difference due to measurement error or chance requires that you analyze the composite scores using the procedure that follows.

Comparing the Composite Scores

Comparing composite scores is a two-step process. The first step is to determine if the difference between the two obtained composite scores is statistically significant. Determining whether the difference between scores is statistically significant is a hypothesis testing process. Using either alpha level (level of significance) .15 or .05 will affect the statistical power (i.e., the sensitivity) and risk level of your hypothesis testing. In the majority of instances, using alpha level .15 will usually increase the power of the test (i.e., the sensitivity). Table 3.4 shows critical values required for statistical significance at the .15 and .05 probability levels by age. When the difference between two scores is equal to or greater than the critical value listed in Table 3.4, the difference can be considered statistically significant and the difference is considered to truly exist (i.e., the difference reflects a true difference in abilities and did not occur as a result of chance fluctuations). To evaluate composite score differences, complete the Discrepancy Comparisons table on page 1 of the Record Form.

If there is a significant difference between the composite scores, the second step is to evaluate how rare the score difference is in the general population. You can determine how frequent or rare the score difference is by determining how prevalent the score difference was in the normative sample. Table 3.5 reports the prevalence of composite score differences between the BBCS–3:R and BBCS:E in the normative sample. The less often that the obtained difference occurs in the normative sample, the greater the likelihood that the difference meaningfully reflects the child's educational development and is a strength or weakness in that skill area.

In the BBCS–3:R and BBCS:E normative sample, the patterns of score differences across ages were consistent. Only 6.1% of the sample showed no difference between Receptive TC and Expressive TC scores, 46.7% of the children earned a higher Receptive TC score, and 47.2% earned a higher Expressive TC score. Similarly, 4.6% of the sample showed no difference between the Receptive SRC and Expressive SRC scores, 47.7% of the children earned a higher Receptive SRC score, and 47.7% earned a higher Expressive SRC score. The larger the difference between any two scores, the smaller the percentage of children who obtained it. For a more detailed description of score discrepancies in the normative sample, see chapter 7.

Follow these steps to determine how frequent or rare the score difference is in the normative sample.

Compare the score difference to the prevalence of score differences reported in Table 3.5. The table shows score differences (discrepancies) required for statistical significance between the following composite score pairs:

1. Receptive TC and Expressive TC; and
2. Receptive SRC and Expressive SRC.

Differences between scores are compared in both directions for each composite pair (i.e., the Receptive TC is less than the Expressive TC and the Receptive TC is greater than the Expressive TC). The first column in Table 3.5 lists the number of standard score points (1 to ≥ 40) that could differ (i.e., amount of discrepancy) between composite scores. The second and third columns list the percentages of the children in the normative sample who obtained the differences between the Receptive TC and the Expressive TC (Receptive TC < Expressive TC [Receptive TC is less than Expressive TC] and Receptive TC > Expressive TC [Receptive TC is greater than Expressive TC]). To determine the percentage of the normative sample that obtained particular score point differences, look for the score point difference (calculated in step 2) in the Amount of Discrepancy column and then find the corresponding percentage in either the Receptive TC < Expressive TC column or the Receptive TC > Expressive TC columns. For example, if a child earned a score of 97 on the Receptive TC and a score of 78 on the Expressive TC, the difference between the two scores is 19 points (97–78 = 19). Look up that amount (i.e., 19) in the Amount of Discrepancy column, and then read across the row to the Receptive TC > Expressive TC column to see that 1.7% of the normative sample had a discrepancy of 19 or more points between their two scores (Receptive TC is greater than Expressive TC). Differences obtained by 5% or less of the normative sample should be considered rare.

If the difference between the two scores is not significantly different and the difference is common in the normative sample, the difference observed may be due to measurement error or chance. Another explanation is that a significant difference was not detected at the current alpha level (level of significance), but may have been detected at a less conservative level (e.g., if alpha level is changed from .05 to .15).

Table 3.4 Differences Between Composite Scores Required for Statistical Significance

Age	Level of Significance	Composite Pair: Receptive TC–Expressive TC	Composite Pair: Receptive SRC–Expressive SRC
3:0–3:2	.15	5	6
	.05	7	8
3:3–3:5	.15	5	6
	.05	7	8
3:6–3:8	.15	5	6
	.05	7	8
3:9–3:11	.15	5	6
	.05	7	8
4:0–4:2	.15	4	6
	.05	5	8
4:3–4:5	.15	4	6
	.05	5	8
4:6–4:8	.15	4	6
	.05	6	8
4:9–4:11	.15	4	6
	.05	6	8
5:0–5:2	.15	4	5
	.05	6	7
5:3–5:5	.15	4	5
	.05	6	7
5:6–5:8	.15	4	6
	.05	6	8
5:9–5:11	.15	4	6
	.05	6	8
6:0–6:2	.15	5	9
	.05	7	12
6:3–6:5	.15	5	9
	.05	7	12
6:6–6:8	.15	6	11
	.05	9	15
6:9–6:11	.15	6	11
	.05	9	15
Overall	.15	5	7
	.05	7	10

Note. Receptive TC = Receptive Total Composite, Expressive TC = Expressive Total Composite, Receptive SRC = Receptive School Readiness Composite, Expressive SRC = Expressive School Readiness Composite

Table 3.5 Prevalence of Differences Between Composite Scores in the Normative Sample

Amount of Discrepancy (points)	Receptive TC – Expressive TC: Receptive TC < Expressive TC (–)	Receptive TC – Expressive TC: Receptive TC > Expressive TC (+)	Receptive SRC – Expressive SRC: Receptive SRC < Expressive SRC (–)	Receptive SRC – Expressive SRC: Receptive SRC > Expressive SRC (+)	Amount of Discrepancy (points)
≥40	0.2	0.0	0.0	0.0	≥40
39	0.2	0.0	0.0	0.0	39
38	0.2	0.0	0.0	0.0	38
37	0.2	0.0	0.0	0.0	37
36	0.3	0.0	0.2	0.0	36
35	0.3	0.2	0.3	0.0	35
34	0.3	0.3	0.3	0.0	34
33	0.3	0.5	0.3	0.0	33
32	0.3	0.5	0.3	0.0	32
31	0.3	0.5	0.3	0.5	31
30	0.3	0.5	0.6	0.5	30
29	0.3	0.5	0.8	0.5	29
28	0.3	0.6	0.8	0.5	28
27	0.3	0.6	1.1	0.5	27
26	0.5	0.6	1.1	0.6	26
25	0.5	0.8	1.4	0.8	25
24	0.6	0.9	1.4	0.9	24
23	0.8	0.9	1.4	1.3	23
22	1.1	1.4	1.4	1.4	22
21	1.3	1.4	1.6	1.9	21
20	1.4	1.6	1.9	2.0	20
19	1.6	1.7	2.0	2.0	19
18	2.2	2.3	3.0	2.5	18
17	2.7	3.4	3.3	3.3	17
16	3.3	4.2	4.4	4.1	16
15	3.8	4.8	5.3	5.3	15
14	4.4	5.9	5.8	6.3	14
13	6.1	6.9	7.3	7.2	13
12	8.3	8.1	8.8	9.5	12
11	10.0	10.0	10.2	11.4	11
10	12.2	12.7	11.6	13.4	10
9	15.0	15.6	13.6	16.3	9
8	17.8	18.1	16.4	18.8	8
7	21.1	20.8	19.1	21.4	7
6	24.7	24.1	23.6	23.8	6
5	28.4	28.1	27.0	27.2	5
4	32.7	32.0	31.6	33.1	4
3	37.8	36.7	37.3	38.6	3
2	42.7	42.2	42.2	42.2	2
1	47.2	46.7	47.7	47.7	1
Mean	7.0	7.2	7.0	7.2	Mean
SD	5.5	5.8	6.1	5.8	*SD*
Median	6.0	6.0	5.0	5.0	Median

Note. Receptive TC = Receptive Total Composite, Expressive TC = Expressive Total Composite, Receptive SRC = Receptive School Readiness Composite, Expressive SRC = Expressive School Readiness Composite

Additional Normative Interpretation Considerations

Interpreting composite scores is a task of determining degree of conceptual understanding, and comparing that degree to the local school context. Because composite scores constitute a range from 40 to 160, children at different points along this continuum might be expected to perform relatively better or less well than other children with lower or higher scores, respectively. Children with scores in the Advanced range of concept development (scores of 115 and above) might be expected to perform well in a typical or average American school. Children who achieve scores in the Average range are likely to perform adequately or better in a typical or average school program. Children who perform well below the average range (scores of 77 or below; Delayed or Very Delayed) may be expected to perform less well in a typical school setting and may be in need of enrichment programs or special educational services.

With children who score in the Delayed conceptual range (i.e., scores of 85 to 78) on the composites, the choice of what to do next is less clear. Children who score in the Delayed or Very Delayed range on the composites should be evaluated further for possible educational, cognitive, or language disorders. Given the complex interaction between assessed intelligence, achievement, and language functioning, you should seek additional information to rule out any of the common reasons for the child's delayed performance (e.g., lack of prior exposure to academic or conceptual content, language delay, central auditory processing disorder, limited English proficiency, hearing loss). To facilitate communication of the child's performance on the BBCS–3:R to parents and teachers, complete the reproducible Parent/Teacher Conference Form in Appendix F. The form will assist you in developing an Individualized Education Plan (IEP), goals, and objectives; consulting and collaborating with classroom teachers to plan instruction; and guiding parents to focus on specific concepts to teach in the home setting.

Curriculum-Based Assessment

The BBCS–3:R is linked instructionally with the *Bracken Concept Development Program* (BCDP). The BBCS–3:R and BCDP can be used together in a curriculum-based assessment paradigm, with the BBCS–3:R constituting the assessment instrument and the BCDP the curriculum. In curriculum-based assessment, it is important that the curriculum and test collectively define the scope and sequence of development, assessment, and instruction. Items on the BBCS–3:R sample the universe of content associated with each subtest's respective content domain. Items are arranged predominantly according to *p*-values (percent correct for all ages), and therefore are hierarchically arranged for instruction by difficulty level. The BCDP provides specific lessons and materials for individual, small group, and large group instruction of the vast majority of concepts assessed by the BBCS–3:R. Refer to Appendix I or go to www.Brackeninfo.net for a sample lesson from the BCDP.

To use the BBCS–3:R and BCDP in curriculum-based assessment, the clinician or teacher should follow these guidelines:

1. After administering and scoring the BBCS–3:R, the clinician or teacher should identify all items below the subtest basal as concepts that most likely have been mastered. All items above the subtest discontinue point should be identified as items that are probably not mastered. Items between a subtest basal and discontinue point represent concepts that the child would likely know in some familiar settings and instances, but not all. Use Appendix F to mark each item as M (Mastered), or NM (Not Mastered). The *Bracken Scoring Assistant* (Bracken, 2006) is a tool that enables you to quickly score and maintain the child's list of concepts mastered and not mastered.

2. Best practice suggests that instruction begin at a level where the child can experience 80% success with instruction. In keeping with best practice, the clinician or teacher should locate the lessons corresponding to the concepts within the BCDP that are associated with the child's basal to provide him or her with a successful start in intervention. Proceed to the items beyond the basal at a rate comfortable for you and the child, based upon your clinical/educational judgment. Lessons and activities related to targeted instructional items should be implemented from the BCDP with enthusiasm and variety until the clinician or teacher believes the child has mastered that subset of concepts. If the child is able to correctly complete the respective items on the BCDP worksheet, mastery is assumed, and the concepts next in the hierarchy can be targeted for instruction and intertwined with the review of recently mastered concepts. If the child fails to demonstrate mastery of the targeted concepts, further instruction is warranted.

3. Instruction should continue in this manner, being guided by the arrangement of items on the BBCS–3:R subtests and matching concepts to the instructional lessons and activities in the BCDP. After the period of time specified in the child's instructional program (e.g., IEP), the BBCS–3:R should be readministered to assess the child's conceptual growth since the last administration.

The BBCS–3:R should continue to guide instruction, with the BCDP providing the activities and lessons, until all of the BBCS–3:R/BCDP concepts have been mastered. BCDP worksheets should be used intermittently to assess the child's short-term progress, while the BBCS–3:R can be used to assess longer-term progress.

Individualized Education Plans (IEPs)

According to the requirements of the Individuals with Disabilities Education Act (IDEA, 1997), those children identified as exceptional must have IEPs developed that will provide guidance for remediation and reevaluation of deficient areas. A child who is deficient in conceptual knowledge may qualify for speech-language therapy or other special education services under the act and would require an IEP to guide remediation. By using the BBCS–3:R for assessment and the BCDP for remedial or instructional purposes, the clinician or teacher can easily link these tools to the child's educational program by identifying and stating: 1) the child's present educational performance; 2) measurable annual goals, including benchmarks or short-term objectives; 3) the special education and related services to be provided; and 4) how the child's progress will be measured and monitored—as required by the law.

To develop behavioral objectives for concept acquisition, the child must be evaluated initially to determine the concepts that he or she does and does not know. Then, in appropriate behavioral terms, a statement is generated that indicates that as a result of conceptual instruction using the BCDP lessons and materials, the child will demonstrate knowledge of the concepts cited in the IEP. Success in concept instruction is then easily measured and documented when the next evaluation is conducted. IDEA requires that IEPs be reviewed at least once per calendar year, if not more often. The BBCS–3:R and the BCDP worksheets are excellent means by which to assess the goals set forth in children's IEPs.

General Guidelines for Instruction and Remediation

Following is a list of 19 principles that should be incorporated into instructional lessons designed to teach basic concepts to young children. These principles are addressed more fully in the BCDP.

Principle 1. Language, examples, materials, and procedures used to teach concepts should be less complex than the concepts being taught.

Because basic concepts are foundational elements of language and communication, it is often difficult to teach these terms without using more advanced synonyms or examples. However, it is important that the basic concept being taught is presented in its simplest terms.

Principle 2. When concepts occur in pairs (e.g., *up-down*) or in series (e.g., *first-second-third-fourth*), maximize the meaningfulness of each concept by teaching all relevant concepts during the same lesson.

It is often easier to teach a concept by using opposite "nonexamples" of that concept. For example, because children learn *hot* very early in their lives, related concepts (e.g., *cold*, *warm*, *cool*) can be taught by contrasting temperatures with what is known to be *hot*.

Principle 3. As much as possible, teach simple concepts, conceptual pairs, and series by using mnemonic strategies that facilitate understanding and enhance memory.

A mnemonic strategy is an intentional "hook" that is attached to information to facilitate it being recalled later. For example, many people remember when America was discovered because of the familiar mnemonic "In fourteen hundred and ninety-two, Columbus sailed the ocean blue." The BCDP uses mnemonics to introduce and teach every concept included in the program.

Principle 4. Concept generalization should be taught initially by instruction with obvious examples of the concept and proceed to less obvious examples.

This instructional format should be followed with cases in which nonexamples are used to teach concept discrimination. Nonexamples should range initially from the apparent to relative nuances in later lessons. When teaching children the concept *dog* the teacher would highlight the salient characteristics of the concept (i.e., wet nose, four legs, wagging tail, barking), and then contrast obvious examples of dogs (e.g., Golden Retrievers, Collies) with obvious nonexamples (e.g., fish, ducks). When the child can effectively discriminate clear examples from nonexamples, the examples and nonexamples should become less obvious. For example, mastiffs and Chihuahuas are less obvious examples of the concept *dog*; cat, raccoon, and fox are less obvious nonexamples of the concept.

Principle 5. Identify the characteristics that define the concept, distinguish which single dimension or group of characteristics are most salient, and provide instruction that initially emphasizes the most important characteristics, while minimizing the less important or irrelevant dimensions.

For example, the single-most important characteristic that is salient to the concept *sister* is female gender. This is the characteristic that is most useful for broad comparisons; more subtle comparisons would employ other less salient characteristics.

Principle 6. Instruction of polar concepts or concepts on a continuum should begin with the positive pole concept.

The positive pole concept is the concept that embodies "more" of the salient characteristics of the concept than the negative pole concept. For example, *loud* has more decibels than *quiet*; *thick* includes more weight or size than *thin*; *hot* features more British Thermal Units (BTUs) than *cold*; and *light* has more lumens than *dark*. Children naturally learn positive pole concepts before negative pole concepts (Bracken, 1988).

Principle 7. Concept pairs should be taught so that children identify positive examples as being the concept and negative examples (nonexamples) as not being the concept (e.g., an object can be *tall* or *not tall*).

Principle 8. Once the positive pole concept is accurately described as the concept or not the concept, the child can be taught initially that when it is not the concept, it is the negative pole concept (e.g., if it is *not tall*, it is *short*).

Principle 9. When both polar concepts are learned, continue to display the logic that if it is not the positive concept, then it is the negative concept and if it is not the negative concept, then it is the positive concept (e.g., if it is *not tall*, it is *short*; if it is *not short*, then it is *tall*).

Principle 10. Considering the sequence in which concepts are acquired, continually teach and assess to ensure that concept instruction is at the appropriate level.

Be sensitive to and assess the level of knowledge the child possesses about each concept being taught. The stages of a child's developing conceptual knowledge include:

1. no understanding of the concept, conceptually or linguistically
2. a vague understanding of some of the attributes associated with the concept
3. partial knowledge of a specific concept or conceptual dichotomy (e.g., *hot/cold*)
4. a behavioral indication of conceptual knowledge (e.g., the child takes the pile with *more* candy when given the choice of two piles of candy)
5. using the positive pole concept exclusively
6. overextending the positive pole concept (e.g., the child says *long* when he means *short*)
7. confusing the positive pole concept in place of the negative pole concept (e.g., the child shakes his or her head negatively and says *more* when he or she doesn't want any)
8. understanding the concept, but not in all settings or under all conditions
9. using the concept correctly in most situations
10. using a more advanced synonym in place of the basic concept

Principle 11. Along with school instruction, provide parents with a list of concepts and helpful suggestions as to how concepts can best be taught at home.

Both the BCDP and Appendix F of the BBCS–3:R enable you to provide parents information about which concepts the child has mastered, and the BCDP provides methods by which they can teach their children concepts that have not yet been mastered.

Principle 12. Conceptual lessons should elicit active participation and allow for multisensory instructional presentations.

Children learn more when they have something to look at while listening to instructions (i.e., auditory + visual stimuli), and they learn even more when they can manipulate materials that are related to the clinician's or teacher's instructions (i.e., auditory + visual + tactile stimuli).

Principle 13. Allow for overlearning in concept instruction by incorporating previously learned concepts in the lessons designed to teach new concepts.

Overlearning is achieved when the child demonstrates mastery of the concept, but instruction continues to include the acquired concept in future instructional lessons.

Principle 14. Concept instructional sessions should be kept appropriately brief.

Young children's short attention spans are best suited for brief, active, fast-paced lessons. Several such lessons a day are more conducive to acquiring concepts than a single long session.

Principle 15. To ensure overlearning of concepts, allow for an adequate review of previously learned concepts before proceeding to new concepts.

Principle 16. Begin instructional sessions at a level that ensures success.

Maintain an instructional difficulty level that guarantees continued success. Instruction of BBCS–3:R concepts should begin at the child's basal level; that is, the latest point at which the child was consistently successful. Instruction should proceed through the items where the child had partial success into the items where the child consistently failed to demonstrate mastery.

Principle 17. Structure instructional sessions so that each has an identifiable beginning and ending, and objectives that are clear.

In addition to brief lessons, young children benefit most when lessons begin with a clear opening (e.g., exposure to a mnemonic), and they are told exactly what they will be doing. Also, because young children typically feel a strong need for "closure," lessons should have clearly identifiable conclusions — preferably with a physical product to show for their efforts.

Principle 18. Concepts should be taught in familiar situations in order to facilitate generalization.

Principle 19. To ensure a thorough understanding of basic concepts as instruction progresses, sessions should include conceptual combinations that are more complex than the instruction of single concepts.

For example, after teaching the concepts of color, shape, and size, the teacher should combine these concepts into instructions such as, "Show me the *small, red, square* block."

Early Childhood Educational Standards and the BBCS–3:R and BBCS:E

Development of current early childhood educational standards has resulted from the personal efforts of individual educators and the coordinated efforts of researchers and educators across national and state levels. This chapter begins with a conceptualization of basic concepts as the foundation of early childhood knowledge (Bracken, 1998a), leading to the current adoption of basic concepts in educational settings across and within each of the 50 states. Appendix G provides a matrix of early childhood educational standards across the 50 United States, and how each of the conceptual categories and the majority of the items included in the *Bracken Basic Concept Scale–Third Edition: Receptive*, *Bracken Basic Concept Scale–Expressive*, and the *Bracken Concept Development Program* (BCDP; Bracken, 1986a) align to those standards. The chapter concludes with a table which serves as a guide to the convergence of early childhood standards across the United States. The table identifies content and conceptual categories of importance, sub-domains of knowledge within these categories, and examples of specific concepts illustrating the content of these foundational categories and sub-domains.

Independent Standards Efforts: The BBCS

When the *Bracken Basic Concept Scale* (BBCS; Bracken, 1984) was first conceived, it was the author's belief that there were some largely unspoken, yet agreed upon, concept-based content standards in early childhood education. While researching conceptual content during the development of the BBCS, the author discovered citations and sources that referred to the universality of many individual basic concepts and concept categories. For example, Berlin and Kay (1969) identified eleven foundational and primary colors as basic color terms used in all languages and cultures.

Among these categories of concepts, some concepts seemed to be more frequently taught intentionally to children by their parents than other concepts prior to the children's enrollment in school. These intentionally taught "school readiness" concepts included colors, letters, numbers, shapes, sizes, and comparison concepts, which were grouped together on the BBCS as the School Readiness Composite (SRC) and later on the *Bracken School Readiness Assessment* (BSRA; Bracken, 2002) as a separate instrument. These readiness concepts have been shown to be sound predictors of early childhood academic success (Panter and Bracken, 2000).

In addition to the concepts assessed in the SRC and BSRA, it was also noted that there were additional categories of concepts that parents generally did not explicitly teach their children (e.g., texture/material, social/emotional, time/sequence), resulting in children enrolling in school with little conceptual knowledge in these important areas. In addition to not knowing all of the important concepts to teach or conceptual categories to cover, conceptual instruction has been confounded further because parents tend not to be well informed of the principles that guide conceptual instruction (Bracken, 1986, 1998b).

Parents and teachers who understand the value of conceptual instruction typically have identified individual concepts or small collections of concepts within the various conceptual categories to teach to their children, but they frequently omit other concepts of equal or even greater importance. For example, in the conceptual category of time/sequence, teachers frequently capitalize on the use of daily classroom schedules and teach concepts such as *morning*, *late*, *first*, *second*, and *third* through related circle time and calendar activities (e.g., asking about what the child did in the *morning* before coming to school; having the child recount what he or she did *last night/late* in the *evening*; reviewing the day's schedule for what activities will occur *first*, *second*, and *third* during the day), but many other time/sequence concepts are missed for instruction because they are not as easily linked to holidays, seasons, regular events, or educational experiences (e.g., *arrive – leave*, *before – after*). Consequently, children learn these latter concepts largely through informal language experiences and by listening to parent or teacher conversations, and not as a result of direct instruction.

The goal during BBCS development was to identify a thorough collection of basic language concepts for parents and teachers to systematically and comprehensively teach to young children. As such, the BBCS stands as one of the first efforts to set informal early childhood instructional standards. To facilitate the instruction of these important and foundational concepts, a unique, curriculum-linked Parent/Teacher Conference Form was provided for parents and teachers as part of every BBCS assessment. This form identified each of the 258 concepts assessed on the BBCS and noted whether the child had mastered or not mastered each concept. Parents and teachers were encouraged to use this information to guide conceptual instruction in the home and classroom, and to promote a systematic, graduated approach to concept instruction.

The 1986 publication of the BCDP provided a curricular link between a comprehensive assessment of children's basic concept knowledge and the potential for direct follow-up instruction of basic concepts. It presented parents and teachers with 19 principles for teaching basic concepts to young children. These guiding instructional principles were derived from the educational and psychological literature and were intended to illustrate empirically-based approaches and techniques for teaching young children about basic concepts. At that point in time, the BBCS and the BCDP essentially had established informal early childhood conceptual standards for assessment and instruction, employing a curriculum-based model. The BBCS was revised in 1998, and the basic concepts identified and assessed on the test were expanded to 308.

Organization Standards

Scott-Little, Kagan, and Frelow (2003) published a research report on behalf of the Southeastern Regional Vision for Education (SERVE) entitled *Standards for Preschool Children's Learning and Development: Who has standards, How were they developed, and How are they used*? This study explored the impetus for the establishment of state standards, which included calling for accountability in education, the "widespread growth of early childhood programs in the late 1990s," and the mounting concern about the "growing divide between the poor and non-poor" (p. 2). The authors cited the efforts of the National Education Goals Panel (NEGP, 1989) to define what *ready to learn* means, concluding that school readiness embodies five principal domains: 1) physical well-being and motor development, 2) social and emotional development, 3) cognition and general knowledge, 4) approaches to learning, and 5) language and communication (Kagan, Moore, and Bredekamp, 1995). This report laid the foundation for the content categories considered by states and early childhood professional organizations that were later developed into early childhood standards.

The National Association for the Education of Young Children (NAEYC) also has been a leader in the development of standards for early childhood education. In 2003, the NAEYC and the National Association of Early Childhood Specialists in State Departments of Education (NAECS/SDE) published a position statement describing the process for establishing standards for early childhood education. This process led the way to the development of curriculum standards for the accreditation of early childhood programs; the organization approved the curriculum standards draft two years later (NAEYC, 2003). In addition to an omnibus collection of 14 standards addressing the integrity of curriculum framework, philosophy, experiences, aesthetics, and daily schedule, the NAEYC standards address several broad curricular categories. These curricular categories overlap with the conceptual categories on the BBCS–3:R and BBCS:E, and include: 1) Social-Emotional Development; 2) Language Development; 3) Literacy Development; 4) Early Mathematics; 5) Scientific Inquiry and Knowledge; 6) Understanding Ourselves, Our Communities, and Our World; 7) Creative Expression and Appreciation for the Arts; and, 8) Physical Development and Skills.

While the NAEYC categories are intended to address more than children's conceptual development (e.g., artistic expression, motion and movement), the foundation for each of these categories is conceptual. For example, Standard 2.15 (Social-Emotional Development) addresses the issue of recognizing one's own and others' feelings. The BBCS–3:R and BBCS:E Self-/Social Awareness subtests address basic feelings and emotion concepts, including *happy, sad, healthy,* and *sick.* Similarly, the NAEYC Early Literacy Development category standards recognize the importance of young children's familiarity with print (Standard 2.31) and the necessity of being able to identify letters and the sounds that letters make as important content standards (Standard 2.35). The BBCS–3:R Letters subtest includes the identification of both upper-case and lower-case letters. The BBCS:E Letters/Sounds subtest assesses individual letter sounds and the sounds that initial consonant blends make. As a final example, the NAEYC Scientific Inquiry and Knowledge and Early Mathematics categories include many concepts from BBCS–3:R and BBCS:E Numbers/Counting, Sizes/Comparisons, Quantity, and Texture/Material subtests. In fact, concepts from all of the BBCS–3:R and BBCS:E subtests are included in the eight basic curricular categories identified in the NAEYC 2004 draft standards.

Governmental Influence

The National Governors Association (2004) published a policy position statement advocating the development of state standards for grades K–12 in the belief that state standards would help ensure that students would receive a uniformly strong, foundational education. Special concern was communicated in the position paper about identifying and closing the gap between more-advantaged students and 'at-risk' students, including minority students and students in poverty.

The most recent presidential administration introduced the early childhood *Good Start, Grow Smart* initiative, emphasizing the importance of cognitive development in youth from birth through age five. The initiative highlights the importance of early childhood letter recognition, as well as other pre-literacy skills and concepts assessed on the BBCS–3:R and BBCS:E. For example, the initiative's report states that a child's knowledge of the alphabet in kindergarten is a substantial predictor of that child's tenth-grade reading ability. Using the *Good Start, Grow Smart* initiative, the federal government employed a downward extension of the *No Child Left Behind* legislation (P. L. 107-110; No Child Left Behind Act, 2002), introducing accountability in education for early childhood and setting the stage for educational standards to guide and standardize instruction during preschool and the primary grades.

Current Practices

At this point a majority of states have early childhood standards or are in the process of developing standards (e.g., Alaska). Review of these early childhood educational state standards reveals the groundwork laid by the BBCS, as well as NAEYC, the SERVE research report, and the early childhood initiatives of the White House and the National Governors Association. In an effort to explore both the common and disparate elements of the states' standards, Bracken and Crawford (2006) conducted a comprehensive review of each state's early childhood educational standards and compared the standards with content (i.e., concepts) assessed on the BBCS–3:R and BBCS:E and taught in the BCDP. Appendix G consolidates these standards to render the language more systematic and consistent across states. The standards are also arranged and presented in a manner consistent with the ten conceptual categories assessed by the BBCS–3:R and BBCS:E.

Examination of Appendix G illustrates that states' standards cite conceptual knowledge from each of the ten BBCS–3:R and BBCS:E categories (i.e., subtests). The standards reported in Appendix G are generally for pre-kindergarten, kindergarten, and first grade. Some states may not include all grade levels or may have collapsed grade levels. It is also generally the case that the same collection of concepts is cited within a specific state's standards across the three grade levels; however, deeper levels of knowledge are expected of children across grade levels. For example, in the area of pre-literacy, pre-kindergarten children might be expected to recognize the letters in their name; kindergarten children might be expected to recognize all upper-case letters; and first grade children might be expected to recognize and name both upper-case and lower-case letters, as well as be able to produce the sounds that correspond to letters. Appendix G provides a consolidation of states' standards and does not specify when a deeper level of knowledge of a concept is warranted for children at different grade levels. For each state's specific standards, go to each state's State Department of Education website.

States' Standards and the BBCS–3:R and BBCS:E

When considering the states' early childhood standards and the BBCS–3:R and BBCS:E conceptual content, a pattern of commonality and universality emerges between the two sources. A second pattern also emerges, illustrating that the BBCS–3:R and BBCS:E content meets or exceeds states' standards.

BBCS–3:R and BBCS:E Categories

In this section, the range of knowledge expected of children in pre-kindergarten, kindergarten, and first grade will be compared across the various states' standards and with the concepts assessed on the BBCS–3:R and BBCS:E. This comparison of different states' standards to the BBCS–3:R and BBCS:E conceptual content will be conducted using the BBCS–3:R and BBCS:E subtest organization.

Colors

Colors are described as primary, secondary, or tertiary, and often are learned by young children in that order. Primary colors are *red*, *yellow*, and *blue*. The colors are considered primary in that no combination of colors is blended to produce those colors. Secondary colors are colors that result from the blending of two primary colors. For example, yellow and blue, when combined, create green. *Orange*, *green*, and *purple* are secondary colors. When primary colors are blended with secondary colors, tertiary colors are created, which vary depending on the proportions of each color added to the mixture (e.g., blue and green combined form the tertiary colors *blue-green*, *aquamarine* or *teal*, depending on the proportions of blue and green added).

In addition to primary, secondary, and tertiary colors, there are the additional 'colors' of *white* and *black*, referred to as absolutes. From a materials perspective, white is the combination of all colors and black is the absence of any color pigmentation. As such, white and black are contributors to the lightening or darkening of primary or secondary colors by degree of addition to the color mixture.

Primary and secondary colors, in addition to white and black, make up the universal colors for all people with normal color vision, and may serve as the educational basis for standards in color recognition and naming. This combination of colors (i.e., primary, secondary, white and black) is the collection of color concepts assessed on the BBCS–3:R and BBCS:E.

When considering the various states' standards summarized in Appendix G, most indicate that young children should be able to describe objects in terms of color, with a few states specifically naming which colors should be known by children. For example, Virginia standards include red, orange, yellow, green, blue, purple, white, violet, brown, and black—all of which are items included in the BBCS–3:R and BBCS:E Colors subtest, except the tertiary color *violet*.

Letters/Sounds

Recognizing and naming the 26 letters of the alphabet appear to be the foundation upon which pre-literacy skills are developed. Difficulty levels achieved for the BBCS–3:R and BBCS:E items during the norming process demonstrate that children generally recognize upper-case (i.e., capital) letters before they recognize lower-case letters; name upper-case before lower-case letters; and finally, produce the individual letter and consonant blend sounds. Most state standards generally follow this sequence. For example, Georgia standards state that children should be able to identify some individual letters of the alphabet (pre-kindergarten); recognize and name all upper-case and lower-case letters (kindergarten); generate the sounds for all letters and letter patterns, and apply knowledge of letter-sound correspondence to decode new words (first grade). In alignment with the states' standards, the BBCS–3:R systematically assesses whether children can identify a random sample of upper-case letters, followed by lower-case letters.

The BBCS:E Letters/Sounds subtest extends the assessment to determine if the child can name a random sample of upper-case letters, followed by a random sample of lower-case letters, and then produce the sound made by a sample of lower-case letters (e.g., *m*, *z*, *b*). Finally, the Letters/Sounds subtest assesses whether the child can produce the sounds made by a sample of initial consonant blends (e.g., *gr*, *ch*, *sw*). As such, the BBCS–3:R and BBCS:E include assessment of all of the letters/sounds that pre-literacy standards cited across the states and extends the standards further to include important phonemic awareness skills and abilities (i.e., letter and initial consonant blend sounds).

Numbers/Counting

States' standards in the domain of counting, number recognition, and number naming are generally as, or more, comprehensive than the case for letter recognition and letter naming. As with pre-literacy skills, pre-math and early-math skills have a predictable developmental progression (Baroody and Ginsburg, 1991). Early on, young children develop a sense of quantity (e.g., *more/less*) and the ability to rote count without a one-to-one number/object correspondence. Later, young children learn to recognize numbers 1–5, followed by 6–9 and zero, and then double-digit numbers. Along the way, young children begin to count to 10 with one-to-one correspondence, and quickly progress to counting to numbers greater than 100. Later still, young children learn to count by twos, fives, and tens.

States' standards generally follow this sequence. Likewise, the BBCS–3:R and BBCS:E follows this sequence quite closely, with item content that assesses a child's number recognition and naming of numerals from 0 through 9, as well as recognition and naming of double digit and triple digit numbers. The Numbers/Counting subtest also assesses a child's ability to count with one-to-one correspondence. The BBCS–3:R and BBCS:E Quantity subtests assess a diverse collection of additional quantitative concepts, which will be discussed later in this chapter.

Sizes/Comparisons

Sizes and comparative knowledge about size can be thought of in a number of ways, including considering objects in terms of their overall, three-dimensional size (e.g., *big*, *small*, *large*, *little*) or two-dimensional size, which may be depicted as vertical (e.g., *tall*, *short*), horizontal (e.g., *long*), or diagonal. Difficulty levels on the BBCS–3:R and BBCS:E support the assertion that children first learn concepts related to gross, three-dimensional size before learning concepts related to two-dimensional size (Bracken, 1998b). The early childhood states' standards focus broadly on children's ability to discern similarities and differences between the many attributes or dimensions of objects in our environment (Bracken, 1998a), including dimensions of relative size (e.g., *same, equal, different*). Many states' standards use the language of *equivalent* and *nonequivalent*, which are important concepts; however, these more advanced concepts are addressed by the more basic BBCS–3:R concepts of *equal* and *unequal*.

States address children's knowledge of size with regard to size-related concepts as salient attributes, including: *small/large, little/big, tall/short/long, same/less than/ greater than*. Interestingly, some states only cite the importance of three-dimensional size concepts (e.g., *small, little, big, large*) while other states include two-dimensional vertical or horizontal concepts (e.g., *tall, short, long*). Many states present these same size-related concepts in their most basic form (e.g., *short*), as well as in their comparative and superlative forms (i.e., *shorter, shortest*).

The BBCS–3:R and BBCS:E thoroughly assess the size and comparison concepts listed in the states' standards. In addition to the specific concepts mentioned in the states' standards, the BBCS–3:R and BBCS:E include additional concepts that provide a more comprehensive assessment of size concepts in unique contexts (e.g., *deep, shallow, thin*) and language referring to comparative size (e.g., *same, not the same, equal, unequal, match, exactly, similar*). Importantly, the BBCS–3:R and BBCS:E concepts were selected to assess knowledge of three-dimensional concepts (e.g., *big, small*), two-dimensional vertical concepts (e.g., *tall, long, short*), and two-dimensional horizontal concepts (e.g., *short, long*)

Shapes

Knowledge about shapes is the conceptual area in the states' standards that is the most thoroughly and uniformly addressed. As the reader reviews the matrix of standards across the various states, it becomes apparent that educators have thought about teaching shapes during the pre-kindergarten, kindergarten, and first grade years. At the most basic level, shapes begin with lines, which may be *straight, curved*, or *angled*. Lines also may run in vertical, horizontal, or diagonal orientations.

Many of the states' standards do not address this aspect of lines as shapes, but begin with lines that have been connected to create a whole object with two dimensions (e.g., *circle, square*) or three dimensions (e.g., *sphere, cube*). Most state standards list an array of common two- and three-dimensional shapes, including: *circle, square, triangle, rectangle, sphere, cube, pyramid, cylinder, cone*. Additionally, some states add other common, but infrequently cited shapes. For example, Montana includes *diamond* and *oval* among its state standards; Arkansas includes *rectangular prism*; Louisiana includes *rhombus*; Kentucky includes *parallelogram, hexagon*, and *trapezoid*; and Georgia includes *pentagon*. California is relatively unique in that it identifies shapes that describe distinct locations (e.g., *edge, corner, curve*).

Although the BBCS–3:R and BBCS:E do not include some of the more age-advanced shape concepts (e.g., *parallelogram, trapezoid*), the tests do assess concepts that define line nature (e.g., *curve, diagonal, angle*), as well as a range of two- and three-dimensional (e.g., *diamond, heart, column, pyramid*) shapes. The BBCS–3:R and BBCS:E also include the shapes included in the California standards that describe distinct locations (e.g., *edge, corner*); however, these appear in the Direction/Position subtest.

Direction/Position

Direction and location (i.e., position) concepts describe the relative location or position of objects in space. From a developmental orientation, children begin by viewing objects in locations from their own perspective (e.g., *right* is from the child's right-hand perspective). Older children progress to having the ability to take another's perspective. They can view locations from the orientation of others (e.g., an opposing orientation where Anna's *right* is understood as the child's *left*). That is, from a basic knowledge point of view, directional concepts are first learned from a self-perspective orientation and later from another person's perspective.

In addition to perspective, direction and position concepts are represented most frequently as prepositions, although they also may include nouns (e.g., *edge, corner*). Early directional knowledge emphasizes a three-dimensional orientation from a self-perspective, and includes concepts that address vertical (e.g., *above, below, up, down, under, over, high, low, top, bottom*), horizontal (e.g., *right, left, beside, next to, sideways*), three-dimensional (e.g., *around, through*), internal/external (e.g., *in, out, between*), relative proximity (e.g., *near, close, far*) concepts, and the child's perception of front or back (e.g., *front, back, forward, backward*).

States' standards collectively cite many of these concepts as knowledge that should be acquired during the early childhood years. BBCS–3:R and BBCS:E assess all of the aforementioned concepts plus many other related directional or positional concepts (e.g., *rising, falling, together, apart, side, toward, away, joined, height, length, opposite, level, space, still, end, open, closed, on, off, upside down, following, ahead, behind*).

Self-/Social Awareness

The domain of self- and social awareness includes a wide array of person-oriented and sociological knowledge, including affective feelings, health and physical condition, gender awareness, familial relationships, relative age, and social mores or correctness. As with academic content areas, children's sense of self and formation of self-concepts are developmental in nature (Bracken, 1996). States' standards individually address some of these topical and developmental issues, but not comprehensively within or across all states. For example, Arizona includes several common feelings (e.g., *sad, happy, mad*), as well as some abstract feelings (e.g., *love, pride, frustration, fear*). Other states such as Arkansas, Vermont, and California include more diverse concepts, including gender terms, familial relations, and base emotions (e.g., *angry, excited*).

As with the other standards categories, the BBCS–3:R and BBCS:E include an extremely comprehensive collection of concepts in the area of self- and social awareness. The BBCS–3:R and BBCS:E assess conceptual knowledge associated with gender (e.g., *man, woman, boy, girl*), familial relations (e.g., *brothers, sisters, mother, father*), age (e.g., *old, young*), health and physical awareness (e.g., *tired, resting, healthy, hurt, relaxing, sleepy, sick*), affective state (e.g., *happy, sad, crying, laughing, smiling, angry, afraid, excited, frowning, worried, curious*), and social mores (e.g., *right, wrong, correct, easy, difficult*). As such, the BBCS–3:R and BBCS:E assess nearly all of the concepts that are included in the various states' standards. Moreover, the tests include many concepts not addressed by any of the various states' standards.

Texture/Material

From a developmental perspective, children from birth begin to learn about their environments, including the attributes that define or characterize the objects in their environments. As infants crawl and toddlers toddle about and handle objects, they begin to develop an awareness of different textures (e.g., *rough, hard, soft, smooth*) and material characteristics or conditions (e.g., *heavy, light, wet, dry*). For safety reasons, parents teach their children at very early ages the concept of *hot*, and by comparison, the opposite concept of *cold*. Later, children begin to learn what the objects in their environments are made of (e.g., *wood, metal, glass, cloth*) and they associate the textures and attributes that are associated with each material (e.g., *wood* is *hard, metal* is *shiny, glass* is *clear, cloth* is *soft*). Finally, children learn about the manmade changing states of objects or materials (e.g., *rough* wood can be sanded *smooth*) or natural changing states of objects and materials (e.g., water can be found in various forms, depending on temperature [i.e., *liquid, solid, gas*]).

Such a comprehensive consideration and treatment of materials and textures as conceptual knowledge ensures that children are better able to use their five senses to identify, name, and discriminate between various object attributes, characteristics, and qualities. Early childhood educational states' standards address conceptual knowledge acquired via the five senses. Most states' standards address the specific concepts of *hot/cold* and *liquid/solid/gas*. They go on to cite broad generalizations of what young children should know about other textures and materials. For example, Florida state standards indicate that children should be able to use their senses to observe and explore materials and natural phenomena by how something feels, how fast or slow it flows, its temperature (e.g., *hot* or *cold*), and weight. Unlike some other categories considered in the states' standards (e.g., shapes), which are very specific about what young children should know, the texture/material category is less specific across states' standards.

The BBCS–3:R and BBCS:E systematically assess conceptual knowledge within the senses of sight, touch, and hearing. Taste and smell are not included because they are not easily depicted in drawings. Within the other senses, however, the BBCS–3:R and BBCS:E comprehensively assess knowledge of materials (e.g., *cloth, wood*), material attributes (e.g., *wet, dry*), material textures (e.g., *rough, smooth, sharp*), states of matter (e.g., *liquid, solid, gas*), temperature (e.g., *boiling*), sound (e.g., *loud, quiet*), and appearance (e.g., *shiny, bright, clear, dull, dark, light*).

Quantity

Quantitative knowledge in early childhood is part of, yet distinct from, children's understanding of numbers and counting. Knowledge of numbers and counting usually (but not always) provides the foundation for much of the quantitative understanding that follows. For example, virtually all young children acquire the concept of *more* before they can identify numbers or count. By placing two unequal piles of candy in front of a young child and allowing him or her to take either of the two piles, a parent or teacher can readily see that young children understand the concept *more* long before they can articulate it or count the pieces of candy in the two piles.

Quantitative concepts, then, represent the understanding of such conditions as part/whole (e.g., *whole, part, piece*), relative quantity (e.g., *lots, few, many, nothing, none, every*), volume (e.g., *full, empty*), comparatives (e.g., *more than, less than*), multiples (e.g., *double, pair, couple, triple, dozen*), fractions (e.g., *half, third*), currency (e.g., *dime, nickel, quarter*), and the use and understanding of mathematical signs (e.g., +, –, =). Quantity concepts provide young children with language that enables them to talk about numbers and counting in ways that communicate and generalize knowledge beyond the number of the objects being measured, weighed, counted, divided, distributed, or otherwise treated mathematically.

States' standards vary considerably in the detail of quantitative knowledge children should know at young ages, beyond their ability to count and identify numbers. Nearly all states address children's knowledge of currency and mathematical signs and share several specific quantitative concepts; however, there appears to be less consistency across states' standards in quantity than in some other categories. That is, many states' standards cite specific quantitative concepts that should be mastered by young children, but there is considerable variability in the number and specific concepts cited in the standards from state to state.

The BBCS–3:R and BBCS:E Quantity subtests assess quantitative knowledge with systematic coverage, including part/whole relations (e.g., *part, whole, piece*), relative quantity (e.g., *many, nothing, all, some, little, few, several, none, every, enough*), volume (e.g., *empty, full*), comparatives/superlatives (e.g., *more than, less than, greatest, least, most*), multiples (e.g., *alone, single, double, pair, both, neither, couple, triple, dozen*), fractions (e.g., *half, whole*), and the use and understanding of mathematical signs (e.g., +, –). Earlier versions of the BBCS (i.e., BBCS; Bracken, 1984 and BBCS–R; Bracken, 1998b) assessed knowledge of U.S. coinage and currency; however, the BBCS–3:R and BBCS:E do not assess children's knowledge in this area because currency changes in appearance over the years.

Time/Sequence

Because life progresses temporally, from morning to night, from breakfast to dinner, from new to old, from yesterday to tomorrow, young children quickly attend to the temporal patterns in their lives, even if they have not acquired the language to describe those patterns. In the domain of time/sequence, the mathematical/quantitative nature of seriation (e.g., *first, second, third*) and frequency (e.g., *once, twice*) must be considered.

Knowledge of time and sequence, however, is more than just a quantitative component. Time and sequence also deal with children's knowledge and awareness of natural events (e.g., *morning, daytime, night*), temporal order of events (e.g., *starting, before, after, over, finished*), temporal absolutes (e.g., *never, always*), scheduling (e.g., *early, late, next, arriving, leaving*), speed (e.g., *fast, slow*), relative age (e.g., *new, old*), and descriptive temporal nuances (e.g., *nearly, just, waiting*).

States' early childhood standards are fairly uniform in mentioning the importance of children knowing the temporal order of events, including *beginning, middle,* and *end.* Most states address time in terms of daily event occurrences (e.g., *morning, day, evening, night*) and annual event occurrences (e.g., changing weather patterns associated with seasons of the year). A few states also identify short periods of time as critical knowledge (e.g., *minutes, hours, quarter-hour*), and yet others include longer and broader temporal episodes in their standards (e.g., *long ago; past-present-future; days, weeks, months,* and *years*). Many states also include the natural linkage between time and sequence and number with standards relating to numerical order, seriation, sequence, magnitude, and weight.

Time and sequence concepts, as assessed on the BBCS–3:R and BBCS:E, address nearly all of the elements included in the states' standards except seasonal changes. Seasons were assessed on the BBCS and BBCS–R, but are not assessed in the

BBCS–3:R or BBCS:E. Items pertaining to seasons could be considered biased toward children who live in climates that experience four distinct seasons. For example, children living in southern California or Florida may have never experienced a snowy winter day.

Both the BBCS–3:R and BBCS:E assess in a comprehensive manner conceptual knowledge associated with the mathematical/quantitative nature of seriation (e.g., *first, next*) and frequency (e.g., *twice*), as well as knowledge related to natural events (e.g., *daytime*), temporal order of events (e.g., *starting, finished*), temporal absolutes (e.g., *always, never*), scheduling (e.g., *early, late*), speed (e.g., *slow*), relative age (e.g., *old, new*), and temporal nuances (e.g., *nearly, just*).

Conclusions

The historic changes in early childhood education have resulted in individuals, organizations, and state and federal governments recognizing that there should be a common body of knowledge acquired by children in the pre-kindergarten, kindergarten, and first grade years and is a commendable and welcome state of educational affairs. A review of the various states' early childhood standards, however, reveals there is variation of the concepts, knowledge, skills, and abilities that children are expected to master. Nevertheless, the fact that there are now early childhood standards either written or being written in each of the fifty states is an outstanding step in the right direction of standardizing early childhood education.

The collective developmental and educational literature and the efforts of individual researchers have identified a comprehensive and unified combination of foundational knowledge that young children should know to ensure that all children possess a common knowledge base before entering advanced grades. This foundational knowledge is necessary to ensure that children have the language and understanding to learn about, talk about, and ask about content they learn in social studies, science, language arts, art, and mathematics. This complete list of content and concepts constitute an extremely important foundation of knowledge.

Whereas Appendix F (Parent/Teacher Conference Form) in this Manual lists all of the concepts assessed on the BBCS–3:R for diagnostic and intervention purposes, Table 4.1, modified from the work of Bracken and Crawford (2006), provides the examiner and parents with a list of the conceptual categories and sub-domains that guided the identification of the concepts assessed on the BBCS–3:R and BBCS:E. This list provides all educators with a useful guide for early childhood instruction.

If all young children had a thorough understanding of how these over-arching categories of content provide the foundational knowledge needed later in life; if they understood how all the elements of the sub-domain knowledge compose these categories; and if they understood each of the more than 280 concepts that describe and comprise this universe of basic knowledge, they would start their formal education on a much more even footing. The knowledge base assessed by the BBCS–3:R and BBCS:E and taught in the BCDP provides a real, non-rhetorical, practical, and proven guide for placing a solid, common, and important foundation under all young children—a foundation that helps to ensure that all children are ready for formal academic instruction.

Table 4.1 Early Childhood Conceptual Categories, Sub-Domains, and Conceptual Examples: A Blueprint for Standards

Content/Concept Category	Sub-Domain	Concept Examples
Colors	Primary Colors	Red, Yellow, Blue
	Secondary Colors	Orange, Green, Purple
	Tertiary Colors	Violet, Teal
	Absolutes	White, Black
Letters/Sounds*	Recognition	
	* Upper-case	Point to M, B, S, D
	* Lower-case	Point to u, v, c, b
	Naming	
	* Upper-case	Name this letter, W, P, R, E
	* Lower-case	Name this letter, a, e, g, k
	Letter Sounds	What sound does b make?
	Letter Blend Sounds	What sound does ch make?
	Letter Production	Print the letter X, J, Z
Numbers/Counting	Rote Counting	Counting without place value
	Place Counting	Counting with one-to-one correspondence
	Number Identification	
	* 0–9	Point to the 1, 5, 8, 0
	* Double Digits	Point to the 22, 58, 95
	* Triple Digits	Point to 138, 395, 783
	Number Naming	
	* 0–9	What is this number? 2, 6, 9
	* Double Digits	What is this number? 44, 78
	* Triple Digits	What is this number? 234, 783
	Number Production	Print the number 6, 33, 245
	Counting by Sets	Count to 100 by 2s, 5s, 10s
Sizes/Comparisons	Three-Dimensional Size	Big, Large, Small, Little
	Two-Dimensional Size	
	* Vertical	Tall, Short
	* Horizontal	Long
	Comparative Sizes	Same, Different, Equal
Shapes	Linear (vertical/horizontal)	
	* Curvilinear Line	Curve
	* Diagonal Line	Diagonal
	* Angular Line	Angle
	Two-Dimensional Shapes	Circle, Square, Triangle
	Three-Dimensional Shapes	Sphere, Cube, Pyramid
Direction/Position	Three-Dimensional Direction	Under, Over
	Internal/External	Inside, Outside, Around, Through
	Relative Proximity	Near, Far, Beside
	Self/Other Perspective	My right, Your right, My left, Your left
	Front/Rear	In Front of, Behind, Forward, Backward
	Specific Locations	Edge, Corner
	Cardinal Directions	North, South, East, West

*BBCS–3:R includes Letters; BBCS:E includes Letters/Sounds.

Table 4.1 Early Childhood Conceptual Categories, Sub-Domains, and Conceptual Examples: A Blueprint for Standards (continued)

Content/Concept Category	Sub-Domain	Concept Examples
Self-/Social Awareness	Affective Feeling	Happy, Sad, Excited, Curious
	Health/Physical	Healthy, Sick, Tired
	Gender	Boy, Girl, Woman, Man
	Familial Relationships	Mother, Father, Brother, Sister
	Age	Old, Young
	Mores	Right, Wrong, Correct
Texture/Material	States of Matter	Solid, Liquid, Gas
	Textures	Rough, Smooth, Sharp
	Materials	Cloth, Wood, Metal
	Material Characteristics	Wet, Dry, Shiny, Dull
	Temperatures	Hot, Cold
Quantity	Part/Whole	Whole, Part, Piece
	Relative Quantity	Lots, Few, Some
	Volume	Full, Empty
	Multiples	Pair, Double, Triple, Dozen
	Comparatives/Superlatives	More, Less, Most, Least
	Fractions	Half, One-Third
	Math Signs/Symbols	+, −, x
Time/Sequence	Mathematical Seriation	First, Second, Third
	Frequency	Once, Twice
	Naturally-occurring Events	Morning, Daytime, Evening, Night
	Temporal Order of Events	Before, After, Finished
	Temporal Absolutes	Never, Always
	Scheduling	Early, Late, Next, Arriving
	Speed	Fast, Slow
	Relative Age	New, Old, Young, Old
	Temporal Nuances	Nearly, Just, Waiting
	Larger Temporal Periods	Days, Weeks, Months, Seasons, Years

Development and Standardization

BBCS–3:R is the second revision of the *Bracken Basic Concept Scale*, originally published in 1984. In the two revisions, items have been refined, color artwork has been added, and norms have been updated. The development of the BBCS–3:R was based on feedback from clinicians and experts in the fields of child language and cognitive development, U.S. and international content reviews, a thorough review of current literature, a nationwide tryout, and a nationwide standardization.

Feedback about the previous edition was obtained from a customer survey; from BBCS–R users' questions about test administration, test items, scoring and interpretation; and from questionnaires completed by examiners (i.e., speech-language pathologists, psychologists, teachers, and educational diagnosticians) who participated in the various stages of field-testing. The customer survey and a comprehensive review of the literature were conducted to examine how clinicians and researchers use BBCS–R to assess language skills in young children. The examiner questionnaires were designed to determine how thoroughly the test covers basic concept development/acquisition and its relationship to educational tasks. Additionally, an expert panel, including international representatives, completed an item and subtest content review. In response to clinicians' needs:

- some items were added, deleted, or revised;
- the age range of the test was modified (ages 2:6–2:11 and 7:0–7:11 were not included in the normative sample);
- a chapter was included describing the relationship between the concept categories included on the BBCS–3:R and BBCS:E and state educational standards for young children.

A nationwide tryout was conducted to evaluate new items and changes to existing items, and to add items to improve both the floor and ceiling of the test across the age-span. A nationwide standardization, with numerous research studies, was conducted to develop norms and provide evidence of reliability, validity, and clinical utility.

Research Guidelines

The *Standards for Educational and Psychological Testing* (hereafter referred to as the Test Standards; AERA, et al., 1999) served as the primary resource through the BBCS–3:R research project and provided criteria for the "evaluation of tests, testing practices, and the effects of test use" (1999, p.2). The reader is referred to the Test Standards for a comprehensive discussion of these and other issues related to test development and evaluation.

Item Refinement

The multiple choice item format remained the same for the BBCS–3:R as in the BBCS–R. The child is shown a page with a choice of several pictures and asked to point to the one picture that depicts what the clinician is describing. Changes were made to specific items in several subtests based on input from customers, examiners, and U.S. and international reviewers to make the item contexts more current and culturally universal, including:

- The paint palette in subtest 1 was replaced with a paint box more typical of what children use in school, home, and daycare settings;
- Artwork depicting culturally sensitive images (e.g., bears) was modified (refer to the Bias and Content Review section in this chapter);
- Items depicting animals from specific regions were modified to depict animals that are more universal (e.g., squirrels and skunks were replaced with birds and rabbits);
- Items depicting sports such as baseball were changed to depict sports that are more international, (e.g., soccer);
- Items assessing U.S. seasons of the year were deleted because familiarity with them varies across the U.S., as well as internationally;
- Items assessing U.S. money/currency were deleted because of its changing appearance;
- Artwork was modified to render automobiles more culturally neutral (e.g. steering wheels were eliminated to avoid left-side vs. right-side orientation issue);
- Clothing and hairstyles of some of the children pictured were changed to make them appear more current;
- Items were also modified to improve the floor and ceiling of subtests or to better depict concepts. For example,
  - To improve the floor of the Letters subtest, the format of letter identification items 1–4 was modified to make the items easier;
  - In the Direction/Position subtest, the concept of *joined* is illustrated using magnets instead of hands.

Tryout Research

The tryout research was conducted from September, 2004 to March, 2005, using 11 subtests with the purpose of meeting the following objectives:

- Evaluate subtest and item performance across different ages;
- Evaluate subtests for range of item difficulty;
- Further refine items and subtest content;
- Identify item performance for children with typically-developing language and children identified with language impairments; and
- Identify items that may contain content, gender, and cultural/ethnic bias via statistical analyses and a panel of bias and content reviewers.

Tryout subtests included: Colors, Letters, Numbers/Counting, Sizes, Comparisons, Shapes, Direction/Position, Self-/Social Awareness, Texture/Material, Quantity, and Time/Sequence.

Tryout testing was conducted by 214 speech-language pathologists, psychologists, educational diagnosticians, and early childhood educators who were experienced in test administration. See Appendix H for a list of examiners who participated in the BBCS–3:R research. To ensure that examiners were experienced in individualized, standardized test administration, each examiner completed a detailed background questionnaire. All examiners were required to complete a practice case before being approved to test for the tryout research study. Practice cases were reviewed for accuracy of administration, recording of responses, and scoring. Throughout tryout testing, examiners received written and telephone support to clarify administration and scoring issues. Newsletters that included information about potential testing problems and progress of the testing were sent to all examiners. After testing, examiners completed a questionnaire evaluating the appropriateness of content revisions and additions, the effectiveness of item presentation, the ease of administration, and the clarity of illustrations and instructions.

Tryout Sample

Tryout testing of the BBCS–3:R involved 529 children, ages 3:0–6:11, from across the United States. None of the children involved in the tryout study had been diagnosed with language impairment or hearing loss, and all children were able to take the test in a standardized fashion without modifications in administration. All children in the sample spoke English as their primary (i.e., first and most frequently used) language. Tables 5.1 and 5.2 present the demographic distribution of the tryout sample. Half of the sample was female; half was male.

Table 5.1 Distribution of the BBCS–3:R Tryout Sample by Age

Age (years:months)	*n*
3:0–3:2	52
3:3–3:5	51
3:6–3:8	51
3:9–3:11	51
4:0–4:5	53
4:6–4:11	55
5:0–5:5	54
5:6–5:11	55
6:0–6:5	54
6:6–6:11	53
Total	**529**

Table 5.2 Distribution of the BBCS-3:R Tryout Sample and the U.S. Population by Race/Ethnicity, Geographic Region, and Parent Education Level

	n	% of Sample	% of U.S. Population
Race/Ethnicity			
African American	95	17.96	14.48
Hispanic	92	17.39	19.08
White	317	59.92	60.71
Other	25	4.73	5.73
Geographic Region			
Midwest	129	24.39	22.25
Northeast	92	17.39	17.97
South	175	33.08	34.94
West	133	25.14	24.84
Parent Education Level			
11 years of school or less	95	17.96	14.87
12 years of school or GED	154	29.11	30.12
13 to 15 years of school	138	26.09	27.69
16 years of school or more	142	26.84	27.32

Note. U.S. Population data are from *Current Population Survey, October 2002: School Enrollment Supplemental File* [CD-ROM] by U.S. Bureau of the Census, 2002, Washington DC: U.S. Bureau of the Census (Producer/Distributor).

In addition to the children included in the tryout sample, a clinical study was conducted with 33 children who had been identified as having language impairments (see Tables 5.3 and 5.4). The clinical study comprised children who had been diagnosed as having receptive and expressive language impairments with a standard score of 76 or lower on a standardized assessment, and who were receiving services for language impairments at the time of testing. As in the non-clinical tryout sample, all participants spoke English as their primary language.

Table 5.3 Distribution of the BBCS-3:R Clinical Tryout Sample by Age

Age (years:months)	*n*
3:0–3:2	3
3:3–3:5	4
3:6–3:8	3
3:9–3:11	3
4:0–4:5	4
4:6–4:11	4
5:0–5:5	2
5:6–5:11	3
6:0–6:5	4
6:6–6:11	3
Total	**33**

Table 5.4 Distribution of the BBCS-3:R Clinical Tryout Sample by Gender, Race/Ethnicity, Geographic Region, and Parent Education Level

	n	% of sample
Gender		
Female	12	36.4
Male	21	63.6
Race/Ethnicity		
African American	14	42.4
Hispanic	3	9.1
White	15	45.5
Other	1	3.0
Geographic Region		
Midwest	9	27.3
Northeast	5	15.2
South	17	51.5
West	2	6.0
Parent Education Level		
11 years of school or less	8	24.2
12 years of school or GED	6	18.2
13 to 15 years of school	10	30.3
16 years of school or more	9	27.3

Bias and Content Review

A panel of speech-language pathologists and education specialists with expertise in assessment of diverse populations reviewed the BBCS–3:R tryout test items for content and cultural bias. The group reviewed the verbal and visual stimuli for perceived gender, racial/ethnic, socioeconomic status, and regional biases. The panel provided written, detailed critiques of all visual and verbal stimuli and evaluations of the items. Examples of the changes that were made to the items/artwork based on bias reviewer input follow:

- In some Native American tribes it is not appropriate to tell stories about animals while they are hibernating; therefore, bears depicted in one of the Numbers/Counting items were replaced with ducks.
- Using the ocean as a depiction of *deep* may be biased against children who don't live near or frequently visit an ocean; therefore, the depiction of *deep* was changed from a ship on an ocean to a girl standing in a swimming pool.
- Additional skin tones/colors were added to reflect ethnic/racial diversity.

Table 5.5 lists the tryout bias and content review panel participants.

Table 5.5 BBCS–3:R Tryout Panel of Bias and Content Reviewers

Carol Westby, Ph.D. University of New Mexico Albuquerque, New Mexico	Toya A. Wyatt, Ph.D. California State University Fullerton, California	Chien J. Wang, MA Harcourt Assessment San Antonio, Texas

Statistical Analysis

During the analysis of the tryout data, all items in each subtest were submitted to several statistical procedures. The percentage of children passing each item (*p*-values) as well as item-to-total correlations were calculated for each age group for both the tryout sample and the clinical tryout study. Items were also submitted to statistical studies of group performance differences with regard to gender, race/ethnicity, and parent education level. Bias analyses were was conducted using both traditional Mantel-Haenszel bias analysis (Holland and Thayer, 1988) and item response theory (IRT) bias analyses methods (Hambleton, 1993). Based on the combined results of statistical analyses, bias panel recommendations, and examiner feedback, items that did not meet requirements for fairness, clinical utility, difficulty, and scoring ease (see Table 5.6) were deleted. Refinements were made to item order based on estimates of relative difficulty. Data collected from the clinical study were used to provide evidence of the differential item functioning of individual items and subtests and the clinical utility of the test. After a complete review of the data accumulated from the tryout research, the standardization edition of the BBCS–3:R was developed.

Table 5.6 Concepts/Items Deleted After BBCS–3:R Tryout Research

Subtest	Concepts/Items Deleted
Direction/Position	*covered*
Self-/Social Awareness	*male, female*

Standardization Research

Norm-referenced data for BBCS–3:R enable you to compare a child's scores to the performances of others of the same age in the normative sample. BBCS–3:R norms presented in this Manual were derived from a sample that is representative of the U.S. population (U.S. Bureau of the Census, 2003) of children ages 3:0–6:11. The sample was stratified on the basis of age, gender, race/ethnicity, geographic region, and parent education level.

Normative Sample

The standardization and related reliability and validity research studies involved more than 750 children. Testing began in September, 2005 and continued through April, 2006. The normative sample included 80 children in each of the six-month age groups (i.e., 160 children per one-year age level). Participants in the non-clinical group of the normative sample met the following requirements.

- Children took the test in a standardized manner without modifications (e.g., BBCS–3:R was not administered using American Sign Language, Signing Exact English, finger spelling, or other variations of signed language).
- Children were not currently diagnosed with a behavioral or emotional disorder.
- Children had the ability to use spoken language to communicate (they were also administered the BBCS:E; the tests were co-normed).

Although the sample included children who were bilingual, English was the primary (i.e., first acquired and most frequently used) language of all participants in the standardization and related reliability, validity, and clinical studies. Approximately 6% of the sample lived in homes in which a language other than English was also spoken: 5.7% Spanish and 0.4% Korean.

According to the National Institute on Deafness and Other Communication Disorders (2004), prevalence of speech/language disorders is estimated at about 8% of American school children. Tomblin, Smith, and Shang (1997) found the prevalence of specific language impairment (SLI) in a group of over 7,000 kindergarten children to be 7.4%. The 2002 congressional report from the Office of Special Education Programs (OSEP, 2002) indicated that speech/language impairment was the most prevalent disability category for children ages 3–5 years, accounting for 55.2% of preschoolers who received special education services in 2000–2001. During data collection, children who were diagnosed with a language impairment were excluded from the typically-developing (non-clinical) sample. However, review of the data indicated that approximately 2% of the children in the non-clinical sample performed very similarly to children diagnosed with a language impairment, leading to the hypothesis that some of the children in the non-clinical sample may have had an unidentified language impairment. Based on this hypothesis, the BBCS–3:R normative sample was stratified to include 4.8% of children with diagnosed language impairment to ensure that the sample would be representative of the general U.S. population of children ages 3:0–6:11 (and not over-represent children with language impairment). The stratification was done by age, gender, race/ethnicity, geographic region, and primary caregiver's education level.

Overall, about 14% of the children in the normative sample were reported to be receiving special services or to be enrolled in special programs: less than 1% received services in gifted and talented/enrichment/advanced placement programs, 1.9% in early childhood programs, 5.9% in Head Start programs, and less than 1% in other programs. Approximately 6.7% of the sample received speech/language services: 1.7% for articulation/phonological disorder, 4.8% for receptive and/or expressive language disorder/delay, and .2% for fluency disorder. About 1.4% of children (in the 14%) were enrolled in more than one special program.

The standardization edition of BBCS–3:R was administered by 186 speech-language pathologists who were state licensed and/or ASHA certified, psychologists, and educational diagnosticians in 43 states. See Appendix H for a list of examiners who conducted BBCS–3:R research. All examiners met the same qualifications as described for the tryout research and were required to submit one sample administration of the BBCS–3:R. The development team reviewed the test sample before the examiner was approved to test for standardization research. Throughout the standardization research, examiners received detailed written and telephone feedback and support. Newsletters clarifying examiners' questions about testing as well as the progress of the standardization research were sent to examiners during collection of the normative data and special studies.

Tables 5.7 and 5.8 report the demographic characteristics of the normative sample, along with national census figures. Fifty percent (50%) of the sample was female; 50% was male. Each child in the normative sample was categorized by his or her primary caregivers as belonging to one of the listed racial/ethnic groups. For sampling purposes, Native American, Eskimo, Aleut, and Pacific Islander examinees were combined into an Other category. The BBCS–3:R normative sample was stratified according to the following four parent education level categories.

- 11 years of school or less
- 12 years of school or GED
- 13–15 years of school (1–3 years of college or technical school)
- 16 years of school or more (college or post-graduate degree)

Parent included biological parent, guardian, or primary caregiver. Information on parent education level was obtained from responses to a question that asked the parent(s) to specify the highest grade completed by each parent, and specify which parent was the primary caregiver. The primary caregiver's education level was used as the stratification variable.

Table 5.7 Distribution of the BBCS–3:R Normative Sample by Age

Age (years:months)	*n*
3:0–3:5	80
3:6–3:11	80
4:0–4:5	80
4:6–4:11	80
5:0–5:5	80
5:6–5:11	80
6:0–6:5	80
6:6–6:11	80
Total	**640**

Table 5.8 Distribution of the BBCS-3:R Normative Sample and the U.S. Population by Race/Ethnicity, Geographic Region, and Parent Education Level

	n	% of Sample	% of U.S. Population
Race/Ethnicity			
African American	88	13.75	14.14
Asian	27	4.22	3.65
Hispanic	125	19.53	19.69
White	378	59.06	59.10
Other	22	3.44	3.42
Geographic Region			
Midwest	140	21.88	22.38
Northeast	104	16.25	17.30
South	246	38.43	35.89
West	150	23.44	24.43
Parent Education Level			
11 years of school or less	92	14.38	15.64
12 years of school or GED	181	28.28	27.45
13 to 15 years of school	187	29.21	28.35
16 years of school or more	180	28.13	28.56

Note. U.S. Population data are from *Current Population Survey, October 2003: School Enrollment Supplemental File* [CD-ROM] by U.S. Bureau of the Census, 2003, Washington DC: U.S. Bureau of the Census (Producer/Distributor).

Scoring

All Record Forms were reviewed by trained staff, and responses to test items were machine scanned. The raw data were scored using SAS software.

Item Analysis and Item Ordering

Based on the data collected during the standardization research, items were analyzed for difficulty, differential item functioning, and ease and reliability of scoring. Based on these statistical analyses, some items were deleted (see Table 5.9) and slight adjustments made to item order within subtests. Once items were arranged hierarchically by difficulty level, it was possible to establish empirically derived start points and basal and discontinue rules.

Table 5.9 Concepts/Items Deleted After BBCS-3:R Standardization Research

Subtest	Concepts/Items Deleted
Letters	*z*
Numbers/Counting	*one*
Direction/Position	*inside, moving*
Self-/Social Awareness	*sick, smiling*
Texture/Material	*hot, cold*
Quantity	*lots*
Time/Sequence	*night, fast, leaving*

Determining Start Points and Discontinue Rules

Some items were determined to be too difficult for the youngest children. To avoid frustrating the child and the examiner by administering items that were too difficult, initial discontinue rules were developed based on tryout data analysis. To ensure a shorter but accurate discontinue rule could be established for the published test, the standardization edition included a longer-than-normal discontinue rule of six consecutive scores of zero (incorrect response or no response). This enabled the child to attempt all items he or she might reasonably be expected to pass, yet limited the number of items presented.

The final start points were established based on empirical studies of the BBCS–3:R normative data. Every child begins each of the subtests that make up the SRC (subtests 1–5) with the first item and then proceeds through the subtest until he or she misses three consecutive items. The total raw score of these five subtests (i.e., SRC) is then used to determine the start points for subtests 6–10. The start points were selected to reduce the chance of beginning the remaining subtests with items that may be too easy for the child but still enable the child to establish a basal of three consecutive correct items.

Every child who participated in the standardization research began testing with Item 1 for each subtest 6–10. For the final edition, the start points for subtests 6–10 were determined empirically from the normative data. The normative sample was grouped into eight ability groups. Corresponding to a range of SRC raw scores, the groups ranged in size from 74 to 121 children. Final rules for start points for subtests 6–10 were developed using the percentages of children in each ability group who passed each of the items. If at least 90% of the children in a particular ability group passed the first several items administered, then the starting point for that group was moved to a more difficult item. If few items in a subtest were passed by 90% of that ability group, that group was assigned to start with Item 1. Using this criterion, children in the lowest ability group always start at Item 1, but children in ability groups 2–8 often start beyond Item 1.

The final discontinue rule was established on a theoretical basis. The majority of BBCS–3:R items are formatted so that the child has a choice of four answers. On those items, the child has a one out of four chance (25%) of responding correctly, even if guessing. The discontinue rule of three consecutive scores of zero (incorrect or no response) was established to reduce the possibility of children getting correct responses based on chance or guessing alone. If the child has reached the point where he or she is guessing on every item, the probability of guessing correctly on three out of four items is low.

Raw Scores

Table 5.10 reports raw score means and standard deviations for each age group in the normative sample. The raw score means increase across ages, reflecting growth and development of the concepts measured by the subtests.

Table 5.10 Raw Score Means and Standard Deviations of the BBCS-3:R Subtest and Composite Scores by Age and Across All Ages for the Normative Sample

	3:0–3:5		3:6–3:11		4:0–4:5		4:6–4:11		5:0–5:5		5:6–5:11		6:0–6:5		6:6–6:11		All Ages	
n	80		80		80		80		80		80		80		80		640	
Subtest	Mean	*SD*	Mean	*SD*	Mean	*SD*	Mean	*SD*	Mean	*SD*	Mean	*SD*	Mean	*SD*	Mean	*SD*	Mean	*SD*
1–5 SRC	27.3	13.8	35.6	14.6	45.4	16.0	54.3	15.8	63.9	13.7	69.6	12.8	76.0	5.9	77.9	5.4	56.2	21.8
6 Direction/Position	15.2	8.0	19.6	10.0	27.7	14.9	32.7	14.2	37.7	15.0	45.5	14.8	50.0	11.8	53.9	8.3	35.3	18.1
7 Self-/Social Awareness	13.2	6.0	15.4	6.3	20.8	6.9	24.8	6.6	25.9	5.6	27.3	6.5	29.9	3.6	31.2	2.5	23.6	8.3
8 Texture/Material	6.7	3.6	9.8	5.6	12.4	6.3	15.6	6.3	18.3	6.1	20.3	6.4	22.9	4.7	24.3	4.2	16.3	8.1
9 Quantity	8.3	6.1	11.8	7.3	17.6	8.5	19.3	7.8	22.2	8.0	25.9	8.0	29.6	7.4	34.1	6.1	21.1	11.0
10 Time/Sequence	4.5	3.4	6.5	4.7	10.1	6.1	13.2	6.1	13.9	7.2	18.0	7.0	20.5	6.7	23.4	5.5	13.8	8.6
Receptive TC	75.1	31.2	98.7	39.4	134.1	50.6	159.9	48.8	182.0	47.5	206.5	48.8	229.0	34.0	244.9	27.0	166.3	70.5
Receptive SRC	27.3	13.8	35.6	14.6	45.4	16.0	54.3	15.8	63.9	13.7	69.6	12.8	76.0	5.9	77.9	5.4	56.2	21.8

Note. Receptive TC = Receptive Total Composite, Receptive SRC = Receptive School Readiness Composite

Norms Development

Standard Scores

The following normative data are reported for BBCS–3:R in Appendixes A–E in this Manual.

- Appendix A — Subtest scaled score equivalents (*M* = 10, *SD* = 3) corresponding to subtest raw scores (SRC and subtests 6–10), percentile ranks, and descriptive classifications by age
- Appendix B — Receptive Total Composite (Receptive TC) score equivalents (*M* = 100, *SD* = 15) corresponding to the sums of **scaled** scores of the SRC and subtests 6–10, confidence intervals, percentile ranks, and descriptive classifications
- Appendix C — Receptive School Readiness Composite (Receptive SRC) score equivalents (*M* = 100, *SD* = 15) corresponding to the sums of **raw** scores of subtests 1–5, percentile ranks, and descriptive classifications by age
- Appendix D — Concept age equivalents corresponding to subtest raw scores and the Receptive TC raw score
- Appendix E — Percentile ranks, normal curve equivalents, and stanines

BBCS–3:R normative information was developed using the method of Inferential Norming (Wilkins, Rolfhus, Weiss, and Zhu, 2005). Various moments of normalcy (i.e., means, standard deviations, and skewness) of each subtest were calculated for each age group of the BBCS–3:R normative sample. The moments were plotted across age, and various polynomial regressions, ranging from linear to 5th degree polynomials, were fit to the moment data. Functions for each subtest moment were selected based on consistency with underlying theoretical expectations and the pattern of growth curves observed in the normative sample. For each subtest, the functions were used to derive estimates of the population moments. The estimated moments were then used to generate theoretical distributions for each of the reported normative age groups, yielding percentiles for each raw score. These percentiles were converted to standard scores with a mean of 10, a standard deviation of 3, and a range of 1–19. The irregularities associated with sampling error were eliminated by smoothing. Appendix A presents the scaled score equivalents of the subtest raw scores for ages 3:0–6:11.

Receptive TC scores were derived by first adding the scaled scores from the SRC and subtests 6–10, then normalizing the distribution to have a mean of 100 and a standard deviation of 15. Some smoothing of the score distribution was done to adjust for small irregularities in scores due to sampling error. Using the sum of subtest scaled scores rather than the sum of subtest raw scores ensures that the Receptive TC represents an equal weighting of the subtests and a more equal score distribution that is a closer approximation to a normal score distribution.

Receptive SRC scores were derived using the same inferential norming method described for the development of subtest norms except with a mean of 100 and a *SD* of 15.

Concept Age Equivalents

Concept age equivalents were derived from each subtest raw score. Median raw scores were computed for each subtest based on the raw scores for each age interval. These median raw scores were plotted across ages expressed in months. A smooth line was then fitted to the plotted points. Concept age equivalents corresponding to each age-month interval were then read from the smooth line. The concept age equivalent represents the median raw score at each age level.

BBCS–3:R Spanish

Overview

The *Bracken Basic Concept Scale–Third Edition: Receptive* Spanish and the BBCS–3:R English assess similar concepts; however, because the BBCS–3:R Spanish was not normed, it is intended to be used as a criterion-referenced or curriculum-based measure. It is interpreted in a criterion-referenced manner because the field research conducted with the instrument involved a sample too small from which to derive norms ($n = 61$). The BBCS–3:R Spanish Record Form is designed for use with the BBCS–3:R Stimulus Book.

Use and Interpretation of the BBCS–3:R Spanish

The BBCS–3:R Spanish is designed to be used as a criterion-referenced test. This means that the information provided about the specific knowledge or skills possessed by a child can be interpreted in comparison to some preset criterion, but not in comparison to a normative population. For example, if a child has mastered 80% of color concepts, no information is provided about that child in comparison to his or her peers. Instead, the child's clinician or teacher specifies the level of mastery required. For example, if the clinician or teacher decided that at least 80% mastery of colors were needed to perform successfully in the classroom, the child who identified 80% or more of the colors presented would meet mastery criterion. Conversely, if the clinician or teacher decided that 95% mastery of colors were necessary in that classroom, the child obtaining 80% would not meet mastery criterion even if his or her score were the highest in the class.

In addition to use as a criterion-referenced measure, the BBCS–3:R Spanish can be used to:

- determine a child's baseline level of performance (pretesting) and then to determine the child's level of mastery after instruction/remediation has occurred (posttesting);
- validate previous test results and observations about a child's receptive concept knowledge;
- deep-test concept categories not fully assessed on another measure; and
- identify specific concepts that the child has not mastered that are in need of instruction/remediation so they can be included in the classroom teacher's lesson plans and/or the child's Individualized Education Plan (IEP).

Limitations of the BBCS–3:R Spanish

Norms were not derived for BBCS–3:R Spanish, so the child's performance cannot be compared to that of peers. Moreover, it is not appropriate to use the BBCS–3:R English norms for children who have been tested with the BBCS–3:R Spanish.

Administration and Scoring of the BBCS–3:R Spanish

The BBCS–3:R Spanish can be administered by Spanish–speaking speech-language pathologists, psychologists, special educators, and diagnosticians who have been trained and are experienced in administration and interpretation of individually administered, standardized language tests. An examiner must be able to speak and read Spanish fluently without hesitations or mispronunciations of the verbal stimuli or the administration directions. Examiners who are not fluent in Spanish could make errors in reading the administration directions and/or the test stimuli, resulting in erroneously low raw scores for the child taking the test. If you are unable to speak and read Spanish fluently, you will need to collaborate with other assessment professionals who do, or train an interpreter to administer the test. Training should include information about normal speech and language development; appropriate testing practices (e.g., communication styles, cues and prompts); scoring; cultural factors (e.g., students' views of teachers' status, students' comfort level in interacting with school staff, dialectal variations); regulations governing testing (e.g., purpose of testing, parents' rights and responsibilities, confidentiality issues); and behavior management (e.g., encouragement, redirection to tasks) to name a few. It is *not* appropriate to enlist the aid of a school staff member, parent, or sibling right before testing to administer the test in Spanish without training in these test administration procedures. A number of excellent resources are available that provide detailed methods for preparing and working with interpreters, including Kayser (1995), Langdon (2002), Langdon and Cheng (2002), Langdon and Saenz (1996), and Roseberry-McKibbin (2002, 2003).

Completing the Record Form

Before you begin testing a child, complete the identifying information section on page 1 of the Spanish Record Form. The Record Form can be used for pretest/posttest. The first time you test the child on a subtest or subtests, fill in the date, the child's chronological age, and the results in the Pre (Pretest) row. After instruction/remediation with the *Bracken Concept Development Program* (BCDP) or a similar curriculum, test the child again, using the Post (Posttest) row to record the date of testing, the child's age, and the results.

General Administration Procedures

The same testing considerations should be taken into account when administering the BBCS–3:R Spanish as when administering the BBCS–3:R English. Refer to Chapter 3 for information on setting up the proper test environment, establishing rapport with the child, providing encouragement and reinforcement, and allowing breaks.

Many of the general administration directions for the BBCS–3:R English also apply to the BBCS–3:R Spanish, and these are listed on page 2 of the Spanish Record Form. However, there are several procedural differences:

1. You may administer the subtests in any order you choose, and you do not need to administer all subtests at any given time. Because the BBCS–3:R Spanish yields criterion-referenced information rather than norm-referenced scores, you can administer only the subtests you need in order to meet your instructional or treatment needs; however, a more complete picture of the child's basic concept knowledge is possible after administration of all subtests.

2. Begin with Item 1 on each subtest, regardless of the child's age. Because the BBCS–3:R Spanish research sample was small, the order by item difficulty could not be determined reliably for Spanish speakers. Therefore, the items on the Spanish Record Form may not be arranged in increasing order of difficulty for Spanish speakers.

3. You will obtain the most accurate and complete information by administering all items in each subtest. On the lengthier subtests, you may decide to discontinue testing after the child has missed several consecutive items (such as four incorrect or no responses in a row) if you can see that the child is becoming frustrated.

4. Use the vocabulary option printed on the Spanish Record Form that best reflects the Spanish understood/spoken by the child. If the child appears not to understand the test item, repeat the item using another vocabulary option presented on the Record Form. It may be helpful to review the vocabulary options with the child's parent and/or teacher to identify the appropriate vocabulary to use before testing begins.

Recording and Computing Scores

Recording and scoring instructions are provided on page 2 of the BBCS–3:R Spanish Record Form in the General Administration Directions section. The recording instructions differ from the English edition because of the pretest/posttest design.

Transfer the subtest raw scores to the Number Correct column on the front page of the Record Form; then calculate the percent mastery by dividing the raw score obtained by the total number of items in the subtest (located in the shaded portion of the Number Correct column) and multiplying that number by 100. For example, if a child earns a raw score of 8 out of the 10 items on subtest 1 Colors, you would record a mastery of 80%. Space is provided for you to list the concepts that the child has not mastered and that you may want to target for instruction or remediation. Sum the subtest raw scores to obtain the Receptive Total score; calculate percent mastery for the total test the same way you did for subtests. Figure 6.1 provides an example of a completed first page of the BBCS–3:R Spanish Record Form.

Spanish Receptive Record Form

Name *Michael Muñoz* ☒ M ☐ F

School/Agency *Whitcomb Elementary* Grade *K*

Teacher *K. Zepeda* Examiner *L. Guerrero*

	Pretest			Posttest		
	Year	Month	Day	Year	Month	Day
Date of Test	06	3	15	06	~~9~~ 8	~~1~~ 31
Date of Birth	01	4	11	01	4	11
Chronological Age	4	11	4	5	4	20

Subtest	Pretest/ Posttest	Date	Age	Number Correct		% Mastery	Concepts to Target for Instruction
1 Colors	Pre	3/15/06	4:11	4	10	× 100 = 40	rosa, blanco, naranja, rojo, morado, café
	Post	9/1/06	5:4	10	10	× 100 = 100	
2 Letters	Pre	3/15/06	4:11	0	15	× 100 = 0	todas las mayúsculas y minúsculas
	Post	9/1/06	5:4	13	15	× 100 = 86	b, g
3 Numbers/Counting	Pre	3/15/06	4:11	1	18	× 100 = 6	0–9
	Post	9/1/06	5:4	14	18	× 100 = 77	numeros de dos digitos
4 Sizes/Comparisons	Pre	3/15/06	4:11	10	22	× 100 = 43	profunda, corta, delgado, ancho
	Post	9/1/06	5:4	22	22	× 100 = 100	
5 Shapes	Pre	3/15/06	4:11	8	20	× 100 = 40	rombo, óvalo, rectángulo, curva
	Post	9/1/06	5:4	18	20	× 100 = 90	
6 Direction/Position	Pre				60	× 100 =	
	Post				60	× 100 =	
7 Self-/Social Awareness	Pre				31	× 100 =	
	Post				31	× 100 =	
8 Texture/Material	Pre				29	× 100 =	
	Post				29	× 100 =	
9 Quantity	Pre				43	× 100 =	
	Post				43	× 100 =	
10 Time/Sequence	Pre				30	× 100 =	
	Post				30	× 100 =	
Receptive Total	Pre				278	× 100 =	
	Post				278	× 100 =	

Figure 6.1 Completed Page 1 of the BBCS–3:R Spanish Record Form

History of the Original BBCS Spanish Translation

The goal of the original BBCS Spanish translation was "to produce a Spanish version that could be administered to Spanish-speaking children regardless of their nation of origin or the U.S. region in which they live" (Bracken and Fouad, 1987). The translation procedure used to develop the original Spanish Record Form involved multiple English-to-Spanish translations and Spanish-to-English back-translations of test items until translations believed to be roughly equivalent were achieved. The resulting test items were then reviewed by a multinational bilingual committee. The committee reviewed the items to ensure that the Spanish items conveyed the same approximate meaning as the English items and that the Spanish items provided regional variations for the words that varied in usage from country to country or region to region. Two pilot studies were conducted during the translation process to further refine the items and evaluate the cross-cultural validity of the translation. The second, more extensive pilot study indicated that the two forms (English and Spanish) demonstrated cross-cultural validity because they showed similar developmental age progressions of concept acquisition (Bracken and Fouad, 1987).

The initial pilot studies and resulting item modifications led to the development of the BBCS Spanish Research Edition. The purpose of the research edition was to determine if the item translations were suitable and if the construct of basic concepts was similar across the Spanish and English languages and cultures. The performance of 293 monolingual Spanish-speaking children from Puerto Rico and Venezuela, and Spanish-dominant bilingual children from Texas was evaluated. The performances of these groups were compared to the performances of the BBCS English normative sample.

The result of the multinational validation study with the Research Edition suggested that 1) the BBCS Spanish and English versions appeared to measure similar constructs across languages and cultures; 2) the BBCS Spanish translation could be used with monolingual and bilingual Spanish speakers; 3) the construct of basic concepts is developmental and the sequence of development for many of the concepts is similar across national samples; and 4) the BBCS Spanish and English appeared to assess similar important conceptual content at similar acquisition rates and in similar sequences (Bracken, Barona, et al., 1990).

Development of the BBCS–R and BBCS–3:R Spanish Items

The BBCS–R Spanish was based on the research conducted with the original BBCS Spanish items. A professional translator who is a native speaker of Spanish reviewed and translated the items in the BBCS–R English standardization edition. All items then were reviewed by a multinational panel of native, bilingual Spanish speakers who were familiar with the Spanish spoken in Mexico, Puerto Rico, Central America, South America, Cuba, and the southwestern United States. The reviewers' goal was to make the translated items as comparable to the English items as possible, using wording in Spanish that would test similar basic concepts and with vocabulary most frequently used in Spanish-speaking countries.

The reviewers examined the test items, administration directions, and stimulus pictures to verify the appropriateness of the item translations/adaptations. Bilingual editors resolved conflicts in wording suggestions provided by the reviewers. The test materials then were submitted for review to a psychologist and a speech-language pathologist who had expertise in multicultural assessment and Spanish-language testing/assessment.

The BBCS–3:R Spanish test items are an outgrowth of the translation work on BBCS and BBCS–R items. Translations and back-translations were conducted for the new test items. Discrepancies in the translations and back-translations were reviewed and resolved by experts in bilingual test development and bilingual editorial staff using reference texts (Larousse, 1993; Martínez, 1999).

Differences Between the English and Spanish Items of the BBCS–3:R

Some of the BBCS–3:R Spanish items were adapted or modified from the English items rather than translated. When a test item is adapted, a comparable Spanish word or phrase is chosen that best expresses the concept in English. When an item is adapted or modified, it cannot be assumed that the item difficulty, familiarity, or age of acquisition is the same in both English and Spanish. Below are some examples of the adaptations and modifications made to the items.

- For many items, the stem (verbal stimuli) was changed so that gender cues are not provided in the BBCS–3:R Spanish. For example, in the BBCS–3:R English, many items have a singular stem "Show me which child ..." This singular stem translates directly as the masculine gender "Enséñame cuál niño ..." in Spanish. Because the Spanish translation could provide a gender cue to the correct or incorrect answer if the correct picture depicts a male child or conversely a female child, the stem was changed to the plural form, "Enséñame cuáles niños..." ("Show me which of the children...").
- Vocabulary choices are encouraged on the BBCS–3:R Spanish for many items, recognizing that the vocabulary a child uses will vary somewhat, depending on the child's (or the child's parents') country of origin and/or the area of the U.S. in which the child's family resides. For example, subtest 4, Item 4, "cuál pelota/bola es pequeña" or "which ball is little," offers the choice of *pelota* or *bola* for *ball.* Another example is subtest 9, Item 24. "Cuál persona está sin sombrero/gorra/cachucha" or "which person is without a hat," offers the choice of *sombrero*, *gorra*, or *cachucha* for *hat.* The examiner should present these item(s) using the word(s) that are best understood by the child.
- Many of the BBCS–3:R Spanish items are adaptations rather than translations because the concept being assessed cannot be expressed in a single word in Spanish. For example, subtest 4, Item 22, "which water is shallow," is "cuál agua es poco profunda," ("which water is a little deep") because that is how shallow water depth is denoted in Spanish. Subtest 6, Item 10, "which child is at the top of the slide" is translated to "cuál de los niños está en la parte de arriba de la resbaladera," or "which of the children is on the top part of the slide.

- A few of the items on the BBCS–3:R Spanish repeat a concept word used in a previous item because the words for the concepts are not differentiated in Spanish but are represented by different words in English. For example, in subtest 4, Item 1 (“which animal is big”) and Item 11 (“which rock is large”) both translate as “cuál … es grande” because *big* and *large* both translate as *grande* in Spanish.
- Some items are not assessed in Spanish because there is no equivalent concept. For example, in subtest 6, Item 5, “which boy has his hat off,” would translate to “which child does not have his hat on.” In this case, the translation would be testing the concept of *not on* instead of *off*.

BBCS–3:R Spanish Field Research

Research using BBCS–3:R Spanish was conducted across the United States from September, 2005, through April, 2006. A total of 61 Spanish-speaking children between the ages of 3 years 0 months and 6 years 11 months participated in the study. Children were included in the sample only if Spanish was the language used most frequently by the child. Parents reported that 56% of children spoke and understood both Spanish and English. Because the research sample was relatively small, it was not stratified by gender, geographic region, or parent education level. All the children in the research sample were identified as Hispanic. Table 6.1 reports the demographic characteristics of the sample.

Examiners were required to fluently speak and read the Spanish item stimuli and administration directions without hesitations or mispronunciations. To verify competency of potential examiners in spoken and written Spanish skills, an interview was conducted by a fluent Spanish speaker from the research team. The screening interview consisted of three tasks: conversing briefly on a familiar topic, reading Spanish text aloud, and transcribing sentences presented in Spanish. The team member conversed with the potential examiner and rated him or her on intelligibility, vocabulary, grammar, fluency, and appropriate social language. The potential examiner was asked to read a brief passage of his or her choice in Spanish, and was rated for pronunciation accuracy and fluency. Finally, the examiner was asked to transcribe orally presented sentences with varying degrees of difficulty. Transcriptions were faxed to the team member, who rated the transcription for accuracy, spelling, and legibility.

Table 6.1 Distribution of the BBCS-3:R Spanish Research Sample by Age, Gender, Geographic Region, and Parent Education Level (n = 61)

Age (years:months)	*n*	% of Sample
3:0–3:11	20	32.8
4:0–4:11	15	24.6
5:0–5:11	14	23.0
6:0–6:11	12	19.6
Gender		
Female	30	49.2
Male	31	50.8
Geographic Region		
Midwest	7	11.5
South	34	55.7
West	20	32.8
Parent Education Level		
11 years of school or less	15	24.6
12 years of school or GED	20	32.8
13 to 15 years of school	10	16.4
16 years of school or more	16	26.2

Results of BBCS–3:R Spanish Field Research

Table 6.2 reports the subtest and total test raw score means and standard deviations for the Spanish research sample across all ages. Testing began with Item 1 on all subtests. Testing was discontinued after six consecutive scores of zero (incorrect or no response). For data analysis purposes, the final discontinue rule was applied (i.e., three consecutive scores of zero).

Table 6.2 Subtest and Total Test Raw Score Means and Standard Deviations for the BBCS-3:R Spanish Research Sample (n = 61) Across All Ages

Subtest/Total	Mean	*SD*
1–5 SRC	41.3	23.5
6 Direction/Position	23.6	15.5
7 Self-/Social Awareness	17.7	8.5
8 Texture/Material	9.8	6.9
9 Quantity	16.4	10.4
10 Time/Sequence	10.7	7.3
Receptive Total	119.5	65.3

Evidence of Reliability of the BBCS–3:R Spanish

For general information about reliability, see chapter 7. The reliability of BBCS–3:R Spanish was estimated using a test of internal consistency (data which estimate the extent to which items within a subtest or group of tests are homogenous).

Evidence of Internal Consistency

Using internal consistency as a measure of reliability implies that items in the domain tested (e.g., a single subtest, group of subtests) measure a single, unified construct. Internal consistency reliability coefficients are used to describe the homogeneity of the items in a subtest.

Table 6.3 reports the internal consistency reliability coefficients (split-half) for the BBCS–3:R Spanish research sample and a matched sample from the BBCS–3:R English normative sample. The samples were matched as closely as possible for age, gender, parent education level, and geographic region. Overall, the strong subtest and total test internal consistencies demonstrate that BBCS–3:R reliably assesses the constructs of basic concepts in Spanish as well as in English. The subtest internal consistencies are high for both samples, ranging from .95 to .99. For this analysis, the internal consistency reliability coefficients were calculated across ages because the sample size at each age is small; therefore, they are higher than the average internal consistency reliability coefficients (calculated by age) of the BBCS–3:R normative sample. The strong internal consistency values are similar to the internal consistencies reported for Venezuelan, Puerto Rican, and Texan Hispanic samples in the BBCS research edition multinational validation study discussed previously (Bracken, et al., 1990), and suggest that the BBCS–3:R can be used reliably for both English- and Spanish-speaking children.

Table 6.3 Internal Consistency Reliability Coefficients (Split-Half) Across All Ages for the BBCS–3:R Spanish Subtest and Receptive Total Scores for a Matched Sample of Spanish and English Speakers (*n* = 61 Matched Pairs)

Subtest/Composite	Spanish	English
1–5 SRC	.99	.99
6 Direction/Position	.99	.99
7 Self-/Social Awareness	.96	.97
8 Texture/Material	.95	.96
9 Quantity	.97	.98
10 Time/Sequence	.95	.95
Receptive Total	.99	.99

Note. The reliability coefficients are split-half correlations corrected by the Spearman-Brown formula.

Evidence of Validity of the BBCS–3:R Spanish

The BBCS–3:R Spanish was developed to assess Spanish-speaking children's comprehension of educationally relevant concepts such as colors, letters, numbers/counting, sizes/comparisons, shapes, direction/position, self-/social awareness, texture/material, quantity, and time/sequence. It may be used in any appropriate setting by a trained Spanish-speaking examiner to assess basic concept skills of young Spanish-speaking children as part of a speech-language evaluation, psychoeducational evaluation, or neuropsychological evaluation. See chapter 7 for evidence of validity of the BBCS–3:R based on content sampling. Because BBCS–3:R Spanish is a translation of the BBCS–3:R English, the test content and constructs assessed are similar across languages. Although the list of concepts assessed on the BBCS–3:R was originally developed for the English edition of the test, reviewers familiar with school programs in the United States and in Spanish-speaking countries agreed that the concepts sampled by the BBCS and BBCS–R Spanish were of the same relative importance in Spanish-language or bilingual school curricula as they were in English-language schools. These sources of validity support the intended interpretation of the BBCS–3:R Spanish for Spanish-speaking children.

In addition to the evidence of validity of the BBCS–3:R English presented in chapter 7, refer to the previous sections in this chapter, Development of the BBCS–R and BBCS–3:R Spanish Items, and Differences Between the English and Spanish Items of the BBCS–3:R, for additional evidence of validity based on test content. These sections describe the development of the Spanish items, including the procedures that were followed to ensure that the Spanish items were as similar as possible to the English items and appropriate for Spanish-speaking children ages 3 years, 0 months to 6 years, 11 months, and that the subtests adequately sample the children's ability to understand basic concepts.

Evidence Based on Internal Structure

Intercorrelation Analyses

Patterns of subtest intercorrelations reflect the degree to which subtests are related. Subtests that measure similar abilities are expected to have moderate-to-high intercorrelations, which provide evidence of the subtests' convergent validity. It was hypothesized that there would be a moderate-to-high correlation among all of the BBCS–3:R subtests, given that each subtest assesses children's understanding of basic language concepts. Table 6.4 reports the subtest and receptive total raw score intercorrelations for a matched sample of Spanish-speaking children who took the BBCS–3:R Spanish and English-speaking children who took the BBCS–3:R English. The samples were matched as closely as possible by age, gender, parent education level, and geographic region. The total test intercorrelations for both samples were moderate-to-high, ranging between .82 and .95 for the Spanish sample and .90 to .95 for the English sample. These correlations suggest that the subtests are measuring a homogenous construct in both Spanish and English.

Table 6.4 BBCS–3:R Intercorrelations of Subtest and Receptive Total Raw Scores for a Matched Sample of Spanish and English Speakers (*n* = 61 Matched Pairs)

Subtest/Composite	1–5 SRC	6 Direction/ Position	7 Self-/Social Awareness	8 Texture/ Material	9 Quantity	10 Time/ Sequence	Receptive Total
1–5 SRC							
6 Direction/Position	.83 (.83)						
7 Self-/Social Awareness	.78 (.86)	.78 (.82)					
8 Texture/Material	.73 (.82)	.72 (.82)	.71 (.84)				
9 Quantity	.78 (.84)	.74 (.86)	.75 (.84)	.76 (.85)			
10 Time/Sequence	.78 (.85)	.76 (.88)	.75 (.85)	.66 (.81)	.83 (.87)		
Receptive Total	.95 (.95)	.92 (.94)	.88 (.92)	.82 (.90)	.89 (.93)	.87 (.93)	
Mean[a]	41.3 (51.2)	23.6 (32.7)	17.7 (21.3)	9.8 (14.6)	16.4 (18.3)	10.7 (12.6)	119.5 (150.7)
SD[b]	23.5 (23.1)	15.5 (18.4)	8.5 (9.5)	6.9 (8.2)	10.4 (10.8)	7.3 (8.6)	65.3 (73.4)

Note. English correlations are shown in parentheses. Correlations were averaged across all ages using Fisher's *z* transformations.

[a] Mean is the arithmetic average across all ages.

[b] *SD* is the pooled standard deviation across all ages.

Summary of Reliability and Validity Evidence

Initial evidence of reliability and validity of BBCS–3:R Spanish and its use in making decisions about young children's ability to understand basic concepts is presented. Internal consistency reliability coefficients and an intercorrelation study with the BBCS–3:R English suggest that the BBCS–3:R Spanish reliably assesses similar constructs (i.e., basic concepts) in Spanish as the BBCS–3:R does in English. Evidence based on test content and internal structure is presented and provides evidence for the validity of BBCS–3:R Spanish. Together with the reliability and validity evidence presented in the previous edition (BBCS–R Spanish), this reliability and validity evidence demonstrates that the BBCS–3:R Spanish is a reliable and valid instrument for criterion-referenced or curriculum-based assessment as one component of a child's comprehensive evaluation.

Evidence of Reliability and Validity

When using a standardized, norm-referenced measure, the examiner must be confident that scores obtained are reliable and valid indicators of the assessed construct, skill, or ability. This chapter explains the methods used to evaluate and provide evidence of the reliability and validity of BBCS–3:R scores in measuring a child's understanding of basic concepts.

Evidence of Reliability

The reliability of a test rests on the accuracy, consistency, and stability of test scores across situations (Anastasi and Urbina, 1997). More specifically, reliability refers to the consistency of scores obtained by repeatedly testing the same individual on the same test under identical conditions (assuming no changes to the individual). Although in reality such testing can never be accomplished, it is possible to obtain various estimates of reliability within a single assessment or a limited number of assessments. An individual's obtained test score is best thought of as an approximation of his or her unobservable and hypothetical "true score." The difference between the individual's obtained score and his or her true score is measurement error. A reliable test and assessment process will yield relatively small measurement error and highly consistent measurable results within one test administration or across repeated administrations. In essence, reliability is a function of how well the test is constructed, how prepared the individual is for the evaluation, how prepared the examiner is for the evaluation, and how conducive the assessment conditions are for a sound evaluation. The reliability of a test score should always be considered when interpreting children's obtained test scores and any differences that exist between test scores across multiple occasions.

The reliability of BBCS–3:R was estimated using test-retest stability (i.e., data which show the BBCS–3:R scores are stable across repeated administrations) and internal consistency (i.e., data that show test items within a subtest or a group of subtests are homogenous and yield consistent estimates of ability).

Evidence of Test-Retest Stability

One way of estimating the reliability of an instrument is to examine the stability of test scores over time and repeated administrations of the test. To examine test stability, the child is administered the same test on two occasions, each time under conditions that are as similar as possible. The interval chosen between the test and retest should be as short as reasonable to minimize true developmental changes in the child (e.g., growth in concept knowledge), while being long enough to dissipate any practice or memory effects resulting from having taken the test previously. Typically, the child will not earn identical scores on each of the two test administrations; however, the scores should be close enough to support the interpretation that the construct is being assessed at comparable levels across the two administrations. To demonstrate test stability, test scores from the first administration are correlated with test scores obtained from the second administration, and mean scores are compared to examine the average score difference resulting from the two test administrations. Tests with good test-retest reliability should provide strong positive test–retest correlations and nonsignificant mean score differences.

BBCS–3:R test-retest stability was evaluated in a study in which the test was administered to 87 children on two separate occasions, and the resulting scores were correlated and compared for mean score differences. After being tested initially as part of the normative sample, the 87 children were administered the test again within 2 to 30 days (M = 7.6, SD = 4.8), with both test administrations conducted by the same examiner. The sample included 39 males and 48 females; 19.5% of the children were African American, 6.9% were Asian, 25.3% were Hispanic, 40.2% were White, and 8.1% were children from other racial/ethnic groups. The education level of the children's primary caregivers included 17.3% with less than a high school education, 26.4% with a high school diploma or GED, 33.3% with one-to-three years of college or technical school, and 23.0% with a college or post-graduate degree.

The test-retest stability was estimated using Pearson's product-moment correlation coefficient for the age bands 3:0–4:11 and 5:0–6:11 and all ages combined. The mean subtest scaled scores and composite scores, and their standard deviations are presented in Table 7.1. The test-retest coefficients for the overall sample (all ages combined) were calculated using Fisher's z transformation (Silver and Dunlap, 1987; Strube, 1988). The stability coefficients were corrected for the variability of the normative sample (Allen and Yen, 1979; Magnusson, 1967). The standard difference (i.e., effect size) between the first and second testing is also reported. The standard difference was calculated using the mean score difference between two testing sessions divided by the pooled sample standard deviation (Cohen, 1996).

As the data in Table 7.1 indicate, BBCS–3:R scores possess adequate to good stability across time for all age bands. The average corrected stability coefficients for all ages for the SRC, Direction/Position, Texture/Material, and Time/Sequence subtests are good (in the .80s) and those for the Self-/Social Awareness and Quantity subtests are adequate (in the .70s). In addition, the average corrected stability coefficients of the Receptive TC and the Receptive SRC scores are good to excellent (.94 and .86, respectively).

The data also indicate that the mean retest scores for all subtests for combined ages are higher than the scores for the first test, with the effect sizes ranging from .11 to .39. In general, test-retest gains are less pronounced for the SRC, Texture/Material, and Time/Sequence subtests than for the Direction/Position, Self-/Social Awareness, and Quantity subtests. The score differences for the combined ages, primarily due to practice effects, are 4.7 points for the Receptive TC score and 3.4 points for the Receptive SRC score and are within the expected range.

Table 7.1 Stability Coefficients for Subtest and Composite Scores by Age Group and Across All Ages

3:0–4:11

		Test		Retest				
Subtest/Composite	***n***	**Mean**	***SD***	**Mean**	***SD***	**Standard Difference**[a]	***r***[b]	***SEM***
1–5 SRC	41	9.0	3.2	9.7	3.7	.20	.93	0.79
6 Direction/Position	41	9.6	3.2	10.3	3.7	.20	.85	1.16
7 Self-/Social Awareness	41	9.9	2.9	10.5	3.4	.19	.78	1.41
8 Texture/Material	41	10.0	2.7	10.1	3.3	.03	.88	1.04
9 Quantity	41	9.1	2.7	10.2	3.4	.36	.76	1.47
10 Time/Sequence	41	9.7	3.4	9.5	3.5	–.06	.72	1.59
Receptive TC	41	97.4	15.4	100.7	18.9	.19	.94	3.67
Receptive SRC	41	95.1	16.4	98.3	18.3	.18	.92	4.24

5:0–6:11

		Test		Retest				
Subtest/Composite	***n***	**Mean**	***SD***	**Mean**	***SD***	**Standard Difference**[a]	***r***[b]	***SEM***
1–5 SRC	46	10.3	3.7	10.6	3.8	.08	.65	1.77
6 Direction/Position	46	9.9	2.9	10.7	3.0	.27	.86	1.12
7 Self-/Social Awareness	46	9.8	2.9	10.6	2.9	.28	.78	1.41
8 Texture/Material	46	9.8	3.1	10.6	3.3	.25	.89	0.99
9 Quantity	46	10.1	3.4	11.7	3.5	.46	.82	1.27
10 Time/Sequence	46	9.9	2.8	11.0	2.7	.40	.87	1.08
Receptive TC	46	99.9	16.8	105.9	17.3	.35	.93	3.97
Receptive SRC	46	100.9	19.1	104.7	16.1	.22	.76	7.35

All Ages

		Test		Retest				
Subtest/Composite	***n***	**Mean**	***SD***	**Mean**	***SD***	**Standard Difference**[a]	***r***[b]	***SEM***
1–5 SRC	87	9.7	3.5	10.1	3.7	.11	.84	1.37
6 Direction/Position	87	9.8	3.0	10.5	3.3	.22	.86	1.14
7 Self-/Social Awareness	87	9.8	2.9	10.6	3.2	.26	.78	1.41
8 Texture/Material	87	9.9	2.9	10.4	3.3	.16	.89	1.02
9 Quantity	87	9.7	3.1	11.0	3.5	.39	.79	1.37
10 Time/Sequence	87	9.8	3.1	10.3	3.2	.16	.81	1.36
Receptive TC	87	98.7	16.1	103.4	18.2	.27	.94	3.82
Receptive SRC	87	98.2	18.0	101.6	17.4	.19	.86	6.00

Note. Receptive TC = Receptive Total Composite, Receptive SRC = Receptive School Readiness Composite

[a] Standard Difference is the difference of the two test means divided by the square root of the pooled variance, computed using Cohen's (1996) Formula 10.4.

[b] Correlations were corrected for the variability of the standardization sample (Allen and Yen, 1979; Magnusson, 1967).

[c] Stability coefficients for all ages were calculated by averaging corrected or uncorrected stability coefficients across all ages with Fisher's *z* transformation.

Evidence of Internal Consistency

Measures of internal consistency also can be used to estimate a test's reliability. Using internal consistency as a measure of reliability implies that items within subtests measure a single, unified construct. Internal consistency reliability coefficients are used to describe the homogeneity of the items within subtests.

Internal consistency information is presented for both the normative sample and for two clinical groups: children identified with a language impairment and children identified with intellectual disability. Reliability data also are presented by race/ethnicity and gender. Reliability is reported based on the results of the split-half method of analysis.

Evidence of Reliability Based on the Split-Half Method

The split-half method of reliability calculation uses two halves of a single administration of a test to estimate the internal consistency reliability of the test. First, test items were rank ordered on the basis of item response theory (IRT) difficulty estimates. Then the items were divided into two half-tests of approximately equal difficulty. The variances for the two half-tests were compared to ensure that the two half-tests were distributed similarly. The split-half reliability coefficient of the subtest is the correlation between the total scores on the two half-tests, corrected by the Spearman-Brown formula to account for test length (Crocker and Algina, 1986; Li, Rosenthal, and Rubin, 1996).

The reliability coefficients of the BBCS–3:R composite scores were calculated with the formula recommended by Guilford (1954) and Nunnally and Bernstein (1994). Table 7.2 presents the internal consistency reliability coefficients for subtest and composite scores by age for the normative sample. The average reliability coefficients were calculated using Fisher's z transformation (Silver and Dunlap, 1987; Strube, 1988). These reliability coefficients and standard errors of measurement were used in the development of critical values for confidence intervals cited in the norms tables.

Reliability of Subtest Scores

The data in Table 7.2 indicate that for the overall normative sample, the average split-half reliability coefficients of BBCS–3:R subtests are excellent ($r_{xx} \geq .90$), ranging from .91 for Self-/Social Awareness, Texture/Material, and Time/Sequence to .97 for Direction/Position. Note that the relatively lower reliability coefficients for the older age groups are likely due to ceiling effects (i.e., older children respond correctly to almost all the items).

Reliability of Composite Scores

The average reliability coefficients are excellent ($r_{xx} \geq .90$) for both composite scores (Receptive TC and Receptive SRC). The reliability coefficients for BBCS–3:R composite scores are .98 (Receptive TC) and .95 (Receptive SRC). The reliability coefficient of the Receptive TC is higher than the individual subtests that compose the composite. This difference occurs because each subtest represents only a narrow portion of a child's concept knowledge. Higher reliability of composite scores is expected because the composite scores are based on more items than are tested in a single subtest. The composite scores summarize the child's performance on a broader sample of basic concept knowledge.

Table 7.2 Internal Consistency Reliability Coefficients (Split-Half) for the BBCS–3:R Subtest and Composite Scores by Age and Across All Ages

	3:0–3:5	3:6–3:11	4:0–4:5	4:6–4:11	5:0–5:5	5:6–5:11	6:0–6:5	6:6–6:11	Average r_{xx}
n	80	80	80	80	80	80	80	80	640
Subtest/Composite									
1–5 SRC	.96	.97	.96	.96	.97	.96	.90	.82	.95
6 Direction/Position	.94	.97	.98	.98	.98	.97	.96	.95	.97
7 Self-/Social Awareness	.89	.92	.94	.93	.91	.95	.88	.85	.91
8 Texture/Material	.81	.93	.93	.92	.93	.93	.90	.85	.91
9 Quantity	.93	.94	.96	.93	.94	.96	.93	.92	.94
10 Time/Sequence	.81	.87	.91	.92	.95	.94	.93	.90	.91
Receptive TC	.97	.98	.99	.99	.99	.99	.98	.97	.98
Receptive SRC	.96	.97	.96	.96	.97	.96	.90	.82	.95

Note. The reliability coefficients for all subtests are split-half correlation corrected by the Spearman-Brown formula.

The reliability coefficients for the Receptive TC and Receptive SRC were calculated with the formula for the reliability of a composite (Guilford, 1954; Nunnally and Bernstein, 1994).

The average r_{xx} was computed with Fisher's z transformation and is the average across all ages.

Receptive TC = Receptive Total Composite, Receptive SRC = Receptive School Readiness Composite

Reliability information was also examined for subsets of the normative population (i.e., by gender and race/ethnicity). Tables 7.3 and 7.4 provide internal consistency reliability coefficients of subtests and composites for these groups. The reliability coefficients were calculated using the same procedure described for Table 7.2, but were examined by two age bands (3:0–4:11 and 5:0–6:11) due to the small sample size at each age. The subtest and composite score reliability coefficients for the male and female groups, although somewhat higher due to the greater range of scores when several ages are combined, are consistent with the reliability coefficients reported for the normative sample by age. This suggests that BBCS–3:R is equally reliable for male and female children. The subtest and composite score reliability coefficients for the African American, Hispanic, and White groups, are also consistent with the coefficients reported for the normative sample. This suggests that BBCS–3:R is equally reliable for children of diverse races/ethnicities.

Table 7.3 Internal Consistency Reliability Coefficients (Split-Half) for the BBCS–3:R Subtest and Composite Scores by Gender

	Male		Female	
Age	**3:0–4:11**	**5:0–6:11**	**3:0–4:11**	**5:0–6:11**
n	159	161	161	159
Subtest/Composite				
1–5 SRC	.98	.96	.97	.97
6 Direction/Position	.98	.97	.98	.98
7 Self-/Social Awareness	.94	.93	.95	.93
8 Texture/Material	.94	.93	.94	.93
9 Quantity	.96	.96	.96	.95
10 Time/Sequence	.94	.95	.91	.95
Receptive TC	.99	.99	.99	.99
Receptive SRC	.98	.96	.97	.97

Note. The reliability coefficients for all subtests are split-half correlations corrected by the Spearman-Brown formula.

The reliability coefficients for the Receptive TC and Receptive SRC were calculated with the formula for the reliability of a composite (Guilford, 1954; Nunnally and Bernstein, 1994).

Receptive TC = Receptive Total Composite, Receptive SRC = Receptive School Readiness Composite

Table 7.4 Internal Consistency Reliability Coefficients (Split-Half) for the BBCS–3:R Subtest and Composite Scores by Race/Ethnicity

	African American		Hispanic		White	
Age	**3:0–4:11**	**5:0–6:11**	**3:0–4:11**	**5:0-6:11**	**3:0-4:11**	**5:0-6:11**
n	42	46	59	66	192	186
Subtest/Composite						
1–5 SRC	.97	.98	.97	.96	.97	.94
6 Direction/Position	.97	.98	.96	.98	.98	.96
7 Self-/Social Awareness	.93	.95	.91	.94	.95	.89
8 Texture/Material	.92	.94	.88	.95	.94	.84
9 Quantity	.94	.97	.92	.93	.96	.94
10 Time/Sequence	.95	.95	.94	.94	.92	.93
Receptive TC	.99	.99	.98	.99	.99	.98
Receptive SRC	.97	.98	.97	.96	.97	.94

Note. The reliability coefficients for all subtests are split-half correlations corrected by the Spearman-Brown formula.

The reliability coefficients for the Receptive TC and Receptive SRC were calculated with the formula for the reliability of a composite (Guilford, 1954; Nunnally and Bernstein, 1994).

Receptive TC = Receptive Total Composite, Receptive SRC = Receptive School Readiness Composite

Evidence of Reliability for Clinical Groups

Reliability information was also examined for groups of children with clinical diagnoses. The evidence of internal consistency reliability for clinical groups was obtained by the split-half method for a sample of 116 children in two groups: 52 children with language impairments and 64 children with intellectual disability. See the Evidence Based on Special Group Studies section in this chapter for detailed demographic information for both clinical groups.

Table 7.5 provides internal consistency reliability coefficients of subtests and composite scores for the two clinical groups. The reliability coefficients were calculated using the same procedure described for Table 7.2. As seen in Table 7.5, the subtest reliability coefficients for the clinical groups are consistent with the coefficients reported for the normative sample. As with the reliability coefficients reported for gender and race/ethnicity, they are somewhat higher than the normative sample reliability coefficients due to the greater range of scores when all ages are combined. This initial evidence suggests that BBCS–3:R is equally reliable for measuring children's understanding of basic concepts whether the children come from the general population or are children diagnosed with language impairments or intellectual disability.

Table 7.5 Internal Consistency Reliability Coefficients (Split-Half) for Subtest and Composite Scores by Clinical Group

	Language Impairment	Intellectual Disability
n	52	64
Subtest/Composite		
1–5 SRC	.98	.97
6 Direction/Position	.99	.99
7 Self-/Social Awareness	.97	.97
8 Texture/Material	.96	.97
9 Quantity	.98	.98
10 Time/Sequence	.98	.97
Receptive TC	.99	.99
Receptive SRC	.98	.97

Note. The reliability coefficients for all subtests are split-half correlations corrected by the Spearman-Brown formula.

The reliability coefficients for the Receptive TC and Receptive SRC were calculated with the formula for the reliability of a composite (Guilford, 1954; Nunnally and Bernstein, 1994).

Receptive TC = Receptive Total Composite, Receptive SRC = Receptive School Readiness Composite

Standard Error of Measurement and Confidence Intervals

Reliability coefficients are useful for evaluating a test's consistency of measurement for a group of children, but are not directly applicable to the interpretation of individual test scores. The standard error of measurement (*SEM*), on the other hand, is a statistic that estimates the amount of error present in an assessment and *SEM* is directly related to the test's reliability coefficients and the variability (standard deviation) of the test scores. The standard error of measurement indicates the variability expected in obtained scores around the hypothetical "true" score. In other words, *SEM* indicates how much a child's score would be expected to vary if the child were repeatedly administered the same instrument under identical circumstances. When BBCS–3:R is administered to a child, the resulting observed scores are estimates of his or her true scores, which include some measurement error. The *SEM* of a test helps users gain a sense of how much variability might be expected around the child's observed or obtained score and the extent to which the child's observed score is likely to differ from his or her hypothetical true score. The *SEM* is inversely related to the reliability of a test, so that the greater the reliability, the smaller the *SEM*, and the greater the confidence you can have in the precision of the test scores. The *SEM*s for BBCS–3:R subtest and composite scores are reported in terms of standard score units in Table 7.6. Note that the relatively larger composite score *SEM*s in the table do not indicate a higher level of error in these scores than in the subtest scores, but rather the greater variability of composite scores and the different score scale employed with composite scores versus subtest scores.

To determine the expected amount of variability around a child's observed score, the standard error of measurement can be used to construct and place a confidence interval around the child's obtained score, resulting in a range of scores within which the child's true score is likely to exist with some level of confidence.

Critical values for developing confidence intervals at 90% and 95% confidence levels for each BBCS–3:R subtest scaled score and Receptive SRC score are reported in the norms tables (refer to Appendix A and Appendix C). Suggestions for interpreting test results using confidence intervals are in chapter 3.

Table 7.6 Standard Errors of Measurement Based on Internal Reliability Coefficients (Split-Half) for BBCS–3:R Subtest and Composite Scores by Age and Across All Ages

	3:0–3:5	3:6–3:11	4:0–4:5	4:6–4:11	5:0–5:5	5:6–5:11	6:0–6:5	6:6–6:11	Average *SEM*
n	80	80	80	80	80	80	80	80	640
Subtest/Composite									
1–5 SRC	0.60	0.52	0.60	0.60	0.52	0.60	0.95	1.27	0.75
6 Direction/Position	0.73	0.52	0.42	0.42	0.42	0.52	0.60	0.67	0.55
7 Self-/Social Awareness	0.99	0.85	0.73	0.79	0.90	0.67	1.04	1.16	0.90
8 Texture/Material	1.31	0.79	0.79	0.85	0.79	0.79	0.95	1.16	0.95
9 Quantity	0.79	0.73	0.60	0.79	0.73	0.60	0.79	0.85	0.74
10 Time/Sequence	1.31	1.08	0.90	0.85	0.67	0.73	0.79	0.95	0.93
Receptive TC	2.60	2.12	1.50	1.50	1.50	1.50	2.12	2.60	1.98
Receptive SRC	3.00	2.60	3.00	3.00	2.60	3.00	4.74	6.36	3.75

Note. The average *SEM*s were calculated by averaging the sum of the squared *SEM*s for each age group and obtaining the square root of the result.

Receptive TC = Receptive Total Composite, Receptive SRC = Receptive School Readiness Composite

Score Differences

The difference between a child's ability to comprehend basic concepts and his or her ability to verbally label basic concepts can be determined by examining the difference between the composite scores of the BBCS–3:R and BBCS:E. Interpretation of score differences across receptive and expressive editions of the test examines two aspects—the statistical significance of the difference and the prevalence, or frequency, of the difference in the population. These aspects are designed to address two questions: (1) Is the existing difference statistically significant and not due to measurement error? and (2) Is the difference clinically meaningful?

Composite Score Differences

Statistical Significance of Composite Score Differences

A statistically significant difference between composite scores, such as the Receptive Total Composite (Receptive TC) and the Expressive Total Composite (Expressive TC), indicates that the difference between the two composites was probably not due to measurement error or chance fluctuation. In other words, when a score discrepancy is statistically significant, one can reasonably assume that this is a true difference (Matarazzo and Herman, 1985) in children's receptive and expressive conceptual knowledge. The difference between scores required for statistical significance is computed from the standard error of the difference *(SEdiff)* statistic. This statistic provides an estimated standard deviation of the sampling distribution of the difference between the two obtained composite scores. Multiplying the standard error of the difference by an appropriate z value yields the amount of difference required for statistical significance at any given level of confidence.

The differences between BBCS–3:R and BBCS:E composite scores required for statistical significance are in Table 3.4. The critical values (the difference in standard score units) are provided for the .15 and .05 levels of significance by age group and for the overall normative sample. Although these differences vary slightly from age group to age group, average difference values for all age groups provide an acceptable approximation for many clinical situations. Average difference values for all age groups are presented in the last row of Table 3.4.

Prevalence of Composite Score Differences

The frequency of an observed score difference in the general population is also referred to as the prevalence (base rate) of the score difference. Often the difference between an individual's composite scores is statistically significant but that magnitude of difference occurs with a relatively high frequency among individuals in the general population. When interpreting the difference between a child's composite scores, you must first determine if the difference in scores is statistically significant and then determine whether that difference occurs frequently or rarely in the general population. Significance and rarity are two different issues and consequently have different implications when interpreting a child's score (see discussion of statistical versus clinical significance in McCauley, 2001).

The Receptive and Expressive School Readiness Composites (Receptive SRC and Expressive SRC) are measures of educationally-relevant concepts children have traditionally needed to know to be adequately prepared for early formal education. (See chapter 4 where the importance of these basic concepts in states' early childhood standards is discussed.) The subtests used to derive the Receptive SRC and Expressive SRC scores include: Colors, Letters/Sounds, Numbers, Sizes/Comparisons, and Shapes. The Receptive and Expressive Total Composites (Receptive TC and Expressive TC) are more comprehensive measures of children's basic concept development and include five other subtests (Direction/Position, Self-/Social Awareness, Texture/ Material, Quantity, and Time/Sequence) in addition to the SRC subtests.

The receptive composites (Receptive TC and Receptive SRC) are measures of the child's comprehension or understanding of basic concepts, while the expressive composites (Expressive TC and Expressive SRC) are measures of a child's ability to verbally label basic concepts. Although the distinction between receptive and expressive language skills may help you better understand the nature of a language disorder, and so better plan intervention, expression of language cannot be completely separated from comprehension of language. Nevertheless, clinicians in school settings are expected to provide information about a child's receptive and expressive language performance and to consider the differences in intervention planning if they are clinically meaningful.

The difference between the Receptive TC and Expressive TC and/or the Receptive SRC and Expressive SRC can be significant in a statistical sense, but may or may not be an unusual or uncommon occurrence. To help interpret composite score differences, the prevalence of composite score differences in the normative sample was studied.

The prevalence of Receptive TC and Expressive TC score differences in the normative sample was studied, and the following patterns of differences were found: 6.1% of the normative sample showed no difference; of those children whose scores differed by one or more standard score points, about half earned higher Receptive TC scores (46.7%); and about half earned higher Expressive TC scores (47.2%). As seen in Table 7.7, more children with language impairments than children in the normative sample showed no difference in Receptive TC and Expressive TC scores (11.5% versus 6.1%), and more children in this sample than the normative sample earned higher Receptive TC scores than earned higher Expressive TC scores that differed by one or more standard score points (55.8% versus 32.7%).

For the Receptive SRC and Expressive SRC composite scores, the following patterns of differences were found: 4.6% of the normative sample showed no difference at all; of the remaining 95.4%, an equal number (47.7%) of all children earned higher Receptive SRC scores as earned higher Expressive SRC scores (47.7%). The results, reported in Table 7.8, demonstrate that the pattern of differences between Receptive SRC and Expressive SRC scores is different for the children with language impairments. In that sample, more children earned higher Expressive SRC scores than earned higher Receptive SRC scores (50.0% versus 44.2%).

Table 7.7 Prevalence of Receptive and Expressive Total Composite Score Discrepancies in the Normative and Language Impaired Samples

Amount of Discrepancy (points)	Normative Sample (n = 640) RTC–ETC		Language Impaired Sample (n = 52) RTC–ETC		Amount of Discrepancy (points)
	RTC < ETC (–)	RTC > ETC (+)	RTC < ETC (–)	RTC > ETC (+)	
≥40	0.2	0.0	0.0	0.0	≥40
39	0.2	0.0	0.0	0.0	39
38	0.2	0.0	0.0	0.0	38
37	0.2	0.0	0.0	0.0	37
36	0.3	0.0	0.0	0.0	36
35	0.3	0.2	0.0	0.0	35
34	0.3	0.3	0.0	0.0	34
33	0.3	0.5	0.0	0.0	33
32	0.3	0.5	0.0	0.0	32
31	0.3	0.5	0.0	0.0	31
30	0.3	0.5	0.0	0.0	30
29	0.3	0.5	0.0	0.0	29
28	0.3	0.6	0.0	0.0	28
27	0.3	0.6	0.0	0.0	27
26	0.5	0.6	0.0	0.0	26
25	0.5	0.8	0.0	0.0	25
24	0.6	0.9	0.0	0.0	24
23	0.8	0.9	0.0	0.0	23
22	1.1	1.4	0.0	0.0	22
21	1.3	1.4	0.0	0.0	21
20	1.4	1.6	0.0	0.0	20
19	1.6	1.7	0.0	0.0	19
18	2.2	2.3	0.0	0.0	18
17	2.7	3.4	0.0	1.9	17
16	3.3	4.2	0.0	0.0	16
15	3.8	4.8	0.0	0.0	15
14	4.4	5.9	0.0	0.0	14
13	6.1	6.9	0.0	3.8	13
12	8.3	8.1	0.0	5.8	12
11	10.0	10.0	1.9	5.8	11
10	12.2	12.7	3.8	7.7	10
9	15.0	15.6	5.8	9.6	9
8	17.8	18.1	7.7	17.3	8
7	21.1	20.8	9.6	19.2	7
6	24.7	24.1	9.6	21.2	6
5	28.4	28.1	15.4	26.9	5
4	32.7	32.0	19.2	30.8	4
3	37.8	36.7	21.2	34.6	3
2	42.7	42.2	26.9	42.3	2
1	47.2	46.7	32.7	55.8	1
Mean	7.0	7.2	4.7	5.2	Mean
SD	5.5	5.8	3.3	4.2	*SD*
Median	6.0	6.0	4.0	4.0	Median

Note. RTC = Receptive Total Composite, ETC = Expressive Total Composite

Table 7.8 Prevalence of Receptive and Expressive School Readiness Composite Score Discrepancies in the Normative and Language Impaired Samples

Amount of Discrepancy (points)	Normative Sample (n = 640) RSRC–ESRC: RSRC < ESRC (–)	RSRC > ESRC (+)	Language Impaired Sample (n = 52) RSRC–ESRC: RSRC < ESRC (–)	RSRC > ESRC (+)	Amount of Discrepancy (points)
≥40	0.0	0.0	0.0	0.0	≥40
39	0.0	0.0	0.0	0.0	39
38	0.0	0.0	0.0	0.0	38
37	0.0	0.0	0.0	0.0	37
36	0.2	0.0	0.0	0.0	36
35	0.3	0.0	0.0	0.0	35
34	0.3	0.0	0.0	0.0	34
33	0.3	0.0	0.0	0.0	33
32	0.3	0.0	0.0	0.0	32
31	0.3	0.5	0.0	0.0	31
30	0.6	0.5	0.0	0.0	30
29	0.8	0.5	0.0	0.0	29
28	0.8	0.5	0.0	0.0	28
27	1.1	0.5	0.0	0.0	27
26	1.1	0.6	0.0	0.0	26
25	1.4	0.8	0.0	0.0	25
24	1.4	0.9	0.0	0.0	24
23	1.4	1.3	0.0	0.0	23
22	1.4	1.4	0.0	0.0	22
21	1.6	1.9	0.0	0.0	21
20	1.9	2.0	1.9	0.0	20
19	2.0	2.0	1.9	0.0	19
18	3.0	2.5	1.9	0.0	18
17	3.3	3.3	3.8	0.0	17
16	4.4	4.1	3.8	0.0	16
15	5.3	5.3	7.7	0.0	15
14	5.8	6.3	11.5	0.0	14
13	7.3	7.2	11.5	0.0	13
12	8.8	9.5	13.5	1.9	12
11	10.2	11.4	17.3	7.7	11
10	11.6	13.4	17.3	7.7	10
9	13.6	16.3	21.2	9.6	9
8	16.4	18.8	25.0	11.5	8
7	19.1	21.4	25.0	13.5	7
6	23.6	23.8	28.8	15.4	6
5	27.0	27.2	30.8	23.1	5
4	31.6	33.1	36.5	25.0	4
3	37.3	38.6	40.4	30.8	3
2	42.2	42.2	42.3	36.5	2
1	47.7	47.7	50.0	44.2	1
Mean	7.0	7.2	7.8	5.1	**Mean**
SD	6.1	5.8	5.6	3.6	***SD***
Median	5.0	5.0	7.0	5.0	**Median**

Note. RSRC = Receptive School Readiness Composite, ESRC = Expressive School Readiness Composite

Evidence of Validity

A test is valid to the extent that it measures what it is intended to measure. There are multiple sources of information required in the process of test validation. Evidence of test validity refers to the degree to which specific data, research, or theory support that a test measures the construct or content it purports to measure and is applicable to the intended population (AERA, et al., 1999). Different sources of evidence represent different aspects of validity; however, these sources do not represent distinct types of validity.

The evidence for valid application of a test includes evaluation of previous versions of the test, evaluation of the updated version of the test, and research that evaluates the utility of the new measure in a variety of clinical contexts. The process of a test's validation is ongoing and occurs throughout the life of the instrument. The applicability of the test also extends to clinical contexts beyond those studied as part of the initial phase of validation.

The studies reported here provide evidence of validity of the BBCS–3:R as a measure of basic concept development in children.

Applicability of the BBCS–3:R

The BBCS–3:R is designed specifically to assess children's comprehension of educationally relevant concepts. In this context, comprehension of educationally relevant concepts refers to a child's ability to understand language concepts such as basic colors, sizes, shapes, direction/position, and so on. The test may be used in any setting in which a trained examiner wants to or is required to assess young children's basic concept acquisition (e.g., a speech-language evaluation, psychoeducational evaluation, neuropsychological evaluation). The following sources of evidence of validity support the intended interpretation of BBCS–3:R results.

Evidence Based on Test Content

Evidence of content validity is based on the degree to which the items adequately represent and relate to content being considered. Test content should reflect the constructs being measured and relate to the proposed application and interpretation of the test. The content of tests used with children must also appropriately reflect developmental aspects of the constructs being measured. Test content also involves the wording and format of items, as well as the procedures for administering and scoring the test. The developmental appropriateness of the assessment is a central aspect of test validity for instruments used with young children.

BBCS–3:R content sampling and subtest construction was designed to address a significant portion of basic concept content appropriate for children ages 3 years, 0 months to 6 years, 11 months. The goal of the revision was to ensure that the subtests adequately sample basic concepts associated with early childhood educationally relevant categories. The BBCS–3:R item content was reviewed by the author, national and international test developers, and an expert panel of speech language pathologists and psychologists for comprehensiveness and appropriateness for young children, and was compared directly to the early childhood educational standards for each of the 50 United States. See chapters 1 and

4 for discussion of the test purpose and design, and chapter 4 for information on the relationship between BBCS–3:R basic concept representation and states' educational standards.

Evidence Based on Response Processes

Evidence of validity based on response processes is evidence that shows the fit between the construct being tested and the format used to elicit the desired behavior (AERA et al., 1999). This type of evidence may be provided by theoretical sources or psychometric analysis and can include an analysis of the construct intended to be assessed, and analysis of the children's responses.

Additional evidence of validity was accumulated through empirical and qualitative examination of response processes during the test's development. For example, the BBCS–3:R items are administered in a multiple choice response format. The items were examined to identify any responses that were commonly given in error. The frequently occurring incorrect responses were examined to determine their plausibility as acceptable answers. Children's responses to tasks were analyzed to determine if the administration directions and/or picture stimuli needed to be modified. Discrepancies in the response mode of children within a task were evaluated, and items were either modified or deleted based on the information obtained.

Evidence Based on Internal Structure

The internal structure of a test refers to the degree to which relationships of items and subtests support the test's ability to measure the intended construct. The relationship among subtests may vary in clinical groups of individuals who have deficits in a specific aspect of language.

Intercorrelation Analyses

Patterns of intercorrelations reflect the degree to which subtests are related. Subtests that measure similar abilities are expected to be moderately-to-highly correlated. Moderate-to-high intercorrelations are one source of convergent validity evidence. It was hypothesized that there would be moderate-to-high correlations among all of the BBCS–3:R subtests given that each subtest is a measure of basic language concepts.

The correlations between subtest and composite scores are affected by the degree to which a subtest contributes to the composite score. These correlations should be high if they represent part-to-whole correlations that are statistically dependent. It was anticipated that the BBCS–3:R subtests would correlate moderately to highly with the composite scores and that a similar relationship would exist between the Receptive TC and Receptive SRC. Table 7.9 presents the intercorrelations between subtests and composites for the BBCS–3:R normative sample by age group and by all ages combined. Due to smaller sample size at each age (n = 80), it is most meaningful to evaluate the All Ages (n = 640) intercorrelations.

There is a high correlation (.79) between the Receptive TC and the Receptive SRC scores across all ages. This is expected, because the concepts on the first five subtests (i.e., the Receptive SRC) are part of the total test score (Receptive TC). At the subtest level, the intercorrelations across all ages are moderate, ranging from .54

to .68. The pattern of correlations is consistent with the expected pattern, and the level of intercorrelation provides strong primary evidence for the instrument's construct validity.

Table 7.9 Intercorrelations of BBCS-3:R Subtest and Composite Scores by Age Group and Across All Ages

3:0–3:5 (*n* = 80)

Subtest/Composite	1–5 SRC	6 Direction/ Position	7 Self-/Social Awareness	8 Texture/ Material	9 Quantity	10 Time/ Sequence	Receptive TC	Receptive SRC
6 Direction/Position	0.45							
7 Self-/Social Awareness	0.38	0.67						
8 Texture/Material	0.41	0.43	0.40					
9 Quantity	0.48	0.55	0.53	0.54				
10 Time/Sequence	0.45	0.40	0.42	0.40	0.51			
Receptive TC	0.71	0.78	0.75	0.70	0.80	0.73		
Receptive SRC	1.00	0.47	0.39	0.39	0.49	0.45	0.71	
Mean[a]	10.0	10.2	10.3	10.1	10.1	10.0	101.0	100.1
SD[b]	3.1	3.3	2.9	3.0	3.1	3.5	14.5	15.4

3:6–3:11 (*n* = 80)

Subtest/Composite	1–5 SRC	6 Direction/ Position	7 Self-/Social Awareness	8 Texture/ Material	9 Quantity	10 Time/ Sequence	Receptive TC	Receptive SRC
6 Direction/Position	0.55							
7 Self-/Social Awareness	0.56	0.55						
8 Texture/Material	0.53	0.58	0.52					
9 Quantity	0.53	0.64	0.56	0.65				
10 Time/Sequence	0.29	0.56	0.43	0.54	0.63			
Receptive TC	0.72	0.82	0.76	0.81	0.85	0.75		
Receptive SRC	0.99	0.55	0.57	0.54	0.54	0.31	0.73	
Mean[a]	9.9	9.7	9.3	10.0	9.6	9.5	98.2	99.7
SD[b]	2.8	2.7	2.7	3.0	2.8	3.2	14.1	13.9

4:0–4:5 (*n* = 80)

Subtest/Composite	1–5 SRC	6 Direction/ Position	7 Self-/Social Awareness	8 Texture/ Material	9 Quantity	10 Time/ Sequence	Receptive TC	Receptive SRC
6 Direction/Position	0.70							
7 Self-/Social Awareness	0.53	0.71						
8 Texture/Material	0.62	0.69	0.61					
9 Quantity	0.67	0.77	0.65	0.76				
10 Time/Sequence	0.59	0.68	0.60	0.61	0.74			
Receptive TC	0.80	0.90	0.81	0.84	0.90	0.83		
Receptive SRC	0.99	0.71	0.55	0.63	0.68	0.60	0.81	
Mean[a]	10.1	10.3	10.2	10.0	10.4	10.2	101.4	100.2
SD[b]	2.8	3.5	3.2	2.9	3.1	3.0	16.3	14.4

Table 7.9 Intercorrelations of BBCS-3:R Subtest and Composite Scores by Age Group and Across All Ages (continued)

4:6–4:11 ($n = 80$)

Subtest/Composite	1–5 SRC	6 Direction/ Position	7 Self-/Social Awareness	8 Texture/ Material	9 Quantity	10 Time/ Sequence	Receptive TC	Receptive SRC
6 Direction/Position	0.62							
7 Self-/Social Awareness	0.67	0.72						
8 Texture/Material	0.67	0.73	0.72					
9 Quantity	0.62	0.74	0.74	0.68				
10 Time/Sequence	0.52	0.70	0.64	0.57	0.70			
Receptive TC	0.80	0.89	0.88	0.85	0.88	0.80		
Receptive SRC	1.00	0.62	0.67	0.67	0.62	0.50	0.80	
Mean[a]	9.9	10.1	10.5	10.1	9.8	10.3	100.8	99.3
SD[b]	3.0	3.2	3.1	2.7	2.8	2.6	15.3	14.7

5:0–5:5 ($n = 80$)

Subtest/Composite	1–5 SRC	6 Direction/ Position	7 Self-/Social Awareness	8 Texture/ Material	9 Quantity	10 Time/ Sequence	Receptive TC	Receptive SRC
6 Direction/Position	0.67							
7 Self-/Social Awareness	0.65	0.67						
8 Texture/Material	0.54	0.65	0.65					
9 Quantity	0.64	0.69	0.77	0.67				
10 Time/Sequence	0.68	0.69	0.70	0.63	0.70			
Receptive TC	0.82	0.86	0.86	0.81	0.88	0.86		
Receptive SRC	0.99	0.67	0.66	0.54	0.64	0.69	0.82	
Mean[a]	10.1	9.8	9.6	10.1	9.8	9.6	99.1	100.4
SD[b]	2.8	3.3	2.4	2.7	3.0	3.0	15.1	14.2

5:6–5:11 ($n = 80$)

Subtest/Composite	1–5 SRC	6 Direction/ Position	7 Self-/Social Awareness	8 Texture/ Material	9 Quantity	10 Time/ Sequence	Receptive TC	Receptive SRC
6 Direction/Position	0.76							
7 Self-/Social Awareness	0.66	0.70						
8 Texture/Material	0.62	0.76	0.71					
9 Quantity	0.72	0.78	0.68	0.65				
10 Time/Sequence	0.65	0.78	0.69	0.71	0.72			
Receptive TC	0.84	0.92	0.85	0.86	0.87	0.87		
Receptive SRC	1.00	0.77	0.66	0.63	0.72	0.66	0.85	
Mean[a]	9.8	10.4	9.4	9.9	10.1	10.1	99.9	98.9
SD[b]	2.9	3.5	2.8	3.1	3.0	2.9	16.4	14.9

Table 7.9 Intercorrelations of BBCS-3:R Subtest and Composite Scores by Age Group and Across All Ages (continued)

6:0–6:5 ($n = 80$)

Subtest/Composite	1–5 SRC	6 Direction/ Position	7 Self-/Social Awareness	8 Texture/ Material	9 Quantity	10 Time/ Sequence	Receptive TC	Receptive SRC
6 Direction/Position	0.67							
7 Self-/Social Awareness	0.68	0.66						
8 Texture/Material	0.43	0.55	0.63					
9 Quantity	0.52	0.67	0.59	0.64				
10 Time/Sequence	0.45	0.61	0.67	0.70	0.72			
Receptive TC	0.76	0.84	0.85	0.80	0.84	0.84		
Receptive SRC	1.00	0.68	0.69	0.45	0.52	0.47	0.77	
Mean[a]	10.1	9.7	10.0	10.0	10.1	9.9	100.1	100.1
SD[b]	2.9	2.7	2.8	2.8	3.0	3.0	14.6	14.7

6:6–6:11 ($n = 80$)

Subtest/Composite	1–5 SRC	6 Direction/ Position	7 Self-/Social Awareness	8 Texture/ Material	9 Quantity	10 Time/ Sequence	Receptive TC	Receptive SRC
6 Direction/Position	0.49							
7 Self-/Social Awareness	0.69	0.57						
8 Texture/Material	0.64	0.59	0.69					
9 Quantity	0.64	0.56	0.58	0.65				
10 Time/Sequence	0.58	0.61	0.62	0.67	0.71			
Receptive TC	0.82	0.76	0.83	0.85	0.85	0.85		
Receptive SRC	0.99	0.50	0.68	0.64	0.62	0.57	0.81	
Mean[a]	10.1	9.9	10.0	9.7	10.0	9.7	99.6	99.8
SD[b]	3.1	2.5	2.7	2.6	3.3	2.8	14.7	15.7

All Ages ($n = 640$)

Subtest/Composite	1–5 SRC	6 Direction/ Position	7 Self-/Social Awareness	8 Texture/ Material	9 Quantity	10 Time/ Sequence	Receptive TC	Receptive SRC
6 Direction/Position	0.62							
7 Self-/Social Awareness	0.61	0.66						
8 Texture/Material	0.56	0.63	0.63					
9 Quantity	0.61	0.68	0.65	0.66				
10 Time/Sequence	0.54	0.64	0.61	0.61	0.68			
Receptive TC	0.79	0.86	0.83	0.82	0.86	0.82		
Receptive SRC	0.99	0.63	0.62	0.57	0.61	0.54	0.79	
Mean[a]	10.0	10.0	9.9	10.0	10.0	9.9	100.0	99.8
SD[b]	2.9	3.1	2.8	2.8	3.0	3.0	15.1	14.7

Note. Correlations were averaged across all ages using Fisher's z transformations.

Receptive TC = Receptive Total Composite, Receptive SRC = Receptive School Readiness Composite

[a] Mean is the arithmetic average across each age group.

[b] *SD* is the pooled standard deviation across each age group.

Evidence Based on Relationships With Other Variables

Understanding how a test relates to other tests designed to measure the same or similar constructs provides additional evidence of the test's validity. It is important to understand how the BBCS–3:R relates to the previous version (BBCS–R) as well as other concurrently administered tests of language ability. In addition, because evidence of a test's clinical utility and specificity is crucial, additional evidence of validity is provided based on the results of special group studies. Much of the validity support for the BBCS–3:R is provided in the wide variety of validity studies conducted with the BBCS, the BBCS–R, and the *Bracken School Readiness Assessment* (BSRA; Bracken, 2002) that have examined the relationship between concept development and intelligence (Howell and Bracken, 1992; McIntosh, Wayland, Gridley, and Barnes, 1995; Rothlisberg, Allen, and D'Amato, 1992), academic achievement (Panter, 1997), and language development (Bracken, 1984; Bracken, Howell, and Crain, 1993; Rhyner and Bracken, 1988). All of these previously conducted studies show that the content assessed on the BBCS and its subsequent editions is a powerful predictor of young children's abilities in several related areas (i.e., intelligence, academic achievement, language development).

Two studies were conducted concurrently with the standardization of BBCS–3:R to examine the relationship between BBCS–3:R scores and other measures of language. The relationships between BBCS–3:R and the BBCS–R, and the BBCS–3:R and *Preschool Language Scale–Fourth Edition* (PLS–4; Zimmerman, Steiner, and Pond, 2002) were examined. Additional evidence of validity is provided by examining the performance of two groups of children: one group of children identified with language impairments, and one group of children diagnosed with intellectual disability.

Correlation With BBCS–R

BBCS–R and BBCS–3:R, like their predecessor the BBCS, are designed to measure young children's receptive understanding of basic concepts. As a revision of BBCS–R, the scores on the two tests should be very similar since they measure the same universe of content (i.e., basic concepts). The BBCS–3:R and BBCS–R were administered to 51 typically developing children. The demographic characteristics of the sample are shown in Table 7.10. The BBCS–3:R and BBCS–R were administered, in that order, between 1 and 25 days apart (M = 5.8, SD = 4.5).

Table 7.10 Distribution of the BBCS–3:R–BBCS–R Validity Sample by Age, Gender, Race/Ethnicity, Geographic Region, and Parent Education Level

n	51
Age	
Mean	4.9
SD	1.2
	% of Sample
Gender	
Female	52.9
Male	47.1
Race/Ethnicity	
African American	21.6
Asian	11.8
Hispanic	17.7
White	43.1
Other	5.8
Geographic Region	
Midwest	25.5
Northeast	19.6
South	35.3
West	19.6
Parent Education Level	
11 years of school or less	15.7
12 years of school or GED	35.3
13 to 15 years of school	25.5
16 years of school or more	23.5

Based on the design and application of BBCS–3:R and BBCS–R, it was anticipated that there would be a high positive correlation between the subtest and composite scores of the two tests. Table 7.11 presents the means, standard deviations, and corrected correlation coefficients.

Correlations (corrected for restriction in range) between BBCS–3:R and BBCS–R subtest scores are high as expected, ranging from .69 (Time/Sequence) to .84 (SRC and Quantity). The highest subtest correlations are found with the SRC and Quantity subtests (both .84). The lowest correlation is with the Time/Sequence subtests (.69).

Also as expected, corrected correlations of BBCS–3:R and BBCS–R composite scores are high (i.e., both are .85). See Table 7.11. As expected, the scaled and composite score means of the BBCS–R scores are higher than the BBCS–3:R scores.

- There is partial item overlap that produces a test-retest effect for some, but not all of the items. Practice effects differ by subtests and may result in higher means. In the BBCS–3:R test-retest study, the second test Receptive SRC mean is approximately 3 standard score points higher and the second test Receptive TC mean is approximately 5 points higher. The BBCS–3:R and BBCS–R study was not counterbalanced, so you can expect a mean change in composite scores of approximately 3 to 5 standard score points due to practice effects alone.

- Mean scores were expected to be lower on the BBCS–3:R due to changes in the norms of ability tests over time (Flynn, 1987). You can expect test scores to be 3 to 5 scaled score points lower on the BBCS–3:R due to the Flynn effect. The BBCS–R and BBCS–3:R samples have somewhat different demographic characteristics, with a shift in parent education levels. On BBCS–3:R, there are 1.34% fewer individuals at the two lower parent education levels and 1.35% more individuals at the highest parent education level. This shift in the demographic characteristics should have resulted in slightly lower means on the BBCS–3:R. In addition to shifts in the population, the Flynn effect reflects societal changes that can affect populations, such as improved nutrition, improved education in the form of early-intervention programs, and improved access to medical treatment.

Table 7.11 Means, Standard Deviations, and Correlation Coefficients Between BBCS–3:R and BBCS–R Subtest and Composite Scores (BBCS–3:R Administered First) (*n* = 51)

	BBCS–3:R		BBCS–R			
Subtest/Composite	**Mean**	***SD***	**Mean**	***SD***	***r***	***rc***
BBCS–3:R 1–5 SRC/ BBCS–R 1–6 SRC	10.1	3.0	11.9	2.9	.84	.84
6/7 Direction/Position	9.5	3.0	10.7	3.2	.74	.74
7/8 Self-/Social Awareness	10.2	2.7	11.4	3.0	.78	.81
8/9 Texture/Material	9.3	3.0	10.3	3.1	.71	.71
9/10 Quantity	9.5	2.6	11.0	3.2	.80	.84
10/11 Time/Sequence	9.5	2.7	10.9	3.4	.65	.69
Receptive TC	98.1	15.0	105.7	16.0	.85	.85
Receptive SRC	100.5	15.1	109.3	14.3	.85	.85

Note. Correlations were corrected for the variability of the BBCS–3:R normative sample (Allen and Yen, 1979; Magnusson, 1967).

Receptive TC = Receptive Total Composite, Receptive SRC = Receptive School Readiness Composite

Correlation With PLS–4

PLS–4 is a test designed to identify children ages birth to 6 years 11 months who have receptive and expressive language impairments. The PLS–4 includes two subscales: Auditory Comprehension and Expressive Language. The BBCS–3:R and PLS–4 were administered, in that order, to 55 typically developing children. Test sessions were completed 0 to 22 days apart (M = 6.5, SD = 4.9). The demographic characteristics of the sample are shown in Table 7.12.

Table 7.12 Distribution of the BBCS–3:R–PLS–4 Validity Sample by Age, Gender, Race/Ethnicity, Geographic Region, and Parent Education Level

n	55
Age	
Mean	4.7
SD	1.3
	% of Sample
Gender	
Female	50.9
Male	49.1
Race/Ethnicity	
African American	25.5
Asian	9.1
Hispanic	27.3
White	36.4
Other	1.7
Geographic Region	
Midwest	21.8
Northeast	23.6
South	31.0
West	23.6
Parent Education Level	
11 years of school or less	20.0
12 years of school or GED	34.6
13 to 15 years of school	27.3
16 years of school or more	18.1

Because both tests assess aspects of language development and there is some overlap in the receptive language concepts assessed on the two tests, it was expected that there would be positive moderate correlation between the scores of the two tests. Table 7.13 presents the means, standard deviations, and corrected correlation coefficients between BBCS–3:R and PLS–4. As expected, the correlations are moderate, ranging from .46 to .77. The standard score means for both tests are slightly below 100 due to the shift from parent education levels in this study and in the BBCS–3:R normative sample. In the BBCS–3:R–PLS–4 study, there are 11.9% more individuals at the two lower parent education levels and 11.9% fewer individuals at the higher parent education levels. This shift in the demographic characteristics should have resulted in slightly lower means on the BBCS–3:R and the PLS–4 (as reported in Table 7.13). The PLS–4 scores are somewhat higher than the BBCS–3:R scores likely due to practice effects (i.e., children being more accustomed to the testing situation) or Flynn effect—changes in ability over time (Flynn, 1987).

Table 7.13 Means, Standard Deviations, and Correlation Coefficients Between BBCS–3:R Subtest and Composite Scores and PLS–4 Standard Scores (*n* = 55)

	PLS–4			BBCS–3:R	
BBCS–3:R Subtest/Composite	**AC**	**EC**	**TLS**	**Mean**	***SD***
1–5 SRC	.68	.62	.68	8.7	2.8
6 Direction/Position	.58	.57	.60	8.5	2.7
7 Self/Social Awareness	.54	.52	.56	8.9	2.9
8 Texture/Material	.56	.71	.66	9.1	2.7
9 Quantity	.62	.58	.64	9.0	2.8
10 Time/Sequence	.46	.46	.51	8.9	3.3
Receptive TC	.73	.73	.77	93.1	13.9
Receptive SRC	.65	.61	.66	93.4	14.2
PLS–4					
Mean	98.2	98.3	98.3		
SD	13.6	17.3	15.7		

Note. Correlations were corrected for the variability of the BBCS–3:R normative sample (Allen and Yen, 1979; Magnusson, 1967).

Receptive TC = Receptive Total Composite, Receptive SRC = Receptive School Readiness Composite, AC = Auditory Comprehension, EC = Expressive Communication, TLS = Total Language Score

Evidence Based on Special Group Studies

On a regular basis, speech-language pathologists evaluate a variety of children for evidence of language impairments that may warrant interventions. Other users of BBCS–3:R, including clinical, school, and neuropsychologists evaluate children with a variety of psychological, developmental, and medical disorders that may have an adverse effect on the normal development of language skills. Some of these children will exhibit developmental delays only in language, while others may exhibit global impairments in cognitive development or overall delayed development in multiple behavioral domains. Language abilities may also be globally impaired or specific aspects of language may be identified as problematic. The vast majority of children who will be evaluated clinically with BBCS–3:R and subsequently receive intervention will have been diagnosed with an impairment. BBCS–3:R is designed to identify varying degrees of impairment in basic concept development among these children, as well as children with other cognitively-related deficits such as intellectual disability or developmental delay. Although the BBCS–3:R was designed to contribute to the diagnosis of language, cognitive, and academic achievement delays, it was also intended to be sensitive to the language difficulties exhibited by children in many other clinical groups (e.g., autistic spectrum disorders, hearing impaired, selective/elective mutism). This section presents the results of clinical research conducted with BBCS–3:R that evaluates the performance of children with language impairments and children with intellectual disability. These studies indicate the utility of the BBCS–3:R in a variety of clinical contexts. Children in both clinical studies used English as their primary language and were not enrolled in ESL or LEP classes. They took the BBCS–3:R in a standardized manner. Children in the studies were not colorblind and had adequate vision to see the stimuli. Table 7.14 reports the demographic characteristics of the clinical samples.

Table 7.14 Distribution of the BBCS-3:R Clinical Samples by Age, Gender, Race/Ethnicity, Geographic Region, and Parent Education Level

	Language Impairment	Intellectual Disability
n	52	64
Age		
Mean	4.7	10.0
SD	1.2	1.7
	% of Sample	**% of Sample**
Gender		
Female	38.5	40.6
Male	61.5	59.4
Race/Ethnicity		
African American	28.8	37.5
Hispanic	5.8	10.9
White	59.6	50.0
Other	5.8	1.6
Geographic Region		
Midwest	50.0	46.9
Northeast	1.9	9.3
South	38.5	31.3
West	9.6	12.5
Parent Education Level		
11 years of school or less	17.3	17.2
12 years of school or GED	36.5	42.2
13 to 15 years of school	28.9	25.0
16 years of school or more	17.3	15.6

Children Diagnosed With Language Impairments

A study of 52 children ages 3:0–6:11 diagnosed with language impairments was completed as part of the validation of BBCS–3:R. These children were recruited from speech-language pathologists in multiple sites across the United States, and each child had earned a score at or below 1.5 standard deviations from the mean on a standardized test of language abilities (i.e., an instrument other than the BBCS–R). Of the 52 cases, 90.3% were identified as having a mixed receptive and expressive language impairment; the other 9.7% did not report if the impairment was primarily receptive or expressive. All children in the study were receiving services for language impairments. The majority of the children in the sample were also diagnosed as having other conditions, (e.g., Attention Deficit Disorder, Articulation Disorder, Pervasive Developmental Disorder, and Behavior Disorder). Of the 52 clinical cases in this study, 83% reported using *Preschool Language Scale–Third* or *Fourth Edition* (Zimmerman, Steiner, and Pond, 1992, 2002) scores to qualify for inclusion in the clinical study; 13% used *Clinical Evaluation of Language Fundamentals®–Preschool* (Wiig, Secord, and Semel, 1992) or *Clinical Evaluation of Language*

Fundamentals® Preschool–Second Edition (Wiig, Secord, and Semel, 2004); 2% used *Clinical Evaluation of Language Fundamentals®–Fourth Edition* (Semel, Wiig, and Secord, 2003); and 2% used *Comprehensive Assessment of Spoken Language* (Carrow-Woolfolk, 1999).

A subset of 35 children from the group of 52 children diagnosed with language impairments was matched with a control group of typically developing children. The matched group was selected such that each child in the language impairments group was matched to a control subject from the normative sample based on age, race/ethnicity, parent education level, and gender.

In the BBCS–3:R study of children with language impairments, the largest differences in subtest mean scores were observed for Direction/Position, Self-/Social Awareness, and Quantity. A large difference was also observed for the Total Test score (Bracken, 1998b). Based on BBCS–R data, it was expected that the BBCS-3:R composite scores would produce large effects (standard differences), and that Direction/Position, Self-/Social Awareness, and Quantity would have the largest effects of any of the subtests.

Descriptive and group comparison statistics are presented in Table 7.15 for the BBCS–3:R language impairments study. The Receptive TC score difference is more than 1 standard deviation between the two groups. There is less than 1 standard deviation difference between the Receptive SRC scores of the typically-developing children and the children with a language impairment. Effect sizes (Cohen's *d*; Cohen, 1996) above .5 are generally considered moderate and those above .8 are typically considered to be large. Both subtest and composite score effect sizes are large, ranging from .88 to 1.31. The Receptive TC has the largest effect size at 1.31. At the subtest level, all the effect sizes are at or above .88, highlighting the ability of the BBCS–3:R to discriminate between typically developing children and those with language impairments. Among subtests, Direction/Position, Self-/Social Awareness, and Quantity have the largest effect sizes (1.15–1.27), mirroring the BBCS–R results.

Table 7.15 Mean Performance and Difference of Subtest and Composite Scores for Children with Language Impairment and a Typically Developing Matched Sample (*n* = 35)

	Language Impairment		Matched Sample		Mean Difference of Two Samples			
Subtest/Composite	Mean	*SD*	Mean	*SD*	Difference	*t* value	*p*	Standard Difference
1–5 SRC	6.6	2.9	9.1	2.7	2.49	4.19	<.001	0.88
6 Direction/Position	5.8	3.2	9.6	2.8	3.74	4.87	<.001	1.24
7 Self-/Social Awareness	5.6	2.7	8.9	2.6	3.34	5.19	<.001	1.27
8 Texture/Material	6.5	2.5	8.9	3.0	2.49	3.63	<.001	0.91
9 Quantity	6.2	3.2	9.7	2.8	3.49	4.27	<.001	1.15
10 Time/Sequence	6.7	3.3	9.6	2.7	2.91	3.65	<.001	0.95
Receptive TC	76.8	14.9	95.9	14.3	19.11	5.10	<.001	1.31
Receptive SRC	82.6	15.5	95.5	13.4	12.86	4.16	<.001	0.89

Note. Standard Difference (i.e., effect size) is the difference of the two test means divided by the square root of the pooled variance, computed using Cohen's (1996) Formula 10.4.

Receptive TC = Receptive Total Composite, Receptive SRC = Receptive School Readiness Composite

Children Identified With Intellectual Disability

A study of 64 children ages 7:1–12:8 diagnosed with intellectual disability was completed as part of the validation of BBCS–3:R. Clinically, the BBCS–3:R is useful with this older population because clinicians often need an inventory of the basic concepts that these children do and do not understand. Clinicians can use the inventories to plan intervention and monitor progress. These children were tested by speech-language pathologists in multiple sites across the United States, and each child had earned a total intelligence quotient of 70 or lower on a standardized test of cognitive abilities administered within the last 36 months.

Of the 64 clinical cases in this study, 58% reported using either the *Weschler Intelligence Scale for Children®–Third* or *Fourth Edition* (Wechsler, 1997, 2003) scores to qualify for inclusion in the clinical study; 11% used the *Differential Ability Scales* (Elliott, 1990); and 31% used other instruments. Of the 64 cases, 90% of the children were identified as having a mixed receptive and expressive language impairment; the other 10% did not report if the impairment was primarily receptive or expressive.

The oldest age group (6:9–6:11) in the normative sample was used as the control sample. It was expected that the children with intellectual disability would perform more poorly than their younger controls on the BBCS–3:R subtests. Table 7.16 presents the comparative statistics between the group with intellectual disability and the control sample. As expected, the effect sizes are large for all subtests and composites. The largest composite effect observed was for the Receptive Total Raw Score. At the subtest level, the largest effect size was observed for the Quantity subtest. Accordingly, the results of the study demonstrated the sensitivity of the BBCS–3:R to the expected basic concept deficits in children with intellectual disability and demonstrated how useful it can be to test children out of age range for the BBCS–3:R.

Table 7.16 Mean Performance and Difference of Subtest and Composite Scores for Children with Intellectual Disability (*n* = 64) and Children Ages 6:6–6:11 from the Normative Sample (*n* = 80)

	Intellectual Disability Sample		Age 6:6–6:11 from Normative Sample		Mean Difference of Two Samples			
Subtest/Composite	Mean	*SD*	Mean	*SD*	Difference	*t* value	*p*	Standard Difference[a]
1–5 SRC	64.8	15.5	77.9	5.4	13.1	7.04	<.001	1.18
6 Direction/Position	35.6	19.6	53.9	8.3	18.3	7.57	<.001	1.27
7 Self-/Social Awareness	23.8	9.5	31.2	2.5	7.5	6.74	<.001	1.13
8 Texture/Material	17.2	8.8	24.3	4.2	7.1	6.38	<.001	1.07
9 Quantity	20.6	12.4	34.1	6.1	13.5	8.48	<.001	1.42
10 Time/Sequence	15.4	9.0	23.4	5.5	8.0	6.59	<.001	1.11
Receptive Total Raw Score	177.5	70.1	244.9	27.0	67.4	7.90	<.001	1.33
Receptive SRC Total Raw Score	64.8	15.5	77.9	5.4	13.1	7.05	<.001	1.18

Note. Total raw scores were used because no scaled scores were available for the Intellectual Disability sample. To make a meaningful comparison between the ID group and the control group, total raw scores were used for both groups.

Receptive SRC = Receptive School Readiness Composite

[a] Standard Difference (i.e., effect size) is the difference of the two test means divided by the square root of the pooled variance, computed using Cohen's (1996) Formula 10.4.

Clinical Utility

Another means for evaluating the clinical utility of a test is to analyze the ability of the test to accurately identify children who have a specific clinical condition of interest and to rule out that diagnosis in individuals who do not have that clinical condition. Classification results based on setting a specific diagnostic cut score, such as –1.0 standard deviation, may be presented as Positive Predictive Power (PPP); that is, identifying the condition when it is present. Also, the criterion can be used to evaluate the Negative Predictive Power (NPP) of a test; that is, to detect when individuals do not have the clinical condition of interest. The PPP and NPP vary as a function of the cut score used, as well as the base rate for the clinical condition of interest.

The base rate of a condition is most commonly thought of as the prevalence of the clinical condition within the population, but it is of more clinical usefulness to think of it as the a priori probability that someone in the clinician's own referral population will have the condition. Obviously this probability varies widely depending on the disorder and the clinical setting. According to the National Information Center for Children and Youth with Disabilities (NICHCY, 2003), about 10% of the school-age population has language delays/disorders. A small sample of speech-language pathologists indicated that they expect to identify approximately 20% of preschool children and 10% of school-age children as being at risk for language impairments and in need of further testing. They estimated that they identify 70% to 90% of their preschool referrals and 60% to 80% of their school-age referrals as having language impairments (personal communication; Mason, Perrin, and Schaffan, March 2003; personal communication; Connors, Tremper, and Green, November 2003). As Table 7.17 indicates, 20% was selected as the base rate for screening the population of children, and a combination of the reported base rates for preschool and school referrals was selected (i.e., 70%, 80%, and 90%). Values of PPP and NPP are provided for five referral base rates (20%, 50%, 70%, 80%, and 90%).

Figure 7.1 shows the possible outcomes of a classification using a test. *D* represents someone who truly has the disorder and *ND* represents someone who truly has no disorder (i.e., a True Negative). The test outcomes are + (prediction of disorder) or – (prediction of no disorder). Positive Predictive Power is calculated using the formula PPP = (a × br) ÷ [(a × br) + (1 – br) × c] where *a* and *c* represent the frequencies indicated in Figure 7.1, and br = base rate. PPP is interpreted as the likelihood that a person with a positive test result actually has the disorder (i.e., a True Positive). Negative Predictive Power is calculated using the formula NPP = (d × (1 – br) ÷ [(d × (1 – br) + (b × br)] and is interpreted as the likelihood that someone with a negative test result actually does not have the disorder (i.e., a True Negative). A PPP = 1 indicates no false positives, while PPP = 0.5 indicates a 50% false positive rate. Similarly an NPP = 1 would indicate no false negatives, whereas an NPP = 0.5 would indicate a 50% false negative rate.

	+	–
D	a	b
ND	c	d

Figure 7.1 Possible Test Outcomes of Positive Predictive Power (+) and Negative Predictive Power (–)

Sensitivity and *specificity* are two additional diagnostic validity statistics that describe how a test performs. Sensitivity is computed as a/(a + b) and specificity is computed as d/(c + d). Sensitivity tells us the probability that someone who has the condition will test positive for it. Specificity tells us the probability that someone who does not have the condition will test negative. These values do not depend on the base rate. However, they are affected by the cut score employed (–1.0 *SD*). This means sensitivity and specificity provide overall summary statistics of how accurately the test can classify children with given disorders, although this overall summary can be misleading for specific base rates. Table 7.17 provides the classification table for language impairment based on a cut score of –1 *SD*. The table also reports diagnostic validity statistics based on different base rates. Considering the purpose of the BBCS–3:R (i.e., as a measure of basic concepts and a supplemental assessment for determining whether a child needs intervention in the area of semantic development – not a comprehensive language test used to determine eligibility), the results indicate good (.71) sensitivity and specificity (.83) at –1 *SD*. For example, regardless of base rate, if the cut score is –1 *SD*, 71% of those with a language impairment were correctly identified as such by BBCS–3:R, and 83% of those without language impairment were correctly classified as not having a language impairment by BBCS–3:R. Of course, in the real world, we only see the test results; how accurate those are depends on the base rate as well as the cut score, which is where we use PPP and NPP. For example, if the base rate is low, such as 20%, which might be observed in screening a normal population, and we use a cut score of –1 *SD*, we have a PPP = .51. This means that 51% of those who are identified as having a language impairment actually have it. Although 49% test as false positives, this may be acceptable in a screening situation where the concern is more on minimizing false negatives. The NPP in this situation equals .92, meaning that 92% of those classified as not having a language impairment indeed do not, leaving only 8% false negatives.

Table 7.17 Classification of Language Impairment by Receptive Total Composite at 1 *SD* Below the Mean and PPP and NPP for Five Base Rates

				Base Rates				
				Screening	Referral			Matched Sample
Receptive TC ≤ *SD*	Sensitivity	Specificity	Predictive Power	20%	90%	80%	70%	50%
–1 *SD*	.71	.83	PPP	.51	.97	.94	.91	.81
			NPP	.92	.24	.42	.55	.74

Note. Receptive TC = Receptive Total Composite

Summary

This chapter has presented initial evidence of the reliability and validity for the use of BBCS–3:R in making decisions about the basic concept ability of young children. The test-retest stability and internal consistency results suggest that BBCS–3:R is highly reliable for measuring the basic concept knowledge of children from diverse races/ethnicities.

The clinical validation studies indicate that BBCS–3:R is sensitive to the difficulties with basic concept development exhibited in two clinical groups. Children diagnosed with language impairments and children diagnosed with intellectual disability demonstrated very poor performance on BBCS–3:R.

The diagnostic sensitivity of BBCS–3:R was illustrated in the evaluation of children with language impairments. Given the purpose of the BBCS–3:R as a measure of basic concepts, diagnostic validity statistics reveal good sensitivity and specificity at 1 *SD* below the mean. Clinicians can use the base rate that most appropriately represents the percentage of children referred for evaluation who are diagnosed with language impairments in their clinical practice.

The initial evidence of validity reported here provides support for the clinical utility of the BBCS–3:R for children with language impairments and children with intellectual disability. Ongoing clinical research may expand our knowledge of the applicability of BBCS–3:R in other groups. Clinicians should evaluate this evidence in light of their clinical practice and expertise to make the most appropriate use of BBCS–3:R. BBCS–3:R scores provide only one piece of information about a child's language skills and should always be integrated with additional information (e.g. comprehensive language test results, criterion referenced measures, case history from family members and teachers, as well as observational information). In keeping with the validation history of the BBCS and BBCS–R, the BBCS–3:R appears to be a valid and useful tool for the assessment of young children's understanding of basic language concepts, cognitive development, and school readiness.

Subtest Scaled Scores

Appendix A 3:0–3:2 Subtest Scaled Scores

Scaled Score	1–5 School Readiness Composite (SRC)	6 Direction/ Position	7 Self-/Social Awareness	8 Texture/ Material	9 Quantity	10 Time/ Sequence	Percentile Rank	Descriptive Classification	Scaled Score
	Subtest Raw Score								
19	69–85	36–62	31–33	17–29	27–43	13–30	99.9	Very Advanced	19
18	63–68	33–35	29–30	15–16	24–26	12	99.6	Very Advanced	18
17	57–62	30–32	26–28	14	21–23	11	99	Very Advanced	17
16	51–56	27–29	24–25	13	18–20	10	98	Very Advanced	16
15	46–50	24–26	21–23	11–12	16–17	9	95	Advanced	15
14	41–45	22–23	19–20	10	14–15	8	91	Advanced	14
13	36–40	19–21	17–18	9	11–13	6–7	84	Advanced	13
12	31–35	16–18	14–16	8	9–10	5	75	Average	12
11	26–30	13–15	12–13	6–7	7–8	4	63	Average	11
10	22–25	11–12	10–11	5	5–6	3	50	Average	10
9	18–21	10	8–9	4	4	—	37	Average	9
8	14–17	9	7	—	3	2	25	Average	8
7	11–13	7–8	5–6	3	2	1	16	Delayed	7
6	9–10	6	3–4	2	1	0	9	Delayed	6
5	6–8	5	2	1	0	—	5	Delayed	5
4	4–5	3–4	1	—	—	—	2	Very Delayed	4
3	2–3	2	0	0	—	—	1	Very Delayed	3
2	1	1	—	—	—	—	0.4	Very Delayed	2
1	0	0	—	—	—	—	0.1	Very Delayed	1

Scaled Score Points for Building Confidence Intervals

Confidence Level	1–5 School Readiness Composite (SRC)	6 Direction/ Position	7 Self-/Social Awareness	8 Texture/ Material	9 Quantity	10 Time/ Sequence	Confidence Level
90%	1	1	2	2	1	2	90%
95%	1	1	2	3	2	3	95%

Appendix A 3:3–3:5 Subtest Scaled Scores

Scaled Score	1–5 School Readiness Composite (SRC)	6 Direction/ Position	7 Self-/Social Awareness	8 Texture/ Material	9 Quantity	10 Time/ Sequence	Percentile Rank	Descriptive Classification	Scaled Score
	Subtest Raw Score								
19	75–85	49–62	33	22–29	33–43	19–30	99.9	Very Advanced	19
18	69–74	45–48	30–32	20–21	29–32	17–18	99.6		18
17	63–68	40–44	28–29	18–19	26–28	15–16	99		17
16	57–62	35–39	26–27	16–17	23–25	13–14	98		16
15	52–56	31–34	24–25	15	20–22	12	95	Advanced	15
14	47–51	28–30	22–23	13–14	18–19	10–11	91		14
13	41–46	24–27	19–21	11–12	15–17	9	84		13
12	36–40	20–23	17–18	10	13–14	7–8	75	Average	12
11	31–35	17–19	15–16	8–9	10–12	5–6	63		11
10	26–30	14–16	13–14	7	8–9	4	50		10
9	22–25	11–13	11–12	5–6	6–7	3	37		9
8	18–21	9–10	9–10	4	4–5	—	25		8
7	13–17	8	7–8	3	3	2	16	Delayed	7
6	10–12	6–7	5–6	2	2	—	9		6
5	7–9	5	3–4	1	1	1	5		5
4	4–6	3–4	2	—	0	—	2	Very Delayed	4
3	2–3	2	1	0	—	0	1		3
2	1	1	0	—	—	—	0.4		2
1	0	0	—	—	—	—	0.1		1

Scaled Score Points for Building Confidence Intervals

Confidence Level	1–5 School Readiness Composite (SRC)	6 Direction/ Position	7 Self-/Social Awareness	8 Texture/ Material	9 Quantity	10 Time/ Sequence	Confidence Level
90%	1	1	2	2	1	2	90%
95%	1	1	2	3	2	3	95%

Appendix A 3:6–3:8 Subtest Scaled Scores

Scaled Score	Subtest Raw Score: 1–5 School Readiness Composite (SRC)	6 Direction/ Position	7 Self-/Social Awareness	8 Texture/ Material	9 Quantity	10 Time/ Sequence	Percentile Rank	Descriptive Classification	Scaled Score
19	81–85	55–62	33	26–29	37–43	23–30	99.9		19
18	75–80	51–54	32	24–25	33–36	21–22	99.6	Very Advanced	18
17	69–74	46–50	30–31	22–23	30–32	18–20	99	Very Advanced	17
16	63–68	41–45	28–29	20–21	27–29	16–17	98	Very Advanced	16
15	58–62	37–40	26–27	18–19	24–26	14–15	95	Advanced	15
14	52–57	33–36	24–25	16–17	21–23	13	91	Advanced	14
13	47–51	29–32	22–23	14–15	18–20	11–12	84	Advanced	13
12	41–46	24–28	20–21	12–13	15–17	9–10	75	Average	12
11	36–40	20–23	18–19	10–11	13–14	7–8	63	Average	11
10	31–35	17–19	15–17	8–9	10–12	5–6	50	Average	10
9	26–30	14–16	13–14	7	8–9	4	37	Average	9
8	21–25	11–13	11–12	5–6	6–7	3	25	Average	8
7	17–20	8–10	9–10	4	4–5	2	16	Delayed	7
6	12–16	6–7	7–8	2–3	2–3	—	9	Delayed	6
5	8–11	5	4–6	1	1	1	5	Delayed	5
4	4–7	3–4	2–3	—	0	—	2	Very Delayed	4
3	2–3	2	1	0	—	0	1	Very Delayed	3
2	1	1	0	—	—	—	0.4	Very Delayed	2
1	0	0	—	—	—	—	0.1	Very Delayed	1

Scaled Score Points for Building Confidence Intervals

Confidence Level	1–5 School Readiness Composite (SRC)	6 Direction/ Position	7 Self-/Social Awareness	8 Texture/ Material	9 Quantity	10 Time/ Sequence	Confidence Level
90%	1	1	1	1	1	2	90%
95%	1	1	2	2	1	2	95%

Appendix A 3:9–3:11 Subtest Scaled Scores

Scaled Score	Subtest Raw Score: 1–5 School Readiness Composite (SRC)	6 Direction/ Position	7 Self-/Social Awareness	8 Texture/ Material	9 Quantity	10 Time/ Sequence	Percentile Rank	Descriptive Classification	Scaled Score
19	83–85	61–62	33	29	39–43	27–30	99.9	Very Advanced	19
18	79–82	57–60	32	27–28	36–38	24–26	99.6	Very Advanced	18
17	74–78	52–56	31	24–26	33–35	21–23	99	Very Advanced	17
16	69–73	47–51	30	22–23	30–32	19–20	98	Very Advanced	16
15	63–68	42–46	28–29	20–21	27–29	17–18	95	Advanced	15
14	58–62	37–41	26–27	18–19	24–26	15–16	91	Advanced	14
13	52–57	33–36	24–25	16–17	21–23	13–14	84	Advanced	13
12	47–51	28–32	22–23	14–15	18–20	10–12	75	Average	12
11	41–46	23–27	20–21	12–13	15–17	8–9	63	Average	11
10	36–40	19–22	18–19	10–11	12–14	6–7	50	Average	10
9	31–35	16–18	15–17	8–9	10–11	5	37	Average	9
8	26–30	12–15	13–14	6–7	7–9	4	25	Average	8
7	20–25	9–11	11–12	4–5	5–6	3	16	Delayed	7
6	15–19	7–8	8–10	3	3–4	2	9	Delayed	6
5	10–14	5–6	6–7	2	2	1	5	Delayed	5
4	6–9	3–4	3–5	1	1	—	2	Very Delayed	4
3	3–5	2	1–2	0	0	0	1	Very Delayed	3
2	1–2	1	0	—	—	—	0.4	Very Delayed	2
1	0	0	—	—	—	—	0.1	Very Delayed	1

Scaled Score Points for Building Confidence Intervals

Confidence Level	1–5 School Readiness Composite (SRC)	6 Direction/ Position	7 Self-/Social Awareness	8 Texture/ Material	9 Quantity	10 Time/ Sequence	Confidence Level
90%	1	1	1	1	1	2	90%
95%	1	1	2	2	1	2	95%

Appendix A 4:0–4:2 Subtest Scaled Scores

Scaled Score	Subtest Raw Score: 1–5 School Readiness Composite (SRC)	6 Direction/ Position	7 Self-/Social Awareness	8 Texture/ Material	9 Quantity	10 Time/ Sequence	Percentile Rank	Descriptive Classification	Scaled Score
19	83–85	62	33	29	40–43	29–30	99.9		19
18	81–82	59–61	—	28	37–39	27–28	99.6	Very Advanced	18
17	76–80	55–58	32	27	34–36	24–26	99		17
16	73–75	50–54	31	25–26	31–33	21–23	98		16
15	68–72	46–49	30	22–24	29–30	19–20	95		15
14	63–67	41–45	28–29	20–21	26–28	17–18	91	Advanced	14
13	57–62	36–40	26–27	18–19	23–25	15–16	84		13
12	52–56	31–35	24–25	15–17	20–22	12–14	75		12
11	46–51	27–30	22–23	13–14	17–19	10–11	63		11
10	41–45	22–26	20–21	11–12	15–16	8–9	50	Average	10
9	36–40	18–21	17–19	9–10	12–14	6–7	37		9
8	30–35	15–17	15–16	7–8	9–11	5	25		8
7	24–29	12–14	12–14	5–6	7–8	3–4	16		7
6	19–23	9–11	10–11	3–4	4–6	2	9	Delayed	6
5	13–18	7–8	7–9	2	2–3	1	5		5
4	8–12	4–6	4–6	1	1	—	2		4
3	3–7	2–3	2–3	0	0	0	1	Very Delayed	3
2	1–2	1	1	—	—	—	0.4		2
1	0	0	0	—	—	—	0.1		1

Scaled Score Points for Building Confidence Intervals

Confidence Level	1–5 School Readiness Composite (SRC)	6 Direction/ Position	7 Self-/Social Awareness	8 Texture/ Material	9 Quantity	10 Time/ Sequence	Confidence Level
90%	1	1	1	1	1	1	90%
95%	1	1	1	2	1	2	95%

Appendix A 4:3–4:5 Subtest Scaled Scores

Scaled Score	1–5 School Readiness Composite (SRC)	6 Direction/ Position	7 Self-/Social Awareness	8 Texture/ Material	9 Quantity	10 Time/ Sequence	Percentile Rank	Descriptive Classification	Scaled Score
	Subtest Raw Score								
19	85	62	33	29	41–43	30	99.9	Very Advanced	19
18	83–84	60–61	—	28	38–40	28–29	99.6		18
17	80–82	57–59	32	27	36–37	26–27	99		17
16	76–79	54–56	—	26	33–35	23–25	98		16
15	71–75	50–53	31	24–25	30–32	21–22	95	Advanced	15
14	67–70	45–49	29–30	22–23	27–29	19–20	91		14
13	62–66	40–44	28	19–21	25–26	16–18	84		13
12	57–61	35–39	26–27	17–18	22–24	14–15	75	Average	12
11	52–56	30–34	24–25	15–16	19–21	12–13	63		11
10	46–51	25–29	22–23	12–14	16–18	9–11	50		10
9	41–45	21–24	19–21	10–11	14–15	7–8	37		9
8	35–40	17–20	16–18	8–9	11–13	6	25		8
7	29–34	13–16	14–15	6–7	8–10	4–5	16	Delayed	7
6	23–28	10–12	11–13	4–5	5–7	2–3	9		6
5	17–22	7–9	8–10	3	3–4	1	5		5
4	11–16	4–6	5–7	2	2	—	2	Very Delayed	4
3	5–10	2–3	3–4	1	1	0	1		3
2	2–4	1	1–2	0	0	—	0.4		2
1	0–1	0	0	—	—	—	0.1		1

Scaled Score Points for Building Confidence Intervals

Confidence Level	1–5 School Readiness Composite (SRC)	6 Direction/ Position	7 Self-/Social Awareness	8 Texture/ Material	9 Quantity	10 Time/ Sequence	Confidence Level
90%	1	1	1	1	1	1	90%
95%	1	1	1	2	1	2	95%

Appendix A 4:6–4:8 Subtest Scaled Scores

	Subtest Raw Score								
Scaled Score	1–5 School Readiness Composite (SRC)	6 Direction/ Position	7 Self-/Social Awareness	8 Texture/ Material	9 Quantity	10 Time/ Sequence	Percentile Rank	Descriptive Classification	Scaled Score
19	85	62	—	—	42–43	—	99.9		19
18	84	61	—	29	39–41	30	99.6	Very Advanced	18
17	82–83	59–60	33	—	37–38	28–29	99		17
16	79–81	56–58	—	28	34–36	25–27	98		16
15	75–78	52–55	32	26–27	32–33	23–24	95		15
14	71–74	48–51	30–31	23–25	29–31	20–22	91	Advanced	14
13	67–70	43–47	29	21–22	26–28	18–19	84		13
12	62–66	38–42	28	19–20	24–25	15–17	75		12
11	57–61	33–37	26–27	16–18	21–23	13–14	63		11
10	52–56	29–32	23–25	14–15	18–20	11–12	50	Average	10
9	46–51	24–28	20–22	12–13	15–17	9–10	37		9
8	40–45	20–23	18–19	10–11	13–14	7–8	25		8
7	34–39	16–19	15–17	7–9	10–12	5–6	16		7
6	28–33	12–15	12–14	5–6	7–9	3–4	9	Delayed	6
5	22–27	9–11	9–11	3–4	4–6	2	5		5
4	15–21	6–8	6–8	2	2–3	1	2		4
3	8–14	3–5	4–5	1	1	0	1		3
2	3–7	1–2	2–3	0	0	—	0.4	Very Delayed	2
1	0–2	0	0–1	—	—	—	0.1		1

Scaled Score Points for Building Confidence Intervals

Confidence Level	1–5 School Readiness Composite (SRC)	6 Direction/ Position	7 Self-/Social Awareness	8 Texture/ Material	9 Quantity	10 Time/ Sequence	Confidence Level
90%	1	1	1	1	1	1	90%
95%	1	1	2	2	2	2	95%

Appendix A 4:9–4:11 Subtest Scaled Scores

Scaled Score	Subtest Raw Score: 1–5 School Readiness Composite (SRC)	6 Direction/ Position	7 Self-/Social Awareness	8 Texture/ Material	9 Quantity	10 Time/ Sequence	Percentile Rank	Descriptive Classification	Scaled Score
19	85	—	—	—	42–43	—	99.9	Very Advanced	19
18	84	—	—	—	40–41	30	99.6	Very Advanced	18
17	83	60–62	33	29	38–39	29	99	Very Advanced	17
16	81–82	58–59	—	28	35–37	27–28	98	Very Advanced	16
15	78–80	55–57	32	27	33–34	25–26	95	Advanced	15
14	75–77	51–54	31	25–26	31–32	22–24	91	Advanced	14
13	71–74	46–50	—	22–24	28–30	19–21	84	Advanced	13
12	67–70	41–45	30	20–21	25–27	17–18	75	Average	12
11	62–66	36–40	28–29	18–19	22–24	14–16	63	Average	11
10	57–61	32–35	25–27	16–17	20–21	12–13	50	Average	10
9	51–56	28–31	22–24	13–15	17–19	10–11	37	Average	9
8	45–50	23–27	19–21	11–12	14–16	8–9	25	Average	8
7	39–44	19–22	16–18	9–10	11–13	5–7	16	Delayed	7
6	33–38	15–18	14–15	6–8	8–10	3–4	9	Delayed	6
5	27–32	11–14	11–13	4–5	5–7	2	5	Delayed	5
4	20–26	8–10	8–10	2–3	3–4	1	2	Very Delayed	4
3	13–19	4–7	5–7	1	2	0	1	Very Delayed	3
2	6–12	1–3	2–4	0	1	—	0.4	Very Delayed	2
1	0–5	0	0–1	—	0	—	0.1	Very Delayed	1

Scaled Score Points for Building Confidence Intervals

Confidence Level	1–5 School Readiness Composite (SRC)	6 Direction/ Position	7 Self-/Social Awareness	8 Texture/ Material	9 Quantity	10 Time/ Sequence	Confidence Level
90%	1	1	1	1	1	1	90%
95%	1	1	2	2	2	2	95%

Appendix A 5:0–5:2 Subtest Scaled Scores

Scaled Score	1–5 School Readiness Composite (SRC)	6 Direction/ Position	7 Self-/Social Awareness	8 Texture/ Material	9 Quantity	10 Time/ Sequence	Percentile Rank	Descriptive Classification	Scaled Score
	Subtest Raw Score								
19	85	—	—	—	42–43	—	99.9		19
18	84	—	—	—	40–41	30	99.6	Very Advanced	18
17	83	62	—	29	38–39	29	99		17
16	82	60–61	33	—	36–37	28	98		16
15	80–81	57–59	—	28	34–35	26–27	95	Advanced	15
14	78–79	54–56	32	26–27	32–33	23–25	91		14
13	74–77	50–53	31	24–25	29–31	21–22	84		13
12	71–73	45–49	30	21–23	27–28	19–20	75	Average	12
11	67–70	40–44	28–29	19–20	24–26	16–18	63		11
10	61–66	36–39	26–27	17–18	21–23	14–15	50		10
9	55–60	31–35	23–25	15–16	18–20	11–13	37		9
8	49–54	27–30	21–22	12–14	16–17	9–10	25		8
7	44–48	22–26	18–20	10–11	13–15	6–8	16	Delayed	7
6	38–43	17–21	15–17	7–9	10–12	4–5	9		6
5	33–37	12–16	12–14	5–6	7–9	2–3	5		5
4	26–32	8–11	9–11	3–4	4–6	1	2	Very Delayed	4
3	18–25	4–7	5–8	1–2	2–3	0	1		3
2	12–17	1–3	2–4	0	1	—	0.4		2
1	0–11	0	0–1	—	0	—	0.1		1

Scaled Score Points for Building Confidence Intervals

Confidence Level	1–5 School Readiness Composite (SRC)	6 Direction/ Position	7 Self-/Social Awareness	8 Texture/ Material	9 Quantity	10 Time/ Sequence	Confidence Level
90%	1	1	1	1	1	1	90%
95%	1	1	2	2	1	1	95%

Appendix A 5:3–5:5 Subtest Scaled Scores

Scaled Score	1–5 School Readiness Composite (SRC)	6 Direction/ Position	7 Self-/Social Awareness	8 Texture/ Material	9 Quantity	10 Time/ Sequence	Percentile Rank	Descriptive Classification	Scaled Score
	Subtest Raw Score								
19	—	—	—	—	42–43	—	99.9	Very Advanced	19
18	85	—	—	—	41	—	99.6	Very Advanced	18
17	84	62	—	—	39–40	30	99	Very Advanced	17
16	82–83	61	—	29	37–38	29	98	Very Advanced	16
15	81	59–60	—	28	35–36	27–28	95	Advanced	15
14	79–80	56–58	33	26–27	33–34	25–26	91	Advanced	14
13	78	52–55	32	25	31–32	22–24	84	Advanced	13
12	74–77	48–51	31	23–24	28–30	20–21	75	Average	12
11	71–73	44–47	30	21–22	26–27	17–19	63	Average	11
10	66–70	40–43	28–29	19–20	23–25	15–16	50	Average	10
9	60–65	35–39	25–27	16–18	20–22	13–14	37	Average	9
8	54–59	30–34	22–24	14–15	17–19	10–12	25	Average	8
7	49–53	25–29	20–21	11–13	14–16	7–9	16	Delayed	7
6	44–48	20–24	17–19	9–10	11–13	5–6	9	Delayed	6
5	38–43	16–19	14–16	7–8	8–10	3–4	5	Delayed	5
4	32–37	11–15	10–13	4–6	5–7	2	2	Very Delayed	4
3	23–31	6–10	6–9	2–3	3–4	1	1	Very Delayed	3
2	16–22	2–5	2–5	1	1–2	0	0.4	Very Delayed	2
1	0–15	0–1	0–1	0	0	—	0.1	Very Delayed	1

Scaled Score Points for Building Confidence Intervals

Confidence Level	1–5 School Readiness Composite (SRC)	6 Direction/ Position	7 Self-/Social Awareness	8 Texture/ Material	9 Quantity	10 Time/ Sequence	Confidence Level
90%	1	1	1	1	1	1	90%
95%	1	1	2	2	1	1	95%

Appendix A 5:6–5:8 Subtest Scaled Scores

Scaled Score	1–5 School Readiness Composite (SRC)	6 Direction/ Position	7 Self-/Social Awareness	8 Texture/ Material	9 Quantity	10 Time/ Sequence	Percentile Rank	Descriptive Classification	Scaled Score
	Subtest Raw Score								
19	—	—	—	—	42–43	—	99.9	Very Advanced	19
18	85	—	—	—	41	—	99.6		18
17	84	62	—	—	40	30	99		17
16	83	61	—	29	38–39	29	98		16
15	82	59–60	—	28	36–37	28	95	Advanced	15
14	81	57–58	33	27	34–35	26–27	91		14
13	80	54–56	—	26	32–33	24–25	84		13
12	78–79	51–53	32	24–25	30–31	21–23	75	Average	12
11	75–77	47–50	31	22–23	27–29	19–20	63		11
10	70–74	43–46	29–30	20–21	24–26	17–18	50		10
9	64–69	39–42	26–28	18–19	22–23	14–16	37		9
8	58–63	34–38	24–25	15–17	19–21	11–13	25		8
7	53–57	29–33	21–23	13–14	16–18	9–10	16	Delayed	7
6	49–52	24–28	18–20	11–12	12–15	6–8	9		6
5	45–48	19–23	15–17	8–10	9–11	4–5	5		5
4	38–44	14–18	12–14	5–7	6–8	2–3	2	Very Delayed	4
3	29–37	8–13	9–11	3–4	3–5	1	1		3
2	23–28	3–7	5–8	1–2	1–2	0	0.4		2
1	0–22	0–2	0–4	0	0	—	0.1		1

Scaled Score Points for Building Confidence Intervals

Confidence Level	1–5 School Readiness Composite (SRC)	6 Direction/ Position	7 Self-/Social Awareness	8 Texture/ Material	9 Quantity	10 Time/ Sequence	Confidence Level
90%	1	1	1	1	1	1	90%
95%	1	1	1	2	1	1	95%

Appendix A 5:9–5:11 Subtest Scaled Scores

Scaled Score	1–5 School Readiness Composite (SRC)	6 Direction/ Position	7 Self-/Social Awareness	8 Texture/ Material	9 Quantity	10 Time/ Sequence	Percentile Rank	Descriptive Classification	Scaled Score
	Subtest Raw Score								
19	—	—	—	—	42–43	—	99.9	Very Advanced	19
18	—	—	—	—	41	—	99.6		18
17	85	62	—	—	40	30	99		17
16	84	61	—	29	39	29	98		16
15	83	60	—	28	38	28	95	Advanced	15
14	81–82	59	33	27	36–37	27	91		14
13	80	57–58	—	—	34–35	25–26	84		13
12	79	54–56	32	26	31–33	23–24	75	Average	12
11	77–78	50–53	31	24–25	29–30	21–22	63		11
10	73–76	46–49	30	22–23	26–28	18–20	50		10
9	68–72	42–45	28–29	19–21	23–25	16–17	37		9
8	62–67	37–41	26–27	17–18	20–22	13–15	25		8
7	58–61	32–36	23–25	14–16	17–19	10–12	16	Delayed	7
6	55–57	27–31	20–22	12–13	14–16	7–9	9		6
5	51–54	22–26	17–19	10–11	11–13	5–6	5		5
4	44–50	16–21	14–16	8–9	8–10	3–4	2	Very Delayed	4
3	36–43	9–15	11–13	5–7	5–7	1–2	1		3
2	31–35	3–8	7–10	2–4	2–4	0	0.4		2
1	0–30	0–2	0–6	0–1	0–1	—	0.1		1

Scaled Score Points for Building Confidence Intervals

Confidence Level	1–5 School Readiness Composite (SRC)	6 Direction/ Position	7 Self-/Social Awareness	8 Texture/ Material	9 Quantity	10 Time/ Sequence	Confidence Level
90%	1	1	1	1	1	1	90%
95%	1	1	1	2	1	1	95%

Appendix A 6:0–6:2 Subtest Scaled Scores

Scaled Score	1–5 School Readiness Composite (SRC)	6 Direction/ Position	7 Self-/Social Awareness	8 Texture/ Material	9 Quantity	10 Time/ Sequence	Percentile Rank	Descriptive Classification	Scaled Score
	Subtest Raw Score								
19	—	—	—	—	43	—	99.9		19
18	—	—	—	—	42	—	99.6	Very Advanced	18
17	85	62	—	—	41	—	99	Very Advanced	17
16	84	—	—	29	40	30	98	Very Advanced	16
15	83	61	—	28	39	29	95	Advanced	15
14	82	60	33	27	37–38	28	91	Advanced	14
13	80–81	59	—	—	35–36	26–27	84	Advanced	13
12	79	57–58	32	26	33–34	24–25	75	Average	12
11	78	54–56	—	25	31–32	22–23	63	Average	11
10	76–77	50–53	31	23–24	28–30	20–21	50	Average	10
9	74–75	45–49	29–30	21–22	25–27	17–19	37	Average	9
8	70–73	40–44	27–28	19–20	22–24	14–16	25	Average	8
7	65–69	35–39	25–26	16–18	19–21	12–13	16	Delayed	7
6	61–64	31–34	22–24	14–15	16–18	9–11	9	Delayed	6
5	59–60	26–30	19–21	11–13	13–15	7–8	5	Delayed	5
4	55–58	20–25	16–18	8–10	10–12	4–6	2	Very Delayed	4
3	45–54	14–19	13–15	5–7	7–9	2–3	1	Very Delayed	3
2	39–44	8–13	10–12	2–4	3–6	1	0.4	Very Delayed	2
1	0–38	0–7	0–9	0–1	0–2	0	0.1	Very Delayed	1

Scaled Score Points for Building Confidence Intervals

Confidence Level	1–5 School Readiness Composite (SRC)	6 Direction/ Position	7 Self-/Social Awareness	8 Texture/ Material	9 Quantity	10 Time/ Sequence	Confidence Level
90%	2	1	2	2	1	1	90%
95%	2	1	2	2	2	2	95%

Appendix A 6:3–6:5 Subtest Scaled Scores

	Subtest Raw Score								
Scaled Score	1–5 School Readiness Composite (SRC)	6 Direction/ Position	7 Self-/Social Awareness	8 Texture/ Material	9 Quantity	10 Time/ Sequence	Percentile Rank	Descriptive Classification	Scaled Score
19	—	—	—	—	43	—	99.9	Very Advanced	19
18	—	—	—	—	42	—	99.6		18
17	—	—	—	—	41	—	99		17
16	84–85	—	—	29	—	30	98		16
15	83	—	—	—	40	29	95	Advanced	15
14	82	62	—	28	39	28	91		14
13	81	61	33	27	37–38	27	84		13
12	80	59–60	—	—	35–36	26	75	Average	12
11	79	56–58	32	26	33–34	24–25	63		11
10	78	52–55	31	24–25	31–32	22–23	50		10
9	76–77	47–51	30	22–23	28–30	19–21	37		9
8	75	43–46	28–29	20–21	25–27	16–18	25		8
7	70–74	38–42	27	18–19	22–24	14–15	16	Delayed	7
6	66–69	34–37	25–26	16–17	19–21	11–13	9		6
5	63–65	29–33	23–24	14–15	16–18	9–10	5		5
4	60–62	23–28	21–22	11–13	13–15	6–8	2	Very Delayed	4
3	54–59	16–22	19–20	7–10	9–12	3–5	1		3
2	47–53	10–15	17–18	4–6	5–8	1–2	0.4		2
1	0–46	0–9	0–16	0–3	0–4	0	0.1		1

Scaled Score Points for Building Confidence Intervals

Confidence Level	1–5 School Readiness Composite (SRC)	6 Direction/ Position	7 Self-/Social Awareness	8 Texture/ Material	9 Quantity	10 Time/ Sequence	Confidence Level
90%	2	1	2	2	1	1	90%
95%	2	1	2	2	2	2	95%

Appendix A 6:6–6:8 Subtest Scaled Scores

Scaled Score	1–5 School Readiness Composite (SRC)	6 Direction/ Position	7 Self-/Social Awareness	8 Texture/ Material	9 Quantity	10 Time/ Sequence	Percentile Rank	Descriptive Classification	Scaled Score
	Subtest Raw Score								
19	—	—	—	—	43	—	99.9		19
18	—	—	—	—	42	—	99.6	Very Advanced	18
17	—	—	—	—	—	—	99		17
16	—	—	—	—	41	30	98		16
15	84–85	—	—	29	—	—	95		15
14	83	62	—	—	40	29	91	Advanced	14
13	82	61	33	28	39	28	84		13
12	81	59–60	—	27	38	27	75		12
11	80	57–58	32	26	36–37	26	63		11
10	78–79	54–56	—	25	34–35	24–25	50	Average	10
9	76–77	50–53	31	23–24	31–33	21–23	37		9
8	75	46–49	30	21–22	28–30	18–20	25		8
7	71–74	42–45	28–29	19–20	25–27	16–17	16		7
6	69–70	38–41	26–27	18	23–24	14–15	9	Delayed	6
5	67–68	34–37	25	16–17	20–22	11–13	5		5
4	64–66	29–33	24	14–15	16–19	8–10	2		4
3	59–63	24–28	22–23	12–13	12–15	5–7	1	Very Delayed	3
2	55–58	18–23	21	10–11	9–11	2–4	0.4		2
1	0–54	0–17	0–20	0–9	0–8	0–1	0.1		1

Scaled Score Points for Building Confidence Intervals

Confidence Level	1–5 School Readiness Composite (SRC)	6 Direction/ Position	7 Self-/Social Awareness	8 Texture/ Material	9 Quantity	10 Time/ Sequence	Confidence Level
90%	2	1	2	2	1	2	90%
95%	2	1	2	2	2	2	95%

Appendix A 6:9–6:11 Subtest Scaled Scores

Scaled Score	1–5 School Readiness Composite (SRC)	6 Direction/ Position	7 Self-/Social Awareness	8 Texture/ Material	9 Quantity	10 Time/ Sequence	Percentile Rank	Descriptive Classification	Scaled Score
	Subtest Raw Score								
19	—	—	—	—	—	—	99.9	Very Advanced	19
18	—	—	—	—	43	—	99.6		18
17	—	—	—	—	—	—	99		17
16	—	—	—	—	—	—	98		16
15	85	—	—	29	42	—	95	Advanced	15
14	84	62	—	—	—	30	91		14
13	83	61	—	28	41	29	84		13
12	81–82	60	33	—	40	—	75	Average	12
11	80	58–59	32	27	39	28	63		11
10	78–79	55–57	—	26	37–38	26–27	50		10
9	77	52–54	31	24–25	34–36	23–25	37		9
8	75–76	49–51	—	22–23	31–33	20–22	25		8
7	74	46–48	30	20–21	29–30	18–19	16	Delayed	7
6	72–73	44–45	29	19	27–28	16–17	9		6
5	71	41–43	28	17–18	25–26	14–15	5		5
4	69–70	37–40	—	15–16	22–24	11–13	2	Very Delayed	4
3	67–68	33–36	27	12–14	18–21	7–10	1		3
2	66	29–32	26	10–11	15–17	3–6	0.4		2
1	0–65	0–28	0–25	0–9	0–14	0–2	0.1		1

Scaled Score Points for Building Confidence Intervals

Confidence Level	1–5 School Readiness Composite (SRC)	6 Direction/ Position	7 Self-/Social Awareness	8 Texture/ Material	9 Quantity	10 Time/ Sequence	Confidence Level
90%	2	1	2	2	1	2	90%
95%	2	1	2	2	2	2	95%

Receptive TC Scores

Appendix B Receptive Total Composite Scores

Sum of Scaled Scores	Composite Score	Confidence Interval 90%	Confidence Interval 95%	Percentile Rank	Descriptive Classification
6	40	38–45	37–45	<0.1	
7	41	39–46	38–46	<0.1	
8	43	41–48	40–48	<0.1	
9	45	43–50	42–50	<0.1	
10	47	45–51	44–52	<0.1	
11	48	46–52	45–53	<0.1	
12	50	48–54	47–55	<0.1	
13	51	49–55	48–56	0.1	
14	52	50–56	49–57	0.1	
15	53	51–57	50–58	0.1	
16	54	52–58	51–59	0.1	
17	55	52–59	52–60	0.1	
18	57	54–61	54–62	0.2	Very Delayed
19	58	55–62	55–63	0.3	
20	59	56–63	56–64	0.3	
21	60	57–64	57–65	0.4	
22	61	58–65	58–66	0.5	
23	62	59–66	59–67	1	
24	63	60–67	60–68	1	
25	64	61–68	61–69	1	
26	65	62–69	62–70	1	
27	66	63–70	63–71	1	
28	67	64–71	64–72	1	
29	68	65–72	65–73	2	
30	69	66–73	66–74	2	
31	70	67–74	67–75	2	
32	71	68–75	68–76	3	
33	72	69–76	68–77	3	
34	73	70–77	69–78	4	
35	74	71–78	70–79	4	
36	75	72–79	71–80	5	
37	76	73–80	72–81	5	
38	78	75–82	74–83	7	
39	79	76–83	75–83	8	Delayed
40	80	77–84	76–84	9	
41	81	78–85	77–85	10	
42	82	79–86	78–86	12	
43	83	80–87	79–87	13	
44	84	81–88	80–88	14	
45	85	82–89	81–89	16	
46	86	83–90	82–90	18	
47	87	84–91	83–91	19	
48	88	85–92	84–92	21	
49	89	86–93	85–93	23	
50	90	87–94	86–94	25	
51	91	88–95	87–95	27	
52	92	89–96	88–96	30	
53	93	90–97	89–97	32	Average
54	94	91–98	90–98	34	
55	95	92–99	91–99	37	
56	96	93–99	92–100	39	
57	97	94–100	93–101	42	
58	98	95–101	94–102	45	
59	99	96–102	95–103	47	
60	100	97–103	96–104	50	
61	101	98–104	97–105	53	
62	102	99–105	98–106	55	
63	103	100–106	99–107	58	
64	104	101–107	100–108	61	
65	105	101–108	101–109	63	
66	106	102–109	102–110	66	
67	107	103–110	103–111	68	Average
68	108	104–111	104–112	70	
69	109	105–112	105–113	73	
70	110	106–113	106–114	75	
71	112	108–115	108–116	79	
72	113	109–116	109–117	81	
73	114	110–117	110–118	82	
74	115	111–118	111–119	84	
75	116	112–119	112–120	86	
76	117	113–120	113–121	87	
77	118	114–121	114–122	88	
78	119	115–122	115–123	90	
79	120	116–123	116–124	91	
80	121	117–124	117–125	92	Advanced
81	122	118–125	117–126	93	
82	123	119–126	118–127	94	
83	124	120–127	119–128	95	
84	125	121–128	120–129	95	
85	126	122–129	121–130	96	
86	127	123–130	122–131	96	
87	128	124–131	123–132	97	
88	130	126–133	125–133	98	
89	131	127–134	126–134	98	
90	132	128–135	127–135	98	
91	133	129–136	128–136	99	
92	134	130–137	129–137	99	
93	135	131–138	130–138	99	
94	136	132–139	131–139	99	
95	137	133–140	132–140	99	
96	138	134–141	133–141	99	
97	139	135–142	134–142	99.5	
98	140	136–143	135–143	99.6	
99	141	137–144	136–144	99.7	
100	142	138–145	137–145	99.7	
101	143	139–146	138–146	99.8	Very Advanced
102	144	140–147	139–147	99.8	
103	145	141–148	140–148	99.9	
104	146	142–148	141–149	99.9	
105	147	143–149	142–150	99.9	
106	148	144–150	143–151	99.9	
107	150	146–152	145–153	>99.9	
108	151	147–153	146–154	>99.9	
109	152	148–154	147–155	>99.9	
110	154	150–156	149–157	>99.9	
111	156	151–158	151–159	>99.9	
112	157	152–159	152–160	>99.9	
113	158	153–160	153–161	>99.9	
114	160	155–162	155–163	>99.9	

Receptive SRC Scores

Appendix C 3:0–3:2 Receptive SRC Scores

Composite Score	RSRC Raw Score	Percentile Rank	Descriptive Classification
40	—	<0.1	
41	—	<0.1	
42	—	<0.1	
43	—	<0.1	
44	—	<0.1	
45	—	<0.1	
46	—	<0.1	
47	—	<0.1	
48	—	<0.1	
49	—	<0.1	
50	—	<0.1	
51	—	0.1	
52	—	0.1	
53	—	0.1	
54	—	0.1	
55	—	0.1	Very Delayed
56	0	0.2	
57	—	0.2	
58	—	0.3	
59	—	0.3	
60	1	0.4	
61	—	0.5	
62	—	1	
63	—	1	
64	2	1	
65	—	1	
66	—	1	
67	3	1	
68	—	2	
69	4	2	
70	—	2	
71	5	3	
72	—	3	
73	6	4	
74	—	4	
75	7	5	
76	—	5	
77	8	6	
78	—	7	Delayed
79	9	8	
80	—	9	
81	10	10	
82	—	12	
83	11	13	
84	12	14	
85	—	16	
86	13	18	
87	—	19	
88	14	21	
89	15	23	
90	16	25	
91	—	27	
92	17	30	
93	18	32	
94	—	34	
95	19	37	
96	20	39	
97	21	42	
98	22	45	
99	—	47	
100	23	50	Average
101	24	53	
102	25	55	
103	26	58	
104	27	61	
105	28	63	
106	29	66	
107	30	68	
108	31	70	
109	32	73	
110	33	75	
111	34	77	
112	35	79	
113	36	81	
114	37	82	
115	38	84	
116	39	86	
117	40	87	
118	41	88	
119	42	90	
120	43	91	
121	44	92	
122	45	93	Advanced
123	46	94	
124	47	95	
125	48	95	
126	49	96	
127	50	96	
128	51	97	
129	52	97	
130	53	98	
131	54	98	
132	55–56	98	
133	57	99	
134	58	99	
135	59	99	
136	60–61	99	
137	62	99	
138	63	99	
139	64–65	99.5	
140	66	99.6	
141	67	99.7	
142	68	99.7	
143	69–70	99.8	
144	71	99.8	
145	72	99.9	Very Advanced
146	73	99.9	
147	74	99.9	
148	75	99.9	
149	76	99.9	
150	77	>99.9	
151	78	>99.9	
152	79	>99.9	
153	80	>99.9	
154	81	>99.9	
155	82	>99.9	
156	83	>99.9	
157	—	>99.9	
158	84	>99.9	
159	—	>99.9	
160	85	>99.9	

Composite Score Points for Building Confidence Intervals

Confidence Level	SRC
90%	5
95%	6

Note. Receptive SRC/RSRC = Receptive School Readiness Composite

Appendix C 3:3–3:5 Receptive SRC Scores

Appendix C 3:3–3:5 Receptive SRC Scores
Appendix C 3:3–3:5 Receptive SRC Scores

Composite Score	RSRC Raw Score	Percentile Rank	Descriptive Classification
40	—	<0.1	
41	—	<0.1	
42	—	<0.1	
43	—	<0.1	
44	—	<0.1	
45	—	<0.1	
46	—	<0.1	
47	—	<0.1	
48	—	<0.1	
49	—	<0.1	
50	—	<0.1	
51	—	0.1	
52	—	0.1	
53	—	0.1	
54	—	0.1	
55	—	0.1	Very Delayed
56	0	0.2	
57	—	0.2	
58	—	0.3	
59	—	0.3	
60	1	0.4	
61	—	0.5	
62	—	1	
63	—	1	
64	2	1	
65	—	1	
66	—	1	
67	3	1	
68	—	2	
69	4	2	
70	—	2	
71	5	3	
72	6	3	
73	—	4	
74	7	4	
75	8	5	
76	—	5	
77	9	6	
78	10	7	Delayed
79	—	8	
80	11	9	
81	12	10	
82	—	12	
83	13	13	
84	14	14	
85	15	16	
86	16	18	
87	17	19	
88	—	21	
89	18	23	
90	19	25	
91	20	27	
92	21	30	
93	22	32	
94	23	34	
95	—	37	
96	24	39	
97	25	42	
98	26	45	
99	27	47	
100	28	50	Average
101	29	53	
102	30	55	
103	31	58	
104	32	61	
105	33	63	
106	34	66	
107	35	68	
108	36	70	
109	37	73	
110	38	75	
111	39	77	
112	40	79	
113	41	81	
114	42	82	
115	43	84	
116	44–45	86	
117	46	87	
118	47	88	
119	48	90	
120	49	91	
121	50	92	
122	51	93	Advanced
123	52	94	
124	53	95	
125	54	95	
126	55	96	
127	56	96	
128	57–58	97	
129	59	97	
130	60	98	
131	61	98	
132	62	98	
133	63	99	
134	64–65	99	
135	66	99	
136	67	99	
137	68	99	
138	69–70	99	
139	71	99.5	
140	72	99.6	
141	73	99.7	
142	74	99.7	
143	75–76	99.8	
144	77	99.8	
145	78	99.9	Very Advanced
146	79	99.9	
147	80	99.9	
148	81	99.9	
149	—	99.9	
150	82	>99.9	
151	—	>99.9	
152	—	>99.9	
153	83	>99.9	
154	—	>99.9	
155	—	>99.9	
156	84	>99.9	
157	—	>99.9	
158	—	>99.9	
159	85	>99.9	
160	—	>99.9	

Composite Score Points for Building Confidence Intervals

Confidence Level	SRC
90%	5
95%	6

Note. Receptive SRC/RSRC = Receptive School Readiness Composite

Appendix C 3:6–3:8 Receptive SRC Scores

Composite Score	RSRC Raw Score	Percentile Rank	Descriptive Classification
40	—	<0.1	
41	—	<0.1	
42	—	<0.1	
43	—	<0.1	
44	—	<0.1	
45	—	<0.1	
46	—	<0.1	
47	—	<0.1	
48	—	<0.1	
49	—	<0.1	
50	—	<0.1	
51	—	0.1	
52	—	0.1	
53	—	0.1	
54	—	0.1	
55	0	0.1	Very Delayed
56	—	0.2	
57	—	0.2	
58	—	0.3	
59	1	0.3	
60	—	0.4	
61	—	0.5	
62	—	1	
63	2	1	
64	—	1	
65	—	1	
66	3	1	
67	—	1	
68	4	2	
69	5	2	
70	6	2	
71	—	3	
72	7	3	
73	8	4	
74	9	4	
75	10	5	
76	—	5	
77	11	6	
78	12	7	Delayed
79	13	8	
80	14	9	
81	15	10	
82	16	12	
83	17	13	
84	18	14	
85	—	16	

Appendix C 3:6–3:8 Receptive SRC Scores

Composite Score	RSRC Raw Score	Percentile Rank	Descriptive Classification
86	19	18	
87	20	19	
88	21	21	
89	22	23	
90	23	25	
91	24	27	
92	25	30	
93	26	32	
94	27	34	
95	28	37	
96	29	39	
97	30	42	
98	31	45	
99	32	47	
100	33	50	Average
101	34	53	
102	35	55	
103	36	58	
104	37	61	
105	38	63	
106	39	66	
107	40	68	
108	41	70	
109	42	73	
110	43	75	
111	44–45	77	
112	46	79	
113	47	81	
114	48	82	
115	49	84	
116	50	86	
117	51	87	
118	52	88	
119	53	90	
120	54	91	
121	55–56	92	
122	57	93	Advanced
123	58	94	
124	59	95	
125	60	95	
126	61	96	
127	62	96	
128	63	97	
129	64–65	97	

Appendix C 3:6–3:8 Receptive SRC Scores

Composite Score	RSRC Raw Score	Percentile Rank	Descriptive Classification
130	66	98	
131	67	98	
132	68	98	
133	69	99	
134	70	99	
135	71–72	99	
136	73	99	
137	74	99	
138	75	99	
139	76	99.5	
140	77–78	99.6	
141	79	99.7	
142	80	99.7	
143	81	99.8	
144	82	99.8	
145	—	99.9	Very Advanced
146	83	99.9	
147	—	99.9	
148	—	99.9	
149	84	99.9	
150	—	>99.9	
151	—	>99.9	
152	—	>99.9	
153	85	>99.9	
154	—	>99.9	
155	—	>99.9	
156	—	>99.9	
157	—	>99.9	
158	—	>99.9	
159	—	>99.9	
160	—	>99.9	

Composite Score Points for Building Confidence Intervals

Confidence Level	SRC
90%	4
95%	5

Note. Receptive SRC/RSRC = Receptive School Readiness Composite

Appendix C 3:9–3:11 Receptive SRC Scores

Appendix C 3:9–3:11 Receptive SRC Scores

Appendix C 3:9–3:11 Receptive SRC Scores

Composite Score	RSRC Raw Score	Percentile Rank	Descriptive Classification
40	—	<0.1	
41	—	<0.1	
42	—	<0.1	
43	—	<0.1	
44	—	<0.1	
45	—	<0.1	
46	—	<0.1	
47	—	<0.1	
48	—	<0.1	
49	—	<0.1	
50	—	<0.1	
51	—	0.1	
52	—	0.1	
53	—	0.1	
54	0	0.1	
55	—	0.1	Very Delayed
56	—	0.2	
57	—	0.2	
58	1	0.3	
59	—	0.3	
60	—	0.4	
61	2	0.5	
62	—	1	
63	—	1	
64	3	1	
65	—	1	
66	4	1	
67	5	1	
68	6	2	
69	7	2	
70	—	2	
71	8	3	
72	9	3	
73	10	4	
74	11	4	
75	12	5	
76	13	5	
77	14	6	
78	15	7	Delayed
79	16	8	
80	17	9	
81	18	10	
82	19	12	
83	20	13	
84	21	14	
85	22	16	
86	23	18	
87	24–25	19	
88	26	21	
89	27	23	
90	28	25	
91	29	27	
92	30	30	
93	31	32	
94	32	34	
95	33	37	
96	34	39	
97	35	42	
98	36	45	
99	37	47	
100	38	50	Average
101	39	53	
102	40	55	
103	41	58	
104	42	61	
105	43	63	
106	44	66	
107	45–46	68	
108	47	70	
109	48	73	
110	49	75	
111	50	77	
112	51	79	
113	52	81	
114	53	82	
115	54	84	
116	55	86	
117	56–57	87	
118	58	88	
119	59	90	
120	60	91	
121	61	92	
122	62	93	Advanced
123	63	94	
124	64	95	
125	65	95	
126	66–67	96	
127	68	96	
128	69	97	
129	70	97	
130	71	98	
131	72	98	
132	73	98	
133	74	99	
134	75	99	
135	76	99	
136	77	99	
137	78	99	
138	79	99	
139	80	99.5	
140	81	99.6	
141	82	99.7	
142	—	99.7	
143	83	99.8	
144	—	99.8	
145	—	99.9	Very Advanced
146	84	99.9	
147	—	99.9	
148	—	99.9	
149	—	99.9	
150	85	>99.9	
151	—	>99.9	
152	—	>99.9	
153	—	>99.9	
154	—	>99.9	
155	—	>99.9	
156	—	>99.9	
157	—	>99.9	
158	—	>99.9	
159	—	>99.9	
160	—	>99.9	

Composite Score Points for Building Confidence Intervals

Confidence Level	SRC
90%	4
95%	5

Note. Receptive SRC/RSRC = Receptive School Readiness Composite

Appendix C 4:0–4:2 Receptive SRC Scores

Composite Score	RSRC Raw Score	Percentile Rank	Descriptive Classification
40	—	<0.1	
41	—	<0.1	
42	—	<0.1	
43	—	<0.1	
44	—	<0.1	
45	—	<0.1	
46	—	<0.1	
47	—	<0.1	
48	—	<0.1	
49	—	<0.1	
50	—	<0.1	
51	—	0.1	
52	—	0.1	
53	—	0.1	
54	0	0.1	
55	—	0.1	Very Delayed
56	—	0.2	
57	—	0.2	
58	1	0.3	
59	—	0.3	
60	—	0.4	
61	2	0.5	
62	—	1	
63	3	1	
64	4	1	
65	5	1	
66	6	1	
67	7	1	
68	8	2	
69	9	2	
70	10	2	
71	11	3	
72	12	3	
73	13	4	
74	14	4	
75	15	5	
76	16–17	5	
77	18	6	
78	19	7	Delayed
79	20	8	
80	21	9	
81	22	10	
82	23	12	
83	24–25	13	
84	26	14	
85	27	16	
86	28	18	
87	29	19	
88	30	21	
89	31	23	
90	32	25	
91	33–34	27	
92	35	30	
93	36	32	
94	37	34	
95	38	37	
96	39	39	
97	40	42	
98	41	45	
99	42	47	
100	43	50	Average
101	44	53	
102	45	55	
103	46–47	58	
104	48	61	
105	49	63	
106	50	66	
107	51	68	
108	52	70	
109	53	73	
110	54	75	
111	55	77	
112	56	79	
113	57	81	
114	58	82	
115	59	84	
116	60	86	
117	61–62	87	
118	63	88	
119	64	90	
120	65	91	
121	66	92	
122	67	93	Advanced
123	68	94	
124	69	95	
125	70	95	
126	71	96	
127	72	96	
128	—	97	
129	73	97	
130	74	98	
131	75	98	
132	—	98	
133	76	99	
134	77	99	
135	78	99	
136	79	99	
137	80	99	
138	—	99	
139	81	99.5	
140	—	99.6	
141	82	99.7	
142	—	99.7	
143	83	99.8	
144	—	99.8	
145	—	99.9	Very Advanced
146	84	99.9	
147	—	99.9	
148	—	99.9	
149	85	99.9	
150	—	>99.9	
151	—	>99.9	
152	—	>99.9	
153	—	>99.9	
154	—	>99.9	
155	—	>99.9	
156	—	>99.9	
157	—	>99.9	
158	—	>99.9	
159	—	>99.9	
160	—	>99.9	

Composite Score Points for Building Confidence Intervals

Confidence Level	SRC
90%	5
95%	6

Note. Receptive SRC/RSRC = Receptive School Readiness Composite

Appendix C 4:3–4:5 Receptive SRC Scores

Composite Score	RSRC Raw Score	Percentile Rank	Descriptive Classification
40	—	<0.1	
41	—	<0.1	
42	—	<0.1	
43	—	<0.1	
44	—	<0.1	
45	—	<0.1	
46	—	<0.1	
47	—	<0.1	
48	—	<0.1	
49	—	<0.1	
50	—	<0.1	
51	—	0.1	
52	0	0.1	
53	—	0.1	
54	—	0.1	
55	—	0.1	Very Delayed
56	1	0.2	
57	—	0.2	
58	—	0.3	
59	2	0.3	
60	—	0.4	
61	3	0.5	
62	4	1	
63	5	1	
64	6	1	
65	7	1	
66	8–9	1	
67	10	1	
68	11	2	
69	12	2	
70	13–14	2	
71	15	3	
72	16	3	
73	17	4	
74	18	4	
75	19–20	5	
76	21	5	
77	22	6	
78	23	7	Delayed
79	24	8	
80	25–26	9	
81	27	10	
82	28	12	
83	29	13	
84	30	14	
85	31–32	16	
86	33	18	
87	34	19	
88	35	21	
89	36	23	
90	37	25	
91	38–39	27	
92	40	30	
93	41	32	
94	42	34	
95	43	37	
96	44	39	
97	45	42	
98	46–47	45	
99	48	47	
100	49	50	Average
101	50	53	
102	51	55	
103	52	58	
104	53	61	
105	54	63	
106	55	66	
107	56	68	
108	57	70	
109	58	73	
110	59	75	
111	60	77	
112	61	79	
113	62	81	
114	63	82	
115	64	84	
116	65	86	
117	66	87	
118	67	88	
119	68	90	
120	69	91	
121	70	92	
122	—	93	Advanced
123	71	94	
124	72	95	
125	73	95	
126	74	96	
127	75	96	
128	—	97	
129	76	97	
130	77	98	
131	78	98	
132	79	98	
133	—	99	
134	80	99	
135	81	99	
136	—	99	
137	82	99	
138	—	99	
139	83	99.5	
140	—	99.6	
141	—	99.7	
142	84	99.7	
143	—	99.8	
144	—	99.8	
145	—	99.9	Very Advanced
146	85	99.9	
147	—	99.9	
148	—	99.9	
149	—	99.9	
150	—	>99.9	
151	—	>99.9	
152	—	>99.9	
153	—	>99.9	
154	—	>99.9	
155	—	>99.9	
156	—	>99.9	
157	—	>99.9	
158	—	>99.9	
159	—	>99.9	
160	—	>99.9	

Composite Score Points for Building Confidence Intervals

Confidence Level	SRC
90%	5
95%	6

Note. Receptive SRC/RSRC = Receptive School Readiness Composite

Appendix C 4:6–4:8 Receptive SRC Scores

Composite Score	RSRC Raw Score	Percentile Rank	Descriptive Classification
40	—	<0.1	
41	—	<0.1	
42	—	<0.1	
43	—	<0.1	
44	—	<0.1	
45	—	<0.1	
46	—	<0.1	
47	—	<0.1	
48	—	<0.1	
49	—	<0.1	
50	0	<0.1	
51	—	0.1	
52	—	0.1	
53	1	0.1	
54	—	0.1	
55	—	0.1	Very Delayed
56	2	0.2	
57	—	0.2	
58	3	0.3	
59	4	0.3	
60	5	0.4	
61	6	0.5	
62	7	1	
63	8–9	1	
64	10	1	
65	11	1	
66	12–13	1	
67	14	1	
68	15	2	
69	16–17	2	
70	18	2	
71	19	3	
72	20–21	3	
73	22	4	
74	23	4	
75	24	5	
76	25–26	5	
77	27	6	
78	28	7	Delayed
79	29	8	
80	30	9	
81	31–32	10	
82	33	12	
83	34	13	
84	35	14	
85	36	16	
86	37–38	18	
87	39	19	
88	40	21	
89	41	23	
90	42	25	
91	43–44	27	
92	45	30	
93	46	32	
94	47	34	
95	48	37	
96	49–50	39	
97	51	42	
98	52	45	
99	53	47	
100	54	50	Average
101	55	53	
102	56	55	
103	57	58	
104	58	61	
105	59	63	
106	60	66	
107	61	68	
108	62	70	
109	63	73	
110	64	75	
111	65	77	
112	66	79	
113	67	81	
114	—	82	
115	68	84	
116	69	86	
117	70	87	
118	71	88	
119	72	90	
120	73	91	
121	—	92	
122	74	93	Advanced
123	75	94	
124	76	95	
125	—	95	
126	77	96	
127	78	96	
128	—	97	
129	79	97	
130	80	98	
131	—	98	
132	81	98	
133	—	99	
134	82	99	
135	—	99	
136	—	99	
137	83	99	
138	—	99	
139	—	99.5	
140	—	99.6	
141	84	99.7	
142	—	99.7	
143	—	99.8	
144	—	99.8	
145	85	99.9	Very Advanced
146	—	99.9	
147	—	99.9	
148	—	99.9	
149	—	99.9	
150	—	>99.9	
151	—	>99.9	
152	—	>99.9	
153	—	>99.9	
154	—	>99.9	
155	—	>99.9	
156	—	>99.9	
157	—	>99.9	
158	—	>99.9	
159	—	>99.9	
160	—	>99.9	

Appendix C 4:6–4:8 Receptive SRC Scores

Appendix C 4:6–4:8 Receptive SRC Scores

Composite Score Points for Building Confidence Intervals

Confidence Level	SRC
90%	5
95%	6

Note. Receptive SRC/RSRC = Receptive School Readiness Composite

Appendix C 4:9–4:11 Receptive SRC Scores

Composite Score	RSRC Raw Score	Percentile Rank	Descriptive Classification
40	—	<0.1	
41	0	<0.1	
42	—	<0.1	
43	—	<0.1	
44	—	<0.1	
45	1	<0.1	
46	—	<0.1	
47	—	<0.1	
48	—	<0.1	
49	2	<0.1	
50	—	<0.1	
51	—	0.1	
52	3	0.1	
53	—	0.1	
54	—	0.1	
55	4	0.1	Very Delayed
56	—	0.2	
57	5	0.2	
58	6	0.3	
59	7–8	0.3	
60	9	0.4	
61	10–11	0.5	
62	12	1	
63	13	1	
64	14–15	1	
65	16	1	
66	17–18	1	
67	19	1	
68	20–21	2	
69	22	2	
70	23	2	
71	24–25	3	
72	26	3	
73	27	4	
74	28	4	
75	29–30	5	
76	31	5	
77	32	6	
78	33	7	Delayed
79	34	8	
80	35	9	
81	36–37	10	
82	38	12	
83	39	13	
84	40	14	
85	41	16	

Appendix C 4:9–4:11 Receptive SRC Scores

Composite Score	RSRC Raw Score	Percentile Rank	Descriptive Classification
86	42	18	
87	43–44	19	
88	45	21	
89	46	23	
90	47	25	
91	48–49	27	
92	50	30	
93	51	32	
94	52	34	
95	53	37	
96	54	39	
97	55–56	42	
98	57	45	
99	58	47	
100	59	50	Average
101	60	53	
102	61	55	
103	62	58	
104	63	61	
105	64	63	
106	65	66	
107	66	68	
108	—	70	
109	67	73	
110	68	75	
111	69	77	
112	70	79	
113	71	81	
114	—	82	
115	72	84	
116	73	86	
117	74	87	
118	—	88	
119	75	90	
120	76	91	
121	—	92	
122	77	93	Advanced
123	78	94	
124	—	95	
125	79	95	
126	—	96	
127	80	96	
128	—	97	
129	81	97	

Appendix C 4:9–4:11 Receptive SRC Scores

Composite Score	RSRC Raw Score	Percentile Rank	Descriptive Classification
130	—	98	
131	—	98	
132	82	98	
133	—	99	
134	—	99	
135	83	99	
136	—	99	
137	—	99	
138	—	99	
139	84	99.5	
140	—	99.6	
141	—	99.7	
142	—	99.7	
143	—	99.8	
144	85	99.8	
145	—	99.9	Very Advanced
146	—	99.9	
147	—	99.9	
148	—	99.9	
149	—	99.9	
150	—	>99.9	
151	—	>99.9	
152	—	>99.9	
153	—	>99.9	
154	—	>99.9	
155	—	>99.9	
156	—	>99.9	
157	—	>99.9	
158	—	>99.9	
159	—	>99.9	
160	—	>99.9	

Composite Score Points for Building Confidence Intervals

Confidence Level	SRC
90%	5
95%	6

Note. Receptive SRC/RSRC = Receptive School Readiness Composite

Appendix C 5:0–5:2 Receptive SRC Scores

Composite Score	RSRC Raw Score	Percentile Rank	Descriptive Classification
40	0	<0.1	
41	—	<0.1	
42	—	<0.1	
43	1	<0.1	
44	—	<0.1	
45	2	<0.1	
46	3	<0.1	
47	4	<0.1	
48	—	<0.1	
49	5	<0.1	
50	—	<0.1	
51	6	0.1	
52	—	0.1	
53	7	0.1	
54	8	0.1	
55	9	0.1	Very Delayed
56	10	0.2	
57	11	0.2	
58	12	0.3	
59	13	0.3	
60	14–15	0.4	
61	16	0.5	
62	17	1	
63	18–19	1	
64	20–21	1	
65	22	1	
66	23–24	1	
67	25	1	
68	26–27	2	
69	28	2	
70	29	2	
71	30	3	
72	31–32	3	
73	33	4	
74	34	4	
75	35	5	
76	36	5	
77	37	6	
78	38	7	Delayed
79	39	8	
80	40	9	
81	41–42	10	
82	43	12	
83	44	13	
84	45	14	
85	46	16	

Appendix C 5:0–5:2 Receptive SRC Scores

Composite Score	RSRC Raw Score	Percentile Rank	Descriptive Classification
86	47	18	
87	48	19	
88	49	21	
89	50–51	23	
90	52	25	
91	53	27	
92	54	30	
93	55–56	32	
94	57	34	
95	58	37	
96	59	39	
97	60	42	
98	61	45	
99	62	47	
100	63–64	50	Average
101	65	53	
102	66	55	
103	—	58	
104	67	61	
105	68	63	
106	69	66	
107	70	68	
108	—	70	
109	71	73	
110	72	75	
111	73	77	
112	—	79	
113	74	81	
114	75	82	
115	—	84	
116	76	86	
117	77	87	
118	—	88	
119	78	90	
120	—	91	
121	79	92	
122	—	93	Advanced
123	80	94	
124	—	95	
125	—	95	
126	81	96	
127	—	96	
128	—	97	
129	82	97	

Appendix C 5:0–5:2 Receptive SRC Scores

Composite Score	RSRC Raw Score	Percentile Rank	Descriptive Classification
130	—	98	
131	—	98	
132	—	98	
133	83	99	
134	—	99	
135	—	99	
136	—	99	
137	—	99	
138	84	99	
139	—	99.5	
140	—	99.6	
141	—	99.7	
142	—	99.7	
143	85	99.8	
144	—	99.8	
145	—	99.9	Very Advanced
146	—	99.9	
147	—	99.9	
148	—	99.9	
149	—	99.9	
150	—	>99.9	
151	—	>99.9	
152	—	>99.9	
153	—	>99.9	
154	—	>99.9	
155	—	>99.9	
156	—	>99.9	
157	—	>99.9	
158	—	>99.9	
159	—	>99.9	
160	—	>99.9	

Composite Score Points for Building Confidence Intervals

Confidence Level	SRC
90%	4
95%	5

Note. Receptive SRC/RSRC = Receptive School Readiness Composite

Appendix C 5:3–5:5 Receptive SRC Scores

Composite Score	RSRC Raw Score	Percentile Rank	Descriptive Classification
40	0	<0.1	
41	—	<0.1	
42	—	<0.1	
43	1	<0.1	
44	—	<0.1	
45	2	<0.1	
46	3	<0.1	
47	4	<0.1	
48	5	<0.1	
49	6	<0.1	
50	7	<0.1	
51	8	0.1	
52	9	0.1	
53	10	0.1	
54	11	0.1	
55	12–13	0.1	Very Delayed
56	14	0.2	
57	15	0.2	
58	16	0.3	
59	17–18	0.3	
60	19	0.4	
61	20	0.5	
62	21–22	1	
63	23–24	1	
64	25	1	
65	26–27	1	
66	28–29	1	
67	30–31	1	
68	32	2	
69	33–34	2	
70	35	2	
71	36	3	
72	37	3	
73	38–39	4	
74	40	4	
75	41	5	
76	42	5	
77	43	6	
78	44	7	Delayed
79	45	8	
80	46	9	
81	47	10	
82	48	12	
83	49	13	
84	50	14	
85	51	16	

Appendix C 5:3–5:5 Receptive SRC Scores

Composite Score	RSRC Raw Score	Percentile Rank	Descriptive Classification
86	52	18	
87	53	19	
88	54	21	
89	55	23	
90	56	25	
91	57–58	27	
92	59	30	
93	60	32	
94	61	34	
95	62	37	
96	63–64	39	
97	65	42	
98	66	45	
99	67	47	
100	68	50	Average
101	69	53	
102	70	55	
103	71	58	
104	72	61	
105	—	63	
106	73	66	
107	—	68	
108	74	70	
109	75	73	
110	76	75	
111	—	77	
112	77	79	
113	—	81	
114	—	82	
115	78	84	
116	—	86	
117	—	87	
118	79	88	
119	—	90	
120	—	91	
121	—	92	
122	80	93	Advanced
123	—	94	
124	—	95	
125	81	95	
126	—	96	
127	—	96	
128	82	97	
129	—	97	

Appendix C 5:3–5:5 Receptive SRC Scores

Composite Score	RSRC Raw Score	Percentile Rank	Descriptive Classification
130	—	98	
131	—	98	
132	83	98	
133	—	99	
134	—	99	
135	—	99	
136	—	99	
137	84	99	
138	—	99	
139	—	99.5	
140	—	99.6	
141	—	99.7	
142	85	99.7	
143	—	99.8	
144	—	99.8	
145	—	99.9	Very Advanced
146	—	99.9	
147	—	99.9	
148	—	99.9	
149	—	99.9	
150	—	>99.9	
151	—	>99.9	
152	—	>99.9	
153	—	>99.9	
154	—	>99.9	
155	—	>99.9	
156	—	>99.9	
157	—	>99.9	
158	—	>99.9	
159	—	>99.9	
160	—	>99.9	

Composite Score Points for Building Confidence Intervals

Confidence Level	SRC
90%	4
95%	5

Note. Receptive SRC/RSRC = Receptive School Readiness Composite

Appendix C 5:6–5:8 Receptive SRC Scores

Composite Score	RSRC Raw Score	Percentile Rank	Descriptive Classification
40	0–6	<0.1	
41	7	<0.1	
42	8	<0.1	
43	9	<0.1	
44	10	<0.1	
45	11	<0.1	
46	12	<0.1	
47	—	<0.1	
48	13	<0.1	
49	14	<0.1	
50	15	<0.1	
51	16	0.1	
52	17	0.1	
53	18	0.1	
54	19	0.1	
55	20	0.1	Very Delayed
56	21	0.2	
57	22	0.2	
58	23	0.3	
59	24	0.3	
60	25	0.4	
61	26–27	0.5	
62	28	1	
63	29–30	1	
64	31	1	
65	32–33	1	
66	34–35	1	
67	36–37	1	
68	38–39	2	
69	40	2	
70	41	2	
71	42–43	3	
72	44	3	
73	45	4	
74	46	4	
75	47	5	
76	—	5	
77	48	6	
78	49	7	Delayed
79	50	8	
80	51	9	
81	52	10	
82	—	12	
83	53	13	
84	54	14	
85	55	16	
86	56	18	
87	57	19	
88	58	21	
89	59	23	
90	60	25	
91	61	27	
92	62–63	30	
93	64	32	
94	65	34	
95	66	37	
96	67–68	39	
97	69	42	
98	70	45	
99	71	47	
100	72	50	Average
101	73	53	
102	74	55	
103	—	58	
104	75	61	
105	76	63	
106	—	66	
107	77	68	
108	—	70	
109	78	73	
110	—	75	
111	—	77	
112	79	79	
113	—	81	
114	—	82	
115	—	84	
116	80	86	
117	—	87	
118	—	88	
119	—	90	
120	81	91	
121	—	92	
122	—	93	Advanced
123	—	94	
124	82	95	
125	—	95	
126	—	96	
127	—	96	
128	—	97	
129	83	97	
130	—	98	
131	—	98	
132	—	98	
133	—	99	
134	84	99	
135	—	99	
136	—	99	
137	—	99	
138	—	99	
139	85	99.5	
140	—	99.6	
141	—	99.7	
142	—	99.7	
143	—	99.8	
144	—	99.8	
145	—	99.9	Very Advanced
146	—	99.9	
147	—	99.9	
148	—	99.9	
149	—	99.9	
150	—	>99.9	
151	—	>99.9	
152	—	>99.9	
153	—	>99.9	
154	—	>99.9	
155	—	>99.9	
156	—	>99.9	
157	—	>99.9	
158	—	>99.9	
159	—	>99.9	
160	—	>99.9	

Composite Score Points for Building Confidence Intervals

Confidence Level	SRC
90%	5
95%	6

Note. Receptive SRC/RSRC = Receptive School Readiness Composite

Appendix C 5:9–5:11 Receptive SRC Scores

Appendix C 5:9–5:11 Receptive SRC Scores

Appendix C 5:9–5:11 Receptive SRC Scores

Composite Score	RSRC Raw Score	Percentile Rank	Descriptive Classification
40	0–16	<0.1	
41	17	<0.1	
42	18	<0.1	
43	19	<0.1	
44	—	<0.1	
45	20	<0.1	
46	21	<0.1	
47	—	<0.1	
48	22	<0.1	
49	23	<0.1	
50	24	<0.1	
51	25	0.1	
52	—	0.1	
53	26	0.1	
54	27	0.1	
55	28	0.1	Very Delayed
56	29	0.2	
57	30	0.2	
58	31	0.3	
59	32	0.3	
60	33	0.4	
61	34	0.5	
62	35	1	
63	36	1	
64	37	1	
65	38–39	1	
66	40–41	1	
67	42–43	1	
68	44–45	2	
69	46–47	2	
70	48	2	
71	49	3	
72	50	3	
73	51	4	
74	—	4	
75	52	5	
76	53	5	
77	54	6	
78	—	7	Delayed
79	55	8	
80	56	9	
81	—	10	
82	57	12	
83	58	13	
84	59	14	
85	—	16	
86	60	18	
87	61	19	
88	62	21	
89	63–64	23	
90	65	25	
91	66	27	
92	67	30	
93	68	32	
94	69	34	
95	70	37	
96	71	39	
97	72	42	
98	73	45	
99	74	47	
100	75	50	Average
101	—	53	
102	76	55	
103	—	58	
104	77	61	
105	—	63	
106	—	66	
107	78	68	
108	—	70	
109	—	73	
110	79	75	
111	—	77	
112	—	79	
113	—	81	
114	80	82	
115	—	84	
116	—	86	
117	—	87	
118	81	88	
119	—	90	
120	—	91	
121	—	92	
122	82	93	Advanced
123	—	94	
124	—	95	
125	—	95	
126	83	96	
127	—	96	
128	—	97	
129	—	97	
130	84	98	
131	—	98	
132	—	98	
133	—	99	
134	85	99	
135	—	99	
136	—	99	
137	—	99	
138	—	99	
139	—	99.5	
140	—	99.6	
141	—	99.7	
142	—	99.7	
143	—	99.8	
144	—	99.8	
145	—	99.9	Very Advanced
146	—	99.9	
147	—	99.9	
148	—	99.9	
149	—	99.9	
150	—	>99.9	
151	—	>99.9	
152	—	>99.9	
153	—	>99.9	
154	—	>99.9	
155	—	>99.9	
156	—	>99.9	
157	—	>99.9	
158	—	>99.9	
159	—	>99.9	
160	—	>99.9	

Composite Score Points for Building Confidence Intervals

Confidence Level	SRC
90%	5
95%	6

Note. Receptive SRC/RSRC = Receptive School Readiness Composite

Appendix C 6:0–6:2 Receptive SRC Scores

Composite Score	RSRC Raw Score	Percentile Rank	Descriptive Classification
40	0–26	<0.1	
41	27	<0.1	
42	28	<0.1	
43	29	<0.1	
44	—	<0.1	
45	30	<0.1	
46	—	<0.1	
47	31	<0.1	
48	32	<0.1	
49	—	<0.1	
50	33	<0.1	
51	34	0.1	
52	—	0.1	
53	35	0.1	
54	36	0.1	
55	—	0.1	Very Delayed
56	37	0.2	
57	38	0.2	
58	39	0.3	
59	—	0.3	
60	40	0.4	
61	41–42	0.5	
62	43–44	1	
63	45–46	1	
64	47–48	1	
65	49–50	1	
66	51–52	1	
67	53–54	1	
68	55–56	2	
69	57	2	
70	—	2	
71	58	3	
72	—	3	
73	59	4	
74	—	4	
75	—	5	
76	60	5	
77	—	6	
78	61	7	Delayed
79	62	8	
80	63	9	
81	64	10	
82	—	12	
83	65	13	
84	66	14	
85	67	16	
86	68	18	
87	69	19	
88	—	21	
89	70	23	
90	71	25	
91	72	27	
92	73	30	
93	74	32	
94	—	34	
95	75	37	
96	—	39	
97	—	42	
98	76	45	
99	—	47	
100	—	50	Average
101	—	53	
102	77	55	
103	—	58	
104	—	61	
105	—	63	
106	78	66	
107	—	68	
108	—	70	
109	79	73	
110	—	75	
111	—	77	
112	—	79	
113	80	81	
114	—	82	
115	—	84	
116	—	86	
117	81	87	
118	—	88	
119	—	90	
120	—	91	
121	82	92	
122	—	93	Advanced
123	—	94	
124	—	95	
125	83	95	
126	—	96	
127	—	96	
128	—	97	
129	84	97	
130	—	98	
131	—	98	
132	—	98	
133	85	99	
134	—	99	
135	—	99	
136	—	99	
137	—	99	
138	—	99	
139	—	99.5	
140	—	99.6	
141	—	99.7	
142	—	99.7	
143	—	99.8	
144	—	99.8	
145	—	99.9	Very Advanced
146	—	99.9	
147	—	99.9	
148	—	99.9	
149	—	99.9	
150	—	>99.9	
151	—	>99.9	
152	—	>99.9	
153	—	>99.9	
154	—	>99.9	
155	—	>99.9	
156	—	>99.9	
157	—	>99.9	
158	—	>99.9	
159	—	>99.9	
160	—	>99.9	

Composite Score Points for Building Confidence Intervals

Confidence Level	SRC
90%	8
95%	9

Note. Receptive SRC/RSRC = Receptive School Readiness Composite

Appendix C 6:3–6:5 Receptive SRC Scores

Composite Score	RSRC Raw Score	Percentile Rank	Descriptive Classification
40	0–37	<0.1	Very Delayed
41	38	<0.1	
42	39	<0.1	
43	—	<0.1	
44	40	<0.1	
45	—	<0.1	
46	41	<0.1	
47	—	<0.1	
48	42	<0.1	
49	—	<0.1	
50	43	<0.1	
51	—	0.1	
52	44	0.1	
53	—	0.1	
54	45	0.1	
55	—	0.1	
56	46	0.2	
57	—	0.2	
58	47	0.3	
59	48	0.3	
60	49	0.4	
61	50–51	0.5	
62	52–53	1	
63	54–55	1	
64	56–57	1	
65	58	1	
66	—	1	
67	59	1	
68	—	2	
69	60	2	
70	—	2	
71	61	3	Delayed
72	62	3	
73	—	4	
74	63	4	
75	—	5	
76	64	5	
77	65	6	
78	66	7	
79	67	8	
80	—	9	
81	68	10	
82	69	12	
83	70	13	
84	71–72	14	
85	73	16	

Appendix C 6:3–6:5 Receptive SRC Scores

Composite Score	RSRC Raw Score	Percentile Rank	Descriptive Classification
86	—	18	Average
87	74	19	
88	—	21	
89	—	23	
90	75	25	
91	—	27	
92	—	30	
93	76	32	
94	—	34	
95	—	37	
96	77	39	
97	—	42	
98	—	45	
99	78	47	
100	—	50	
101	—	53	
102	—	55	
103	79	58	
104	—	61	
105	—	63	
106	—	66	
107	—	68	
108	80	70	
109	—	73	
110	—	75	
111	—	77	
112	—	79	
113	81	81	
114	—	82	
115	—	84	Advanced
116	—	86	
117	—	87	
118	—	88	
119	82	90	
120	—	91	
121	—	92	
122	—	93	
123	—	94	
124	83	95	
125	—	95	
126	—	96	
127	—	96	
128	84	97	
129	—	97	

Appendix C 6:3–6:5 Receptive SRC Scores

Composite Score	RSRC Raw Score	Percentile Rank	Descriptive Classification
130	—	98	Very Advanced
131	—	98	
132	85	98	
133	—	99	
134	—	99	
135	—	99	
136	—	99	
137	—	99	
138	—	99	
139	—	99.5	
140	—	99.6	
141	—	99.7	
142	—	99.7	
143	—	99.8	
144	—	99.8	
145	—	99.9	
146	—	99.9	
147	—	99.9	
148	—	99.9	
149	—	99.9	
150	—	>99.9	
151	—	>99.9	
152	—	>99.9	
153	—	>99.9	
154	—	>99.9	
155	—	>99.9	
156	—	>99.9	
157	—	>99.9	
158	—	>99.9	
159	—	>99.9	
160	—	>99.9	

Composite Score Points for Building Confidence Intervals

Confidence Level	SRC
90%	8
95%	9

Note. Receptive SRC/RSRC = Receptive School Readiness Composite

Appendix C 6:6–6:8 Receptive SRC Scores

Composite Score	RSRC Raw Score	Percentile Rank	Descriptive Classification
40	0–48	<0.1	
41	49	<0.1	
42	—	<0.1	
43	50	<0.1	
44	—	<0.1	
45	—	<0.1	
46	51	<0.1	
47	—	<0.1	
48	—	<0.1	
49	52	<0.1	
50	—	<0.1	
51	—	0.1	
52	—	0.1	
53	53	0.1	
54	—	0.1	
55	—	0.1	Very Delayed
56	54	0.2	
57	—	0.2	
58	55	0.3	
59	56	0.3	
60	57	0.4	
61	—	0.5	
62	58	1	
63	—	1	
64	59	1	
65	60	1	
66	61–62	1	
67	63	1	
68	64	2	
69	65	2	
70	—	2	
71	66	3	
72	—	3	
73	67	4	
74	—	4	
75	—	5	
76	68	5	
77	—	6	
78	—	7	Delayed
79	69	8	
80	—	9	
81	70	10	
82	—	12	
83	71	13	
84	72	14	
85	73	16	

Appendix C 6:6–6:8 Receptive SRC Scores

Composite Score	RSRC Raw Score	Percentile Rank	Descriptive Classification
86	—	18	
87	74	19	
88	—	21	
89	—	23	
90	75	25	
91	—	27	
92	—	30	
93	76	32	
94	—	34	
95	—	37	
96	77	39	
97	—	42	
98	—	45	
99	78	47	
100	—	50	Average
101	79	53	
102	—	55	
103	—	58	
104	80	61	
105	—	63	
106	—	66	
107	—	68	
108	81	70	
109	—	73	
110	—	75	
111	—	77	
112	—	79	
113	82	81	
114	—	82	
115	—	84	
116	—	86	
117	—	87	
118	83	88	
119	—	90	
120	—	91	
121	—	92	
122	—	93	Advanced
123	84	94	
124	—	95	
125	—	95	
126	—	96	
127	85	96	
128	—	97	
129	—	97	

Appendix C 6:6–6:8 Receptive SRC Scores

Composite Score	RSRC Raw Score	Percentile Rank	Descriptive Classification
130	—	98	
131	—	98	
132	—	98	
133	—	99	
134	—	99	
135	—	99	
136	—	99	
137	—	99	
138	—	99	
139	—	99.5	
140	—	99.6	
141	—	99.7	
142	—	99.7	
143	—	99.8	
144	—	99.8	
145	—	99.9	Very Advanced
146	—	99.9	
147	—	99.9	
148	—	99.9	
149	—	99.9	
150	—	>99.9	
151	—	>99.9	
152	—	>99.9	
153	—	>99.9	
154	—	>99.9	
155	—	>99.9	
156	—	>99.9	
157	—	>99.9	
158	—	>99.9	
159	—	>99.9	
160	—	>99.9	

Composite Score Points for Building Confidence Intervals

Confidence Level	SRC
90%	10
95%	12

Note. Receptive SRC/RSRC = Receptive School Readiness Composite

Appendix C 6:9–6:11 Receptive SRC Scores

Composite Score	RSRC Raw Score	Percentile Rank	Descriptive Classification
40	0–52	<0.1	
41	53	<0.1	
42	54	<0.1	
43	55	<0.1	
44	56	<0.1	
45	57	<0.1	
46	58	<0.1	
47	59	<0.1	
48	60	<0.1	
49	61	<0.1	
50	62	<0.1	
51	63	0.1	
52	—	0.1	
53	64	0.1	
54	—	0.1	
55	—	0.1	Very Delayed
56	65	0.2	
57	—	0.2	
58	—	0.3	
59	66	0.3	
60	—	0.4	
61	—	0.5	
62	—	1	
63	67	1	
64	—	1	
65	—	1	
66	—	1	
67	68	1	
68	—	2	
69	—	2	
70	69	2	
71	—	3	
72	70	3	
73	—	4	
74	—	4	
75	71	5	
76	—	5	
77	—	6	
78	72	7	Delayed
79	—	8	
80	—	9	
81	73	10	
82	—	12	
83	—	13	
84	74	14	
85	—	16	

Appendix C 6:9–6:11 Receptive SRC Scores

Composite Score	RSRC Raw Score	Percentile Rank	Descriptive Classification
86	—	18	
87	—	19	
88	75	21	
89	—	23	
90	—	25	
91	—	27	
92	76	30	
93	—	32	
94	—	34	
95	77	37	
96	—	39	
97	—	42	
98	78	45	
99	—	47	
100	—	50	Average
101	79	53	
102	—	55	
103	—	58	
104	80	61	
105	—	63	
106	—	66	
107	—	68	
108	81	70	
109	—	73	
110	—	75	
111	—	77	
112	82	79	
113	—	81	
114	—	82	
115	—	84	
116	—	86	
117	83	87	
118	—	88	
119	—	90	
120	—	91	
121	—	92	
122	84	93	Advanced
123	—	94	
124	—	95	
125	—	95	
126	85	96	
127	—	96	
128	—	97	
129	—	97	

Appendix C 6:9–6:11 Receptive SRC Scores

Composite Score	RSRC Raw Score	Percentile Rank	Descriptive Classification
130	—	98	
131	—	98	
132	—	98	
133	—	99	
134	—	99	
135	—	99	
136	—	99	
137	—	99	
138	—	99	
139	—	99.5	
140	—	99.6	
141	—	99.7	
142	—	99.7	
143	—	99.8	
144	—	99.8	
145	—	99.9	Very Advanced
146	—	99.9	
147	—	99.9	
148	—	99.9	
149	—	99.9	
150	—	>99.9	
151	—	>99.9	
152	—	>99.9	
153	—	>99.9	
154	—	>99.9	
155	—	>99.9	
156	—	>99.9	
157	—	>99.9	
158	—	>99.9	
159	—	>99.9	
160	—	>99.9	

Composite Score Points for Building Confidence Intervals

Confidence Level	SRC
90%	10
95%	12

Note. Receptive SRC/RSRC = Receptive School Readiness Composite

Concept Age Equivalents

Appendix D Concept Age Equivalents in One-Month Intervals

Concept Age Equivalent	Subtest Raw Score						Receptive TC Raw Score	Concept Age Equivalent
	1–5 SRC	6 Direction/ Position	7 Self-/Social Awareness	8 Texture/ Material	9 Quantity	10 Time/ Sequence		
>6:11	81–85	58–62	—	27–29	40–43	28–30	270–282	>6:11
6:11	—	—	33	—	39	—	265–269	6:11
6:10	80	57	—	26	38	27	261–264	6:10
6:9	—	—	—	—	37	26	257–260	6:9
6:8	—	56	—	—	36	—	252–256	6:8
6:7	79	—	32	—	35	25	248–251	6:7
6:6	—	55	—	—	34	24	243–247	6:6
6:5	—	—	—	—	33	—	239–242	6:5
6:4	78	54	—	25	32	23	233–238	6:4
6:3	—	53	—	—	31	22	229–232	6:3
6:2	—	—	—	—	30	—	226–228	6:2
6:1	77	52	31	24	29	21	222–225	6:1
6:0	76	50–51	—	—	—	—	218–221	6:0
5:11	—	49	—	—	28	20	215–217	5:11
5:10	75	48	—	23	27	—	211–214	5:10
5:9	74	47	—	22	—	19	207–210	5:9
5:8	73	46	—	—	26	—	203–206	5:8
5:7	72	45	30	21	—	18	200–202	5:7
5:6	70–71	44	—	—	25	17	196–199	5:6
5:5	68–69	43	—	—	—	—	192–195	5:5
5:4	66–67	42	29	20	24	16	188–191	5:4
5:3	65	40–41	28	19	—	—	183–187	5:3
5:2	—	39	—	—	23	—	179–182	5:2
5:1	64	38	27	18	—	15	175–178	5:1
5:0	62–63	36–37	—	—	22	14	171–174	5:0
4:11	61	35	—	—	—	—	167–170	4:11
4:10	59–60	34	26	17	21	13	162–166	4:10
4:9	57–58	33	—	16	—	—	158–161	4:9
4:8	56	32	25	—	20	—	153–157	4:8
4:7	54–55	31	—	15	19	12	149–152	4:7
4:6	52–53	29–30	24	—	—	—	144–148	4:6
4:5	50–51	28	—	14	18	11	140–143	4:5
4:4	49	27	23	—	—	—	135–139	4:4
4:3	47–48	26	22	13	17	10	130–134	4:3
4:2	45–46	25	—	—	—	—	126–129	4:2
4:1	43–44	24	21	12	16	9	121–125	4:1
4:0	41–42	23	20	—	15	8	116–120	4:0
3:11	40	22	—	—	14	—	111–115	3:11
3:10	38–39	21	19	11	13	7	106–110	3:10
3:9	36–37	20	18	10	—	—	100–105	3:9
3:8	35	19	17	—	12	—	96–99	3:8
3:7	33–34	18	16	9	11	6	91–95	3:7
3:6	31–32	17	15	—	10	—	86–90	3:6
3:5	30	16	—	8	—	5	81–85	3:5
3:4	28–29	15	14	7	9	4	75–80	3:4
3:3	27	14	13	—	8	—	70–74	3:3
3:2	25–26	13	12	6	7	—	65–69	3:2
3:1	24	11–12	11	5	6	3	59–64	3:1
3:0	22–23	9–10	10	—	5	—	54–58	3:0
<3:0	0–21	0–8	0–9	0–4	0–4	0–2	0–53	<3:0

Percentile Ranks, Normal Curve Equivalents, and Stanines

Appendix E Percentile Ranks, Normal Curve Equivalents, and Stanines

Subtest Scaled Score	Composite Score	Percentile Rank	Normal Curve Equivalent	Stanine
	160	>99.9	99	9
	159	>99.9	99	9
	158	>99.9	99	9
	157	>99.9	99	9
	156	>99.9	99	9
	155	>99.9	99	9
	154	>99.9	99	9
	153	>99.9	99	9
	152	>99.9	99	9
	151	>99.9	99	9
	150	>99.9	99	9
	149	99.9	99	9
	148	99.9	99	9
	147	99.9	99	9
	146	99.9	99	9
19	145	99.9	99	9
	144	99.8	99	9
	143	99.8	99	9
	142	99.7	99	9
	141	99.7	99	9
18	140	99.6	99	9
	139	99.5	99	9
	138	99	99	9
	137	99	99	9
	136	99	99	9
17	135	99	99	9
	134	99	98	9
	133	99	96	9
	132	98	95	9
	131	98	94	9
16	130	98	92	9
	129	97	91	9
	128	97	89	9
	127	96	88	9
	126	96	87	9
15	125	95	85	8
	124	95	84	8
	123	94	82	8
	122	93	81	8
	121	92	79	8
14	120	91	78	8
	119	90	77	8
	118	88	75	7
	117	87	74	7
	116	86	72	7
13	115	84	71	7
	114	82	70	7
	113	81	68	7
	112	79	67	7
	111	77	65	7
12	110	75	64	6
	109	73	63	6
	108	70	61	6
	107	68	60	6
	106	66	58	6
11	105	63	57	6
	104	61	56	6
	103	58	54	5
	102	55	53	5
	101	53	51	5
10	100	50	50	5
	99	47	49	5
	98	45	47	5
	97	42	46	5
	96	39	44	4
9	95	37	43	4
	94	34	42	4
	93	32	40	4
	92	30	39	4
	91	27	37	4
8	90	25	36	4
	89	23	35	4
	88	21	33	3
	87	19	32	3
	86	18	30	3
7	85	16	29	3
	84	14	28	3
	83	13	26	3
	82	12	25	3
	81	10	23	2
6	80	9	22	2
	79	8	21	2
	78	7	19	2
	77	6	18	2
	76	5	16	2
5	75	5	15	2
	74	4	13	2
	73	4	12	2
	72	3	11	1
	71	3	9	1
4	70	2	8	1
	69	2	6	1
	68	2	5	1
	67	1	4	1
	66	1	2	1
3	65	1	1	1
	64	1	1	1
	63	1	1	1
	62	1	1	1
	61	0.5	1	1
2	60	0.4	1	1
	59	0.3	1	1
	58	0.3	1	1
	57	0.2	1	1
	56	0.2	1	1
1	55	0.1	1	1
	54	0.1	1	1
	53	0.1	1	1
	52	0.1	1	1
	51	0.1	1	1
	50	<0.1	1	1
	49	<0.1	1	1
	48	<0.1	1	1
	47	<0.1	1	1
	46	<0.1	1	1
	45	<0.1	1	1
	44	<0.1	1	1
	43	<0.1	1	1
	42	<0.1	1	1
	41	<0.1	1	1
	40	<0.1	1	1

Parent/Teacher Conference Form (English and Spanish)

Parent/Teacher Conference Form (English)

Date ____________

______________________________________ was recently given the BBCS–3:R. The test assesses knowledge of important concepts. To assist you in teaching these important concepts, the items that the child did or did not know are identified as follows:

M = The child probably understands the concept in most situations (Mastered).

NM = The child probably does not understand the concept in most situations (Not Mastered).

Colors

Concept	M	NM
red	☐	☐
blue	☐	☐
green	☐	☐
black	☐	☐
yellow	☐	☐
pink	☐	☐
orange	☐	☐
purple	☐	☐
white	☐	☐
brown	☐	☐

Letters

Concept	M	NM
A	☐	☐
W	☐	☐
X	☐	☐
S	☐	☐
K	☐	☐
H	☐	☐
Q	☐	☐
D	☐	☐
m	☐	☐
i	☐	☐
b	☐	☐
e	☐	☐
t	☐	☐
j	☐	☐
g	☐	☐

Numbers/Counting

Concept	M	NM
one	☐	☐
three	☐	☐
two	☐	☐
four	☐	☐
zero	☐	☐
three	☐	☐
six	☐	☐
nine	☐	☐
five	☐	☐
seven	☐	☐
eight	☐	☐
six	☐	☐
nine	☐	☐
forty-one	☐	☐
eleven	☐	☐
ninety-five	☐	☐
twenty-seven	☐	☐
fifty-three	☐	☐

Sizes/Comparisons

Concept	M	NM
big	☐	☐
small	☐	☐
long	☐	☐
little	☐	☐
not the same	☐	☐
short	☐	☐
match	☐	☐
different	☐	☐
tall	☐	☐
deep	☐	☐
large	☐	☐
same	☐	☐
alike	☐	☐
wide	☐	☐
exactly	☐	☐
other than	☐	☐
similar	☐	☐
equal	☐	☐
thin	☐	☐
narrow	☐	☐
unequal	☐	☐
shallow	☐	☐

Shapes

Concept	M	NM
star	☐	☐
heart	☐	☐
circle	☐	☐
line	☐	☐
square	☐	☐
triangle	☐	☐
cone	☐	☐
round	☐	☐
diamond	☐	☐
oval	☐	☐
rectangle	☐	☐
check mark	☐	☐
row	☐	☐
pyramid	☐	☐
cylinder	☐	☐
cube	☐	☐
curve	☐	☐
column	☐	☐
diagonal	☐	☐
angle	☐	☐

Direction/Position

Concept	M	NM
on	☐	☐
open	☐	☐
in	☐	☐
closed	☐	☐
off	☐	☐
under	☐	☐
up	☐	☐
upside down	☐	☐
behind	☐	☐
top	☐	☐
out	☐	☐
high	☐	☐
apart	☐	☐
close	☐	☐
around	☐	☐
next to	☐	☐
outside	☐	☐
near	☐	☐
in front	☐	☐
together	☐	☐
away	☐	☐
middle	☐	☐
bottom	☐	☐
into	☐	☐
down	☐	☐
following	☐	☐
side	☐	☐
through	☐	☐
between	☐	☐
front	☐	☐
backward	☐	☐
beside	☐	☐
edge	☐	☐
back	☐	☐
low	☐	☐
straight	☐	☐
corner	☐	☐
toward	☐	☐
falling	☐	☐
end	☐	☐
still	☐	☐
joined	☐	☐
below	☐	☐
above	☐	☐
across from	☐	☐
forward	☐	☐
turn	☐	☐
space	☐	☐
over	☐	☐
underlined	☐	☐
sideways	☐	☐
inside-out	☐	☐
ahead	☐	☐
center	☐	☐
level	☐	☐
separated	☐	☐
rising	☐	☐
height	☐	☐
opposite	☐	☐
right	☐	☐
length	☐	☐
left	☐	☐

Self-/Social Awareness

Concept	M	NM
crying	☐	☐
laughing	☐	☐
sad	☐	☐
man	☐	☐
girl	☐	☐
boy	☐	☐
afraid	☐	☐
angry	☐	☐
brothers	☐	☐
hurt	☐	☐
sisters	☐	☐
happy	☐	☐
relaxing	☐	☐
resting	☐	☐
tired	☐	☐
woman	☐	☐
old	☐	☐
excited	☐	☐
mother	☐	☐
wrong	☐	☐
sleepy	☐	☐
father	☐	☐
friendly	☐	☐
frowning	☐	☐
worried	☐	☐
right	☐	☐
healthy	☐	☐
easy	☐	☐
difficult	☐	☐
disappointed	☐	☐
young	☐	☐
correct	☐	☐
curious	☐	☐

Texture/Material

Concept	M	NM
wet	☐	☐
heavy	☐	☐
loud	☐	☐
dark	☐	☐
quiet	☐	☐
soft	☐	☐
wood	☐	☐
sharp	☐	☐
hard	☐	☐
glass	☐	☐
shiny	☐	☐
light	☐	☐
boiling	☐	☐
flat	☐	☐
bright	☐	☐
gas	☐	☐
metal	☐	☐
reflection	☐	☐
smooth	☐	☐
cloth	☐	☐
rough	☐	☐
clear	☐	☐
dry	☐	☐
tight	☐	☐
loose	☐	☐
light	☐	☐
solid	☐	☐
dull	☐	☐
liquid	☐	☐

Quantity

Concept	M	NM
many	☐	☐
whole	☐	☐
empty	☐	☐
full	☐	☐
none	☐	☐
nothing	☐	☐
both	☐	☐
all	☐	☐
most	☐	☐
enough	☐	☐
alone	☐	☐
every	☐	☐
with	☐	☐
missing	☐	☐
piece	☐	☐
almost	☐	☐
each	☐	☐
left	☐	☐
greatest	☐	☐
part	☐	☐
little	☐	☐
except	☐	☐
dozen	☐	☐
without	☐	☐
half	☐	☐
more than	☐	☐
several	☐	☐
least	☐	☐
less than	☐	☐
pair	☐	☐
another	☐	☐
divided	☐	☐
double	☐	☐
single	☐	☐
add	☐	☐
neither	☐	☐
couple	☐	☐
some	☐	☐
few	☐	☐
weight	☐	☐
subtract	☐	☐
as many as	☐	☐
triple	☐	☐

Time/Sequence

Concept	M	NM
new	☐	☐
old	☐	☐
finished	☐	☐
last	☐	☐
daytime	☐	☐
waiting	☐	☐
through	☐	☐
starting	☐	☐
skipped	☐	☐
quit	☐	☐
next	☐	☐
beginning	☐	☐
order	☐	☐
morning	☐	☐
before	☐	☐
first	☐	☐
slow	☐	☐
twice	☐	☐
third	☐	☐
always	☐	☐
second	☐	☐
never	☐	☐
late	☐	☐
after	☐	☐
arriving	☐	☐
just	☐	☐
over	☐	☐
fourth	☐	☐
early	☐	☐
nearly	☐	☐

Parent/Teacher Conference Form (Spanish)

Feche __________

A ______________________________________ se le administró recientement la prueba BBCS–3:R. El examen determina el conocimento de conceptos importantes. Para ayudarle a enseñar estos conceptos, los conceptos que su niño(a) sabe (S) y no sabe (NS) estan identificados abajo:

S = El niño(a) probalmente entiende los conceptos in mayor parte del tiempo (Sabe).

NS = El niño(a) probalmente no entiende los conceptos in mayor parte del tiempo (No Sabe).

Colors

Concept	S	NS
rojo	☐	☐
azul	☐	☐
verde	☐	☐
negro	☐	☐
amarillo	☐	☐
rosa	☐	☐
anaranjado/naranja	☐	☐
morado/violeta	☐	☐
blanco	☐	☐
café/marrón	☐	☐

Letters

Concept	S	NS
A	☐	☐
W	☐	☐
X	☐	☐
S	☐	☐
K	☐	☐
H	☐	☐
Q	☐	☐
D	☐	☐
m	☐	☐
i	☐	☐
b	☐	☐
e	☐	☐
t	☐	☐
j	☐	☐
g	☐	☐

Numbers/Counting

Concept	S	NS
uno	☐	☐
tres	☐	☐
dos	☐	☐
cuatro	☐	☐
cero	☐	☐
tres flores	☐	☐
seis patos	☐	☐
nueve hormigas	☐	☐
cinco	☐	☐
siete	☐	☐
ocho	☐	☐
seis	☐	☐
nueve	☐	☐
cuarenta y uno	☐	☐
once	☐	☐
noventa y cinco	☐	☐
veintisiete	☐	☐
cincuenta y tres	☐	☐

Sizes/Comparisons

Concept	S	NS
grande	☐	☐
chiquito	☐	☐
largo	☐	☐
pequeña	☐	☐
no son iguales	☐	☐
cortos	☐	☐
hacen el par	☐	☐
diferentes	☐	☐
alta	☐	☐
profunda	☐	☐
iguales	☐	☐
se parecen	☐	☐
ancho	☐	☐
exactamente	☐	☐
algo que no es	☐	☐
similares	☐	☐
igual	☐	☐
delgado	☐	☐
angosto	☐	☐
desiguales	☐	☐
poco profunda	☐	☐

Shapes

Concept	S	NS
estrella	☐	☐
corazón	☐	☐
círculo	☐	☐
fila	☐	☐
cuadrado	☐	☐
triángulo	☐	☐
cono	☐	☐
redondo	☐	☐
diamante/rombo	☐	☐
óvalo	☐	☐
rectángulo	☐	☐
signo de marca/ palomita	☐	☐
línea	☐	☐
pirámide	☐	☐
cilindro	☐	☐
cubo	☐	☐
curva	☐	☐
columna	☐	☐
diagonal	☐	☐
ángulo	☐	☐

Direction/Position

Concept	S	NS
en	☐	☐
abierta	☐	☐
dentro de	☐	☐
cerrada	☐	☐
debajo de	☐	☐
subiendo	☐	☐
de cabeza	☐	☐
detrás de	☐	☐
parte de arriba	☐	☐
fuera	☐	☐
en lo alto	☐	☐
desarmado	☐	☐
cerca	☐	☐
alrededor	☐	☐
al lado de	☐	☐
afuera	☐	☐
cerca	☐	☐
en frente	☐	☐
juntos	☐	☐
se está alejando	☐	☐
en medio	☐	☐
el fondo	☐	☐
al	☐	☐
bajando	☐	☐
siguiendo	☐	☐
el lado	☐	☐
por	☐	☐
entre	☐	☐
parte delantera	☐	☐
hacia atrás	☐	☐
al lado	☐	☐
orilla	☐	☐
parte trasera	☐	☐
baja	☐	☐
estirada/o	☐	☐
esquina	☐	☐
hacia	☐	☐
cayendo	☐	☐
al final	☐	☐
quieto	☐	☐
unidos	☐	☐
debajo	☐	☐
sobre	☐	☐
hacia adelante	☐	☐
voltear	☐	☐
espacio	☐	☐
encima	☐	☐
subrayado	☐	☐
de lado	☐	☐
al revés	☐	☐
adelante	☐	☐
centro	☐	☐
a nivel	☐	☐
separadas	☐	☐
subiendo	☐	☐
altura	☐	☐
opuesta	☐	☐
derecha	☐	☐
lo largo	☐	☐
izquierdo	☐	☐

Self-/Social Awareness

Concept	S	NS
llorando	☐	☐
riéndose	☐	☐
triste	☐	☐
hombre	☐	☐
niña	☐	☐
niño	☐	☐
miedo	☐	☐
enojada	☐	☐
hermanos	☐	☐
lastimado	☐	☐
hermanas	☐	☐
feliz	☐	☐
relajándose	☐	☐
descansado	☐	☐
cansada	☐	☐
mujer	☐	☐
vieja	☐	☐
emocionado	☐	☐
madre	☐	☐
tiene sueño	☐	☐
padre	☐	☐
amigables	☐	☐
preocupado	☐	☐
lo debido	☐	☐
saludable	☐	☐
fácil	☐	☐
difícil	☐	☐
decepcionado	☐	☐
joven	☐	☐
correcto	☐	☐
tiene curiosidad	☐	☐

Texture/Material

Concept	S	NS
mojado	☐	☐
pesado	☐	☐
ruido fuerte	☐	☐
oscura	☐	☐
quieto	☐	☐
suave	☐	☐
madera	☐	☐
filoso	☐	☐
duro	☐	☐
vidrio	☐	☐
brillante	☐	☐
claro	☐	☐
hirviendo	☐	☐
plano	☐	☐
brillante	☐	☐
gas	☐	☐
metal	☐	☐
reflejo	☐	☐
lisa	☐	☐
tela	☐	☐
áspero	☐	☐
clara	☐	☐
seco	☐	☐
estirada/o	☐	☐
floja/o	☐	☐
ligero	☐	☐
sólido	☐	☐
no tiene filo	☐	☐
líquido	☐	☐

Quantity

Concept	S	NS
muchas	☐	☐
entera	☐	☐
vacía	☐	☐
lleno	☐	☐
ninguno	☐	☐
nada	☐	☐
ambos	☐	☐
todas	☐	☐
más	☐	☐
suficiente	☐	☐
sola	☐	☐
todos	☐	☐
con	☐	☐
falta	☐	☐
pedazo	☐	☐
casi	☐	☐
cada	☐	☐
sobra	☐	☐
mayor	☐	☐
parte	☐	☐
poca	☐	☐
excepto	☐	☐
docena	☐	☐
sin	☐	☐
mitad	☐	☐
más que	☐	☐
varias	☐	☐
menos	☐	☐
par	☐	☐
otro	☐	☐
dividido	☐	☐
doble	☐	☐
solo	☐	☐
suma	☐	☐
ninguno	☐	☐
par	☐	☐
algunos	☐	☐
pocas	☐	☐
peso	☐	☐
sustracción	☐	☐
tantos	☐	☐
triple	☐	☐

Time/Sequence

Concept	S	NS
nuevos	☐	☐
viejo	☐	☐
terminado	☐	☐
última	☐	☐
de día	☐	☐
esperando	☐	☐
terminado	☐	☐
comenzando	☐	☐
saltado	☐	☐
dejado	☐	☐
después	☐	☐
empezando a	☐	☐
orden	☐	☐
mañana	☐	☐
antes	☐	☐
primera	☐	☐
lento	☐	☐
dos veces	☐	☐
tercera	☐	☐
siempre	☐	☐
segunda	☐	☐
nunca	☐	☐
tarde	☐	☐
después	☐	☐
llegando	☐	☐
apenas	☐	☐
terminado	☐	☐
cuarto	☐	☐
temprano	☐	☐
casi	☐	☐

Summary of Early Childhood State Standards Addressed by the BBCS–3:R, BBCS:E, and BCDP

Domain	Standards	AL	AK	AZ	AR	CA	CO	CT	DE	FL	GA	HI	ID	IA	KS	KY	LA
1. Colors	1. Sorts and classifies objects by color	●		●	●	●	●	●	●	●	●	●	●	●	●	●	●
	2. Recognizes/Creates/Extends patterns using colors					●	●			●				●			●
	3. Recognizes specific colors *(e.g., red, yellow, blue, green)*	●							●						●		
	4. Describes objects by color	●		●	●	●	●	●	●	●	●	●	●				●
2. Letters	1. Identifies letters	●		●	●	●			●	●	●	●	●	●	●	●	●
	2. Names letters	●		●		●			●	●	●		●		●	●	●
	3. Letter-sound correspondence	●		●			●	●			●	●	●		●	●	●
	4. Writes letters	●			●			●	●				●		●	●	●
3. Numbers	1. Counts to 10	●		●	●	●	●	●	●	●	●	●	●	●	●	●	●
	2. Recognizes numerals 0–9	●		●	●	●	●	●	●	●	●		●	●	●	●	●
	3. One-to-one correspondence	●			●		●		●		●	●	●	●	●	●	
	4. Writes numerals 0–10					●				●			●		●	●	●
4. Sizes/ Comparisons	1. Sorts/Classifies/Orders objects according to physical attributes *(e.g., size, weight, length, volume, height)*	●		●	●	●	●	●	●	●	●	●	●	●	●	●	●
	2. Describes/Compares how two objects are different and alike	●			●		●	●	●	●	●	●	●	●	●	●	●
	3. Familiar with/Uses vocabulary for comparisons *(e.g., as tall as, taller, equal, same)*	●		●	●	●	●	●	●	●	●	●	●	●	●	●	●
5. Shapes	1. Sorts/Classifies/Orders objects by shape	●		●	●	●	●	●	●	●	●	●	●	●	●	●	●
	2. Identifies/Names common shapes *(e.g., circle)*	●		●		●	●	●	●	●	●	●	●	●	●	●	●
	3. Identifies/Names 3-D common attributes *(e.g., sphere)*	●		●		●		●		●	●	●	●		●	●	●
	4. Uses/Recognizes shapes in repeating patterns	●				●						●			●		●
6. Direction/ Position	1. Understands/Uses positional words *(e.g., inside, outside, above)*	●		●	●	●	●	●	●	●	●	●	●	●	●	●	●
	2. Understands/Uses directional words *(e.g., near/far, right/left)*	●		●	●	●	●	●	●	●	●	●	●		●	●	●
	3. Identifies properties of motion *(e.g., backward, side-to-side)*	●		●	●			●	●	●	●		●	●		●	
	4. Understands/Demonstrates different objects in space	●		●	●	●		●	●		●	●	●	●	●	●	
7. Self-/Social Awareness	1. Recognizes personal characteristics *(e.g., gender, age)*	●		●	●	●			●	●		●	●			●	
	2. Identifies roles of family	●			●	●	●		●	●	●		●		●	●	
	3. Recognizes roles of people in society				●		●				●				●	●	
	4. Understands feelings/emotions	●		●	●	●	●	●	●		●	●	●	●	●	●	●
8. Texture/ Material	1. Has awareness of changes in matter *(e.g., liquid/solid)*	●					●		●					●		●	
	2. Recognizes/Identifies different textures and materials *(e.g., smooth, rough)*	●		●		●	●		●	●	●	●	●	●	●	●	●
	3. Sorts by textures	●		●	●	●	●	●	●	●	●	●	●		●	●	●
	4. Identifies/Classifies solids, liquids, and gases	●		●	●	●			●			●			●	●	●
9. Quantity	1. Recognizes part/whole relationships *(e.g., whole, half, piece)*	●			●		●	●	●	●	●	●			●	●	
	2. Uses language to compare quantitiy *(e.g., more, serveral, less, greater than)*	●		●	●	●	●	●	●	●		●	●	●	●	●	●
	3. Identifies symbols associated with math *(e.g., + and – for add and subtract)*	●		●	●	●			●				●	●			
	4. Compares objects according to capacity/volume *(e.g., empty, full, enough)*	●			●	●		●	●	●	●	●	●	●		●	●
10. Time/ Sequence	1. Shows understanding of time of day *(e.g., morning/night)*					●	●	●	●	●	●						●
	2. Uses vocabulary related to time *(e.g., before, after)*	●		●	●	●		●		●	●	●	●		●		●
	3. Identifies relative position sequence *(e.g., 1st, 2nd, 3rd, 4th— ordinal numbers)*	●		●	●			●		●	●				●		●
	4. Recalls sequence of events or story sequence *(e.g., beginning, middle, end)*	●			●	●	●	●	●	●	●	●	●		●	●	●

Note. Alaska was in the process of developing early childhood state standards at the time of publication. Therefore, Alaska's standards are not included.

ME	MD	MA	MI	MN	MS	MO	MT	NE	NV	NH	NJ	NM	NY	NC	ND	OH	OK	OR	PA	RI	SC	SD	TN	TX	UT	VT	VA	WA	WV	WI	WY
●	●	●	●	●	●	●	●	●	●	●	●		●	●	●	●	●	●	●		●	●	●	●	●	●	●	●	●		●
		●				●	●	●			●	●	●		●		●			●	●	●	●	●		●					
●		●			●	●			●																●		●		●		
●	●	●	●	●	●	●	●	●	●		●		●	●			●					●		●		●	●		●	●	●
●	●	●	●	●		●	●	●	●		●		●	●	●	●	●	●	●	●	●	●	●	●	●	●	●	●	●		●
	●	●	●	●	●	●							●	●	●	●	●	●		●	●	●	●	●	●	●	●	●	●		●
●	●	●	●	●		●	●	●	●	●		●			●		●				●	●								●	●
		●	●	●		●		●	●			●	●	●		●				●		●			●				●		
●	●	●	●	●	●	●	●	●	●	●	●	●	●	●	●	●	●	●	●		●	●	●	●	●		●	●	●	●	●
	●	●			●	●		●	●		●	●	●	●	●	●	●	●	●			●	●	●	●		●		●	●	●
●			●	●	●	●	●	●	●	●	●	●			●	●	●		●	●	●	●		●		●	●		●		●
		●		●	●	●		●	●	●		●		●	●	●	●	●				●	●	●	●		●		●		
●	●	●	●	●	●	●	●	●	●	●	●	●	●	●	●	●	●	●	●	●	●	●	●	●	●	●	●	●	●	●	●
●	●		●	●	●	●	●	●	●	●	●	●	●	●		●	●	●	●	●	●	●	●	●	●	●	●	●		●	●
●	●	●	●	●	●	●	●	●	●		●	●	●			●	●				●	●		●		●	●	●	●	●	
●	●	●	●	●	●	●	●	●	●	●	●	●	●	●	●	●	●	●	●	●	●	●	●		●	●	●	●	●	●	●
●	●	●	●	●	●	●	●	●	●	●	●	●	●	●	●	●	●	●	●	●	●	●	●	●	●	●	●	●	●	●	●
●	●	●	●	●	●	●	●			●	●	●	●	●	●	●			●		●		●	●	●	●			●	●	●
		●	●			●		●		●			●								●		●								
●	●	●	●	●	●	●	●	●	●	●	●	●	●	●	●	●	●	●	●	●	●	●	●	●	●	●	●	●	●	●	●
●	●	●	●	●	●			●	●		●	●		●	●	●	●	●	●		●		●	●	●	●	●		●	●	●
●	●		●						●	●		●		●	●			●	●	●	●					●		●		●	
●		●	●			●	●	●			●	●			●	●	●	●				●	●	●		●	●	●	●		●
			●	●		●	●	●			●	●		●			●					●				●				●	●
	●	●	●	●	●	●	●	●	●	●	●		●	●		●	●			●	●	●	●			●		●	●		●
		●	●	●				●		●			●			●	●			●									●		
●	●	●	●	●	●	●	●	●	●		●	●	●	●	●	●	●	●	●	●	●	●	●	●	●	●	●	●	●	●	●
	●		●								●	●	●		●	●	●		●								●		●	●	●
●	●	●	●	●	●	●	●	●	●	●	●	●	●	●	●	●	●	●	●	●	●	●	●	●	●	●	●	●	●	●	●
●		●	●		●	●	●	●	●	●	●			●	●	●	●	●	●		●		●	●	●		●	●	●	●	●
		●			●		●	●		●	●	●	●	●					●	●	●		●		●	●	●	●	●	●	
●	●	●		●	●	●	●	●	●	●					●		●		●	●	●	●	●	●	●	●	●		●	●	
●	●	●	●	●	●	●		●	●	●	●	●	●	●		●	●	●	●	●	●	●	●	●	●	●	●	●	●	●	●
●	●	●	●					●							●	●	●	●				●			●					●	
●	●	●	●	●	●	●	●			●		●	●	●		●			●	●	●	●	●	●	●	●	●			●	
●	●	●	●				●		●			●	●	●		●	●	●				●	●		●			●	●		●
●	●	●	●	●	●	●	●	●				●	●			●		●						●		●		●	●		
●	●	●	●		●	●		●		●			●	●	●	●	●	●	●		●	●	●	●	●		●	●	●		
●	●	●	●	●	●	●	●	●	●		●	●	●	●	●	●	●	●	●		●	●	●	●		●	●	●	●	●	●

List of Examiners

Alabama

Florence
Judy H. Ennis

Arizona

Scottsdale
Catherine Rasmussen

Tucson
Mary Jo Bates

Arkansas

Conway
Shannon Cormier

Jonesboro
Emmett Paul Milam

Malvern
Jill Sullivan

California

Chico
Katherine H. Todd

Grass Valley
Barbara Matiska

Los Angeles
Eleanor Kaplan Jurist

Oakland
Kathy Castaneda

Rancho Palos Verdes
Karin Gregerson

Rocklin
Melanie Rivera

San Diego
H. Hellen Williams

San Leandro
Nelida Pinilla

Saugus
Paulynn Riggen

Sunnyvale
D. Ashley Cohen

Colorado

Centennial
Rita Hanneman
Rhonda Johns

Florida

Apollo Beach
James G. Kessler

Coconut Creek
Jennifer Wells
Joni Zislin

Coral Springs
Meryl S. Braverman

Gainesville
Mary B. Flaitz

Hollywood
Karen Zaidman

Land O Lakes
Kimberly Blanding-Hodges

Leesburg
Susan Andrews

Longwood
Terry H. Mattingly

Miami
Cary Ballesteros
Maria Alejandra Bustillos
Raquel E. Santana
Maria Elena Soto Rodriguez

Orlando
Magaly Aldana
Monica Murray

St. Cloud
Maria T. Torres

Georgia

Auburn
Margaret Yebra

Camilla
Deborah T. Murphy

Cumming
Allyson Jacobi
Megan J. Unger

Evans
Billi Bromer

Idaho

Boise
Amber Romriell
Brenee K. Williams
Nicole L. Wyke

Illinois

Bloomington
Tammy Claypool

Chicago
Myra Gardner
Cynthia Scubla

Glen Carbon
Kristi Halverson Duelm

Palos Park
Marjorie Aitken

Saint Joseph
Jennifer Dahman

Indiana

Carmel
Kathryn J. Gadbury

Elkhart
Laura A. Krause

Hobart
Nancy Starewicz

South Bend
Gina M. Piraccini

Iowa

Cedar Falls
Dennis E. Ford

Kansas

Dodge City
Jimmy Neufeld

Lawrence
Carleen Franz

Leon
Ana Paula G. Mumy

Kentucky

Louisville
Melissa Granger

Paducah
Karen L. Garrett
Candice B. Griffin

Versailles
Nancy Alspach

Lousiana

Calhoun
Angela Sherman

Maine

Biddeford
Lee Ann B. Dutremble

Maryland

Baltimore
Donna Azman

Massachussetts

Agawam
Beth Martin

Assonet
Louise A. Gauthier

Leeds
Elizabeth Aponte Perez

Mattapoisett
Maureen McQuillan

Roxbury
Sunday Taylor

Wellesley
Elyse Gustin Fishkin

Michigan

Bloomfield Hills
Philip R. Owen

Detroit
Gwendolyn D. Persons

Grand Blanc
Melissa Ann Lamb

Minnesota

Brooklyn Park
Leanne C. Goth

Minneapolis
Kristan Angerhofer

Minnetonka
Stephanie Horton

Wayzata
Michele Willert

Mississippi

Quitman
Cynthia Weathers

Missouri

Barnhart
Jane Dycus

Cape Girardeau
Nancy Ann Uzoaru

Hillsboro
Pamela S. Howard

Pevely
Jenna Hale Hodges

Montana

Billings
Loris Friesen

Deer Lodge
Marylou Coutts

Nebraska

Columbus
Mike Goos

Lincoln
Elizabeth Turner

Nevada

Sparks
Sandra Martin

New Hampshire

Keene
Donna Borynack

New Jersey

Hamilton
Colleen A. Morrison

North Arlington
Keri Giordano

Scotch Plains
Amy J Clayman

New Mexico

Albuquerque
Linda S. Meyers-Mitchell

Belen
Diola E. Garcia

Roswell
Gwyn O. Burd

New York

Albany
Rebecca McDonald

Ballston Spa
Ceil M. Drosky

Bronx
Cristina M. Laureano

Cortland
Joanne Finn

East Meadow
Barbra Stein

Fairport
Tracey Green

Farmingdale
Lisa Esposito

Gansevoort
Suzanne Pearce

Macedon
Lisa M. Brockhuizen

Mechanicville
Cindy J. D'Alberto

Newark
Tracy Larson

Ossining
Evelyn Mazzella

Penfield
Michelle Bucenec

Queensbury
Heather Normandin

Rochester
Rebecca Etlinger
Marcie L. Huertas

Saratoga Springs
Lisa Callahan

Slingerlands
Carrie Shapiro

West Henrietta
Amy Way

North Carolina

Asheville
Ruby Drew

Charlotte
Gloria Duarte McCaskill
Magbis N. Love

Graham
Jordana Duncan

High Point
Jo Ellen Ryan

North Dakota

Bismarck
Tamara Waters Wheeler

Ohio

Mentor
Gary Silbiger

Springfield
Angela R. K. Whip

Tiffin
Julie Wiggins

Youngstown
Paula Kempe

Oklahoma

Oklahoma City
Mona Ryan

Seminole
Kathye Easley

Stillwater
Linda B. Johnson

Tulsa
Mary Commer
Karen Copeland

Oregon

Forest Grove
Jana Swedo

Portland
Beverly Mylin

Pennsylvania

Bridgeville
Daniel Moore

Huntingdon Valley
Robin Kushner

Montoursville
Eve A. Hilsher

Punxsutawney
Melissa Shepler

South Carolina

Goose Creek
Kyndra Ford

Seneca
Annette M. Halbig

Summerville
Andrew Preston

South Dakota

Sioux Falls
Vickie Appino Bain

Sisseton
Diane Odland

Tennessee

Helenwood
Debby Sexton

Jackson
Pat Lewelling

Texas

Allen
Jennifer A. Doran

Arlington
Janet Sullivan

Boerne
Shirley S. Wolfe

College Station
Doris Hermann

Dallas
Heather Towell
Alicia Young

El Paso
Mariel E. Aguirre
Lisa Segarra

Hondo
Brenda Vavricek

Houston
Nicole Webb

Huffman
Maria Bianco

Humble
Jill Chappell Zylker

Lindale
Dawn Darden

Los Fresnos
Susi Clark

Lubbock
Brandye Boyd

Lufkin
Nelda Horton

Rancho Viejo
Michele Lazorko

San Antonio
Rose Marie Esparza
Julie M. Fox
Kathy L. Shapley
Jennifer Warzecha

Spring Branch
Dawn Magers

Tyler
Jason L. Stewart

Weslaco
Raquel E. Elizondo

Wichita Falls
John Conway
Tracy L. Otto

Utah

Oakley
Melanie M. Bowen

Riverton
Lori Heaton

Salt Lake City
Nina Lozier
Eunice Zee-Chen

Virginia

Amissville
Marie Clore

Chesterfield
Renia E. B. Cobb

New Castle
Elaine S. King

Virginia Beach
Mary Katherine Canupp

Washington

Yakima
Elsa Judith Riggin
Sylvia B. Sanchez

West Virgina

Elkview
Charles Szasz

Wisconsin

Appleton
Jodi Frailing

Burlington
Deborah Marquardt

Franksville
Linda Townsend Christ

Kenosha
Lorraine E. Vogel

Oshkosh
Dave H. Schaumann

Stanley
Nicole M. Holden

Mexico

Chihuahua
Claudia Alexandra Trevino

Puerto Rico

Rio Piedras
Nury Marcelino

San Juan
Ana Josefina Groneau

Sample BCDP Lesson Plan

Lesson 39

Targeted Concepts

big little large small

Introductory Activity

Note. Medium sized is presented as a targeted concept in Lesson 41 in this unit. Although not targeted here in Lesson 39, you will find its inclusion appropriate in your presentation of the Introductory Activity.

Materials needed:

Storybook of *Goldilocks and the Three Bears* (There are many versions of this story, so choose your own favorite. The size concepts are the important features.)

Flannel board and story characters for *Goldilocks and the Three Bears* (available commercially or make your own)

Three bowls, various sizes

Classroom furniture

Read Goldilocks and the Three Bears to the group, emphasizing the concepts targeted. Manipulate the flannel board pieces as you read, emphasizing and comparing the targeted concepts as you present the story. Read the story a second time and select children to manipulate the flannel pieces. Now that the children are familiar with the story and the concepts large, big, small, little, and medium sized for Papa, Mama, and Baby Bear, have them pantomime the story as you read it a third time. Before presentation of this third reading, have the group work to select appropriate classroom furnishings for:

Three Chairs:

Small for Baby Bear (child's seat)

Medium sized for Mama Bear (folding chair)

Large for Papa Bear (teacher's chair)

Three Beds:

1 chair for Baby's bed

2 chairs, lined together, for Mama's bed

3 chairs, lined together, for Papa's bed

Provide 3 bowls of appropriate sizes for the children to use in the story. Have the class discuss and decide which size bowl will be used by each member of the bear family.

During the above activities, initiate the discussion but let the children decide which sizes to select and why. Doing so will encourage them to use the concept words in their discussion. Select children to do the pantomiming. After both the flannel board and pantomimed versions of the story have been presented, the children will be able to tell the story (without actually reading the book), manipulate the flannel pieces, and pantomime the characters as other children tell the story. Repeat the story until all have had a chance to be involved in telling the story, pantomiming a character, or manipulating the flannel pieces. Each child does not need to tell or act an entire story, but each must have a part in the activity to feel included and to experience the story. Place as many versions and copies of this story as possible on the reading table for the children to see and compare during free time.

Mnemonic Use

A **big** clown with a **small** car,

Wears a **large** hat with a **little** star.

Distribute copies of the mnemonic for Lesson 39. Master is provided in Appendix B. Discuss the picture with the class emphasizing the big, little, large, and small items depicted. Have the children put a finger on the big clown and then on the little car. Check to see that everyone has found the correct pictures. Then have the children point to the clown's large hat and the small star. Read the rhyme with an enthusiastic sing-song rhythm. Use hand and body gestures to emphasize the concepts. Have the children stand at their seats or in a circle and copy the physical movements as they recite the mnemonic with you. Recite and act out the mnemonic again. You may wish to have the class color the pictures.

Poster Use

Introduce the Beach Poster and guide the discussion to cover the situation, event, and activities depicted. Have the children find examples of the concepts targeted, e.g., big, large, little, and small. Guide the discussion to compare and contrast the different-sized items selected. At the close of this activity or as a transition to another activity (lining up for lunch or recess, going back to seats, to reading corner, etc.), have each child choose from the poster one example of one of the targeted concepts and tell about it. Then he/she may proceed to the next activity.

Concept Card Use

For entire class or small-group drill with students who need further practice in identifying and using these concepts; use any of the suggested cards. Generate a discussion of the event and activities pictured in each.

Concept Card 3, Woodworking Shop

Introduce the card and generate a discussion among the children about what is pictured. Have them find and tell about items that demonstrate the concepts targeted and discuss differences in the size of:

scissors	screwdrivers
saws	boards
paint cans	holes in cylindrical pipes
glass stacks	stacks of wood

Concept Card 4, Gnome Workshop

During the discussion of this card, you may want to elicit the points of fantasy and reality depicted. Have the children find examples of the targeted concepts and discuss differences in their sizes.

people	pliers
board	screwdrivers
paint cans	sawdust piles

Concept Card 19, Planting Trees

Have the children cite differences in the sizes of:

trees	holes
dirt piles	people
hills	

Additional suggestions for cards to use are listed in Appendix A.

Worksheet Use

Introduce Worksheets 63 and 64. Repeat the mnemonic, and have the children recite it with the accompanying gestures and review the targeted concepts pictured. Have the children point to the pictures as they recite the rhyme again. Frequently the children will remember the rhyme in its entirety. Then direct attention to the first row of pictures with the small star. Elicit what is pictured. Then have the children find the big tree and put a finger on it. Now read the directions to mark the big tree. Complete the Worksheet giving the directions orally. Observe the children as they complete the Worksheets, noting any difficulty. If needed, introduce additional examples of the concepts using the other Poster and Concept Cards.

Multiple Applications

When teaching the concepts big, small, large, and little, it is important to note relative sizes (e.g., a two-bedroom house is large relative to a book, but small relative to a mountain).

NAIL
BOLTS
DRILL BITS
PAINT
PAINT
RED
Always wear
Safety Glasses

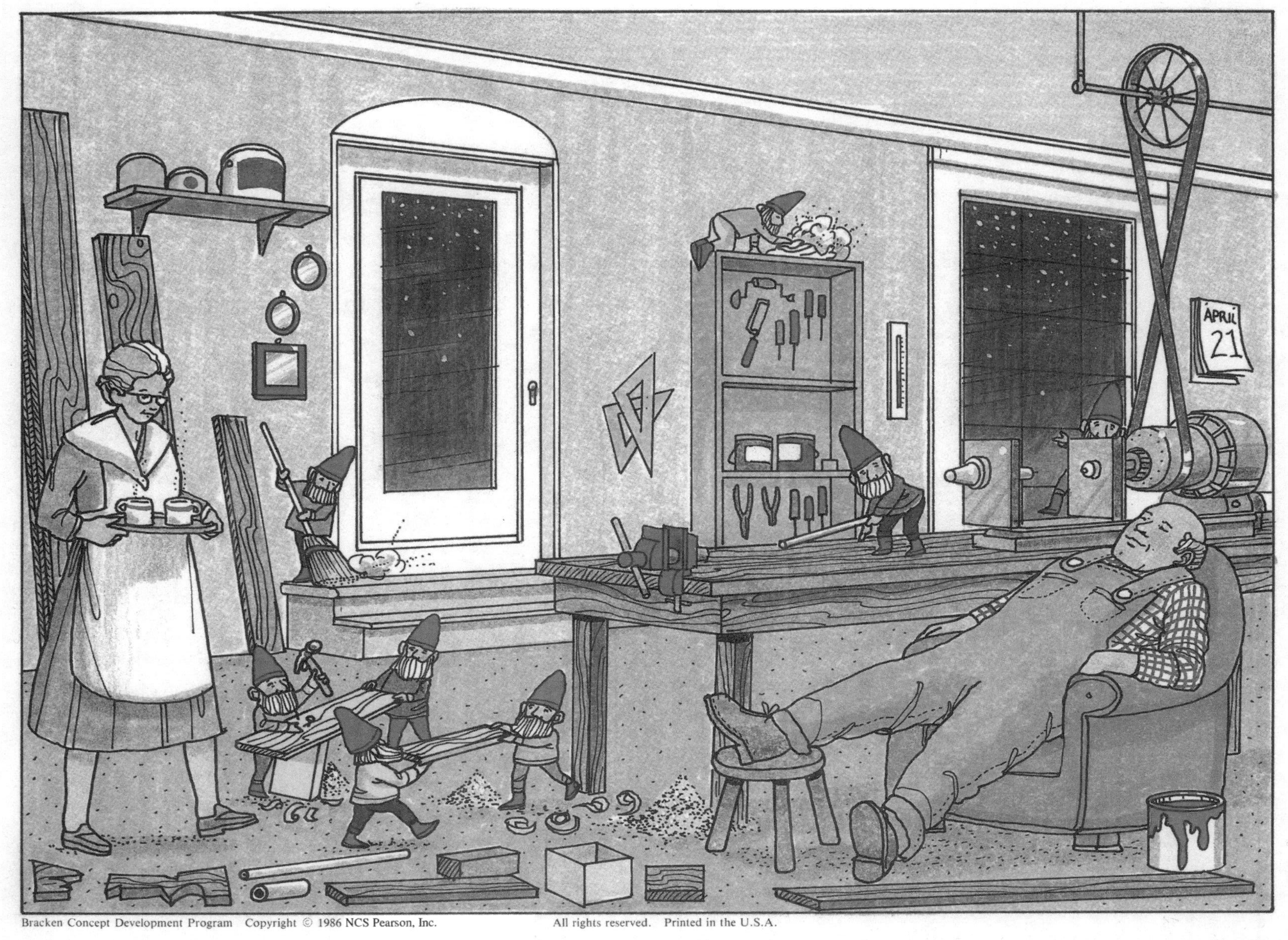
APRIL
21

Concept Card 19
Bracken Concept Development Program Copyright © 1986 NCS Pearson, Inc. All rights reserved. Printed in the U.S.A.

Name ____________________

UNIT 6: Size
LESSON 39: big, little, large, small

A **big** clown with a **small** car, Wears a **large** hat with a **little** star.

★

Mark the **big** tree.

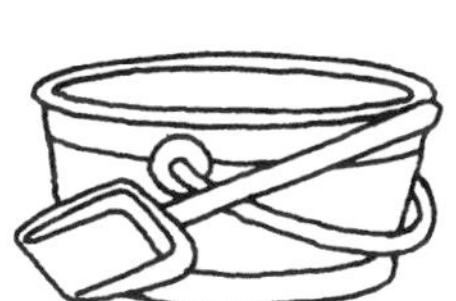

Mark the **small** sand pail.

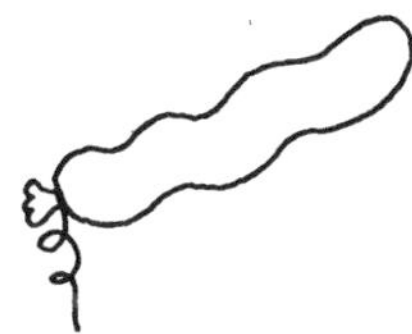

Mark the **large** balloon.

AT HOME ACTIVITIES

- Your child should realize that **big** and **large** mean the same, as do **small** and **little**. You can reinforce this by comparing large and small objects in your home. As your child sets the table, compare **large** and **small** glasses, forks, bottles, etc. Ask him/her to choose **large** and **small** items of each. Have your child point out **large** and **small** objects in your home, yard, and workshop. You can give explicit directions: "Bring me the **small** box," "Pick only the **large** tomatoes," etc.

Worksheet 63

Name ____________________

UNIT 6: Size
LESSON 39: big, little, large, small

Worksheet 64

Mark the **little** snail.

   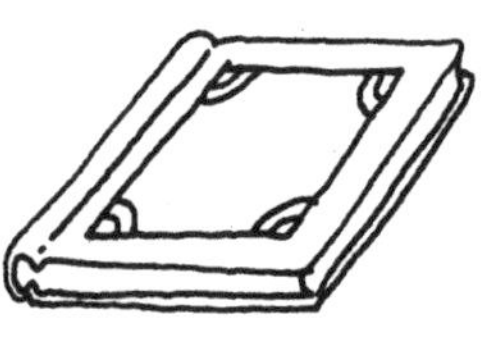

Mark the **big** book.

Mark the **small** balloon.

Mark the **large** sandwich.

Mark the **little** pencil.

References

Allen, M. J., & Yen, W. M. (1979). *Introduction to measurement theory.* Monterey, CA: Brooks/Cole Publishing Company.

American Educational Research Association, American Psychological Association, & National Council on Measurement in Education (AERA, APA, & NCME). (1999). *Standards for educational and psychological testing.* Washington, DC: Author.

Anastasi, A., & Urbina, S. (1997). *Psychological testing* (7th ed.). Upper Saddle River, NJ: Prentice Hall.

Baroody, A., & Ginsburg, H. (1991) A cognitive approach to assessing the mathematical difficulties of children labeled "learning disabled." In H.L Swanson (Ed.). *Handbook on the assessment of learning disabilities.* Austin, TX: Pro-Ed.

Berlin, B., & Kay, P. (1969). *Basic color terms: Their universality and evolution.* Berkeley, CA: University of California Press.

Bracken, B. A. (1984). *Bracken basic concept scale.* San Antonio, TX: The Psychological Corporation.

Bracken, B. A. (1986). *Bracken concept development program.* San Antonio, TX: The Psychological Corporation.

Bracken, B. A. (1988). Rate and sequence of positive and negative poles in basic concept acquisition. *Language, Speech, and Hearing in Schools, 19,* 410–417.

Bracken, B. A. (Ed.). (1996). *Handbook of self-concept: Developmental, social, and clinical considerations* (pp. 463–505). New York: John Wiley and Sons.

Bracken, B. A. (1998a). Basic concept acquisition and assessment: A celebration of our world's many dimensions. *Clinicians' Forum, 8*(2), 1–7.

Bracken, B. A. (1998b). *Bracken basic concept scale–revised* (BBCS-R). San Antonio, TX: Harcourt Assessment, Inc.

Bracken, B. A. (2002). *Bracken school readiness assessment* (BSRA). San Antonio, TX: Harcourt Assessment, Inc.

Bracken, B. A. (2006). *Bracken basic concept scale: Expressive* (BBCS:E). San Antonio, TX: Harcourt Assessment, Inc.

Bracken, B. A., Barona, A., Bauermeister, J. J., Howell, K. K., Poggioli, L., & Puente, A. (1990). Multinational validation of the Bracken Basic Concept Scale for cross-cultural assessments. *Journal of School Psychology, 28*, 325–341.

Bracken, B. A., & Crawford, E. (2006). *A comprehensive review of early childhood state educational standards.* Unpublished manuscript.

Bracken, B. A., & Fouad, N. (1987). Spanish translation and validation of the Bracken Basic Concept Scale. *School Psychology Review, 16*(1), 94–102.

Bracken, B. A., Howell, K. K., & Crain, R. M. (1993). Prediction of Caucasian and African-American preschool children's fluid and crystallized intelligence: Contributions of maternal characteristics and home environment. *Journal of Clinical Child Psychology, 22*(4), 455–464.

Breen, M. J. (1984). *Cognitive patterns of learning disabled as measured by the Woodcock-Johnson psycho-educational battery.* University of Denver, 1984. (University Microfilms International.)

Carrow-Woolfolk, E. (1999). *Comprehensive assessment of spoken language.* Circle Pines, MN: American Guidance Service, Inc.

Cohen, B. H. (1996). *Explaining psychological statistics.* Pacific Grove, CA: Brooks & Cole.

Crocker, L. M., & Algina, J. (1986). *Introduction to classical and modern test theory.* New York: Holt, Rinehart, and Winston.

Elliott, C. D. (1990). *Differential ability scales.* San Antonio, TX: The Psychological Corporation.

Flynn, J. R. (1987). Massive IQ gains in 14 nations: What IQ tests really measure. *Psychological Bulletin, 95*(1), 29–51.

Guilford, J. P. (1954). *Psychometric methods* (2nd ed.). New York: McGraw-Hill Book Company.

Hambleton, R. K. (1993). Translating achievement tests for use in cross-national studies. *European Journal of Psychological Assessment, 9*(1), 57–68.

Holland, P. W., & Thayer, D. T. (1988). Differential item performance and the Mantel-Haenszel Procedure. In H. Wainer & H. I. Braun (Eds.), *Test validity* (pp. 129–145). Hillsdale, NJ: Lawrence Erlbaum Associates.

Howell, K. K., & Bracken, B. A. (1992). Clinical utility of the Bracken Basic Concept Scale as a preschool intellectual screener: Comparison with the Standford-Binet for African-American children. *Journal of Clinical Child Psychology, 21*(3), 255–261.

Individuals with Disabilities Education Act (IDEA) Amendments of 1997, 20 U.S.C. 1431 et seq. (Fed. Reg. 34, 1997).

Kagan, S. L., Moore, E., & Bredekamp, S. (Eds.). (1995). *Reconsidering children's early development and learning: Toward common views and vocabulary.* (Report of the National Education Goals Panel: Goal 1 Technical Planning Group.). Washington, DC: U. S. Government Printing Office.

Kayser, H. (1989). Speech and language assessment of Spanish-English speaking children. *Language Speech and Hearing Services in Schools, 20*(1), 226–244.

Kayser, H. (1995). The language assessment of primarily Spanish-speaking children. *Bilingual speech and language pathology: An Hispanic focus.* San Diego, CA: Singular Publishing.

Langdon, H. W. (2002). Factors affecting special education services for English learners with suspected language-learning impairments. *Multiple Voices for Ethnically Diverse Learners, 5*(1), 66–82.

Langdon, H. W., & Cheng, L. (2002). *Collaborating with interpreters and translators: A guide for communication disorders professionals in the communications disorders field.* Eau Claire, WI: Thinking Publications.

Langdon, H. W., & Merino, B. J. (1992). Acquisitions and development of a second language in the Spanish speaker. In H. W. Langdon, and L. Lilly Cheng (Eds.), *Hispanic children and adults with communication disorders: Assessment and intervention.* Aspen, CO Publishing.

Langdon, H. W., & Saenz T. I. (1996). *Language assessment and intervention with multicultural students: A guide for speech-language-hearing professionals.* Oceanside, CA: Academic Communication Associates.

Larousse Spanish – English / English – Spanish dictionary: Unabridged edition. (1993). Paris, France: Larousse.

Lawrence, C. W. (1992). Assessing the use of age-equivalent scores in clinical management. *Language, Speech, and Hearing Services in Schools, 23*, 6–8.

Li, H., Rosenthal, R., & Rubin, D. B. (1996). Reliability of measurement in psychology: From Spearman-Brown to maximal reliability. *Psychological Methods, 1*(1), 98–107.

Magnusson, D. (1967). *Test theory.* Reading, MA: Addison-Wesley Publishing Co.

Martínez, Agustín (Ed.). (1999). *Multicultural Spanish dictionary.* Rockville, MD: Schreiber Publishing, Inc.

Matarazzo, J. D., & Herman, D. O. (1985). Clinical uses of the WAIS–R: Base rates of differences between VIQ and PIQ in the WAIS–R standardization sample (pp. 899–932). In B. B. Wolman (Ed.), *Handbook of intelligence: Theories, measurements and applications.* New York: John Wiley & Sons, Ltd.

McCauley, R. J. (2001). *Assessment of language disorders in children.* Mahwah, NJ: Lawrence Erlbaum Associates.

McCauley, R. J., & Swisher, L. (1984). Psychometric review of language and articulation tests for preschoolers. *Journal of Speech and Hearing Disorders, 49*, 34–42.

McIntosh, D. E., Wayland, S. J., Gridley, B., & Barnes, L. L. B. (1995). The relationship between the Bracken Basic Concept Scale and the Differential Ability Scales with a preschool sample. *Journal of Psychoeducational Assessment, 13*(1), 39–48.

National Association of Early Childhood Specialists in State Departments of Education (NAECS/SDE), & National Association of the Education of Young Children (NAEYC). (2003). *Early Childhood Curriculum, Assessment and Program Evaluation: Building an effective, accountable system in programs for children birth through age 8.* Retrieved July 6, 2006, from http://www.naeyc.org

National Education Goals Panel (NEGP). (1989). Retrieved July 6, 2006, from http://govinfo.library.unt.edu/negp

National Governors Association. (2004) *ECW-05: Great expectations: The importance of rigorous education standards and K–12/postsecondary alignment.* Retrieved July 6, 2006, from http://www.nga.org/portal/site/nga

National Information Center for Children and Youth with Disabilities (NICHCY). (2003). Retrieved July 6, 2006, from http://www.nichcy.org

National Institute on Deafness and Other Communication Disorders. (2004). Retrieved July 6, 2006, from http://www.nidcd.nih.gov/health/voice

No Child Left Behind Act of 2001, Public Law 107–110. U.S. Statues at Large 115 (2002): 1425.

Nunnally, J., & Bernstein, I. H. (1994). *Psychometric theory* (3rd ed.). New York: McGraw-Hill.

Office of Special Education Programs (OSEP). (2002). *Twenty-third annual report to congress on the implementation of the Individuals with Disabilities Education Act.* Washington, DC.

Panter, J. (1997). *Assessing the school readiness of kindergarten children.* Unpublished doctoral dissertation, University of Memphis, Memphis, TN.

Panter, J. E., & Bracken, B. A. (2000). Promoting school readiness. In K. M. Minke & G. G. Bear (Eds), *Preventing school problems–promoting school success: Strategies and programs that work.* Bethesda, MD: National Association of School Psychologists.

Rhyner, P. M. P., & Bracken, B. A. (1988). Concurrent validity of the Bracken Basic Concept Scale with language and intelligence measures. *Journal of Communication Disorders, 21,* 479–489.

Roseberry-McKibbin, C. (2002). *Multicultural students with special language needs: Practical strategies for assessment and intervention.* Oceanside, CA: Academic Communication Associates.

Roseberry-McKibbin, C. (2003). *Assessment of bilingual learners: language difference or disorder?* [Video]. Rockville, MD: American Speech-Language-Hearing Association.

Rothlisberg, B. A., Allen, C. L., & D'Amato, R. C. (1992, August). *The DAS's relation to basic concepts in kindergartners.* Paper presented at the American Psychological Association's Annual Conference, Washington, DC.

Scott-Little, C., Kagan, S. L., & Frelow, V. S. (2003). *Standards for preschool children's learning and development: Who has standards, how were they developed, and how are they used.* Greensboro, NC: SERVE.

Semel, E., Wiig, E. H., & Secord, W. (2003). *Clinical Evaluation of Language Fundamentals–Fourth Edition.* San Antonio, TX: The Psychological Corporation.

Silver, N. C., & Dunlap, W. P. (1987). Averaging correlation coefficients: Should Fisher's *z* transformation be used? *Journal of Applied Psychology, 72*(1), 146–148.

Sterner, A. G., & McCallum, R. S. (1988). Relationship of the Gessell Developmental Exam and the Basic Concept Scale to academic achievement. *Journal of School Psychology, 26,* 297–300.

Strube, M. J. (1988). Some comments on the use of magnitude-of-effect estimates. *Journal of Counseling Psychology, 35*(3), 342–345.

The American Heritage Spanish Dictionary. (1986). Boston, MA: Houghton Mifflin Compnay

Tomblin, J. B., Smith, E., & Shang, X. (1997). Epidemiology of specific language impairment: Prenatal and perinatal risk factors. *Journal of Communication Disorders, 30,* 325-344.

U.S. Bureau of the Census. (2003). *Current population survey, March 2003.* (Machine-readable data file). Washington, DC: Author

Wechsler, D. (1997). *Wechsler intelligence scale for children—Third edition* (WISC–III). San Antonio, TX: The Psychological Corporation.

Wechsler, D. (2002). *Wechsler preschool and primary scale of intelligence—Third edition* (WPPSI–III). San Antonio, TX: The Psychological Corporation.

Wechsler, David. (2003). *Wechsler intelligence scale for children—Fourth edition* (WISC–IV). San Antonio, TX: Harcourt Assessment, Inc.

Wiig, E. H., & Secord, W. A. (1992). *Measurement and assessment: Making the most of test results.* Chicago: Riverside Publishing Company.

Wiig, E. H., Secord, W. A., & Semel, E. (1992). *Clinical evaluation of language fundamentals preschool.* San Antonio, TX: The Psychological Corporation.

Wiig, E. H., Secord, W. A., & Semel, E. (2004). *Clinical evaluation of language fundamentals preschool–Second edition.* San Antonio, TX: Harcourt Assessment, Inc.

Wilkins, C., Rolfhus, E., Weiss, L., & Zhu, J. (2005). *A simulation study comparing inferential and traditional norming with small sample sizes.* Paper presented at the 2005 Annual Meeting of the American Educational Research Association, Montreal, Canada.

Wyatt, T. A., Brown, G., Brown, M., Dabney, M., Wiley, P., & Weddington, G. (2001, October). *The assessment of African-American children: An update on Larry P.* California Speech-Language-Hearing Association Task Force.

Zimmerman, I. L., Steiner, V. G., & Pond, R. E. (1992). *Preschool language scale–Third edition* (PLS–3). San Antonio, TX: The Psychological Corporation.

Zimmerman, I. L, Steiner V. G., & Pond, R. E. (2002). *Preschool language scale–Fourth edition* (PLS–4) San Antonio, TX: The Psychological Corporation.

Zucker, S., & Riordan, J. (1990). One-year predictive validity of new and revised and conceptual measurement. *Journal of Psychoeducational Assessment, 8*, 4–8.